Reducing Terrorism
Through Situational Crime Prevention

Crime Prevention Studies
Volume 25

Reducing Terrorism Through Situational Crime Prevention

edited by
Joshua D. Freilich &
Graeme R. Newman

LYNNE
RIENNER
PUBLISHERS

BOULDER
LONDON

Published in the United States of America in 2010 by
Lynne Rienner Publishers, Inc.
1800 30th Street, Boulder, Colorado 80301
www.rienner.com

and in the United Kingdom by
Lynne Rienner Publishers, Inc.
3 Henrietta Street, Covent Garden, London WC2E 8LU

ISBN: 978-1-881798-94-1 (pb : alk. paper)

First published in 2009 by Criminal Justice Press.
Reprinted here from the original edition.

Printed and bound in the United States of America

The paper used in this publication meets the requirements
of the American National Standard for Permanence of
Paper for Printed Library Materials Z39.48-1992.

5 4 3 2

CONTENTS

continued

Contents

INTRODUCTION

Joshua D. Freilich
John Jay College of Criminal Justice
National Consortium for the Study of Terrorism and
Responses to Terrorism (START)

Graeme R. Newman
University at Albany, SUNY

Situational Crime Prevention (SCP) is a versatile approach that seeks to prevent criminal behavior by either implementing strategies to manipulate specific situations to make it impossible for the crime to be committed, or by reducing cues that increase a person's motivation to commit a crime during specific types of events. SCP's reach has expanded tremendously in recent years and the number of its techniques has increased from 12 to 25. Importantly, these techniques have been effectively applied to a variety of "new" crimes, such as identity theft, cyber crime, organized crime, and illegal migration, to name but a few. The prevalence of these new crimes has grown out of the new opportunities provided by globalization and the revolution in information technology (see Newman, this volume). This expansion continues to demonstrate the widely recognized practical relevance of SCP to solving crime problems. It also illustrates its unique ability as a theory of crime causation and control to understand the constantly changing environment of crime and the new opportunities for crime that emerge with these changes. It is little wonder, therefore, that SCP should

Crime Prevention Studies, volume 25 (2009), pp. 1–7.

emerge as a significant approach to solving the problem of terrorism. It is an approach that is so practical and so focused on protecting individuals, locations and groups from victimization. It has *always* been primarily concerned with making our world safe and secure.

Why should it be any different when it comes to terrorism? Until recently, a major part of the approach to terrorism has been the province of political scientists, who, naturally, see terrorism as a political problem requiring a political solution. But international bodies such as the United Nations have been unable to agree on a definition of terrorism. This incapacity is quintessentially political. Indeed, the United States Government is unable to agree on a single definition, as various departments and agencies such as the Federal Bureau of Investigation (FBI), the State Department and the Defense Department have their own competing definitions (Freilich, Chermak and Simone, 2009). Although terrorism may appear to be a political problem, its solution does not necessarily lie in politics. In fact, it may be that thinking of terrorism solely in political terms inhibits one from understanding what it is, and worse, presupposes what should be done in response to it.

Clarke and Newman (2006) argued that we should approach terrorism *as if* it were crime, and break it down into its components and processes just as we do in SCP. Their definition (suggested by Nick Ross, a contributor to this volume) was that terrorism is crime with a political motive. Politicians and political scientists can argue whether those who carry out terrorist activities are criminals, murderers, freedom fighters or whatever else. The actual mechanics and operational constraints and contingencies are the same, no matter what political goal is being sought. Thus, as stated in Shane Johnson and Alex Braithwaite's chapter in this volume, the patterned activities of insurgent attacks are open to scientific analysis and discovery, which contribute to our understanding of how insurgents plan and carry out their attacks. Their chapter analyzes unique data from Iraq to examine the spatial and temporal patterns of both Improvised Explosive Device attacks (IED) and non-IED attacks. Johnson and Braithwaite found that both attack types clustered in space and time more than would be expected if their timing and location were independent. Following an attack at one location, other attacks were more likely nearby within a short interval of time, but the risk of attack within the vicinity diminished with time. Importantly, the precise patterns vary by attack type, suggesting that they are generated by different types of insurgent strategy and that different counter-insurgent tactics will therefore be appropriate for different types of attack. The Johnson and Braithwaite study has the useful effect of demystifying terrorism by showing that terrorists face real-life challenges just like any other actors, and that their activities are dominated by primarily operational constraints and opportunities.

But if we must take sides against terrorists, and fight them, who better to tell us how to do this than military scientists whose specialty is fighting? Yet it is probably also true that the military establishments of many countries, especially those who have fought so many wars in Europe over the past century, have had great difficulty in adapting their standard approach to war. World War II brought this approach to its zenith: massive armies confronting each other in a defined field or location using massive firepower to overcome the other. Terrorists avoid this confrontation since they are weak in firepower. Instead, they use the strategies of "asymmetrical warfare." As Graeme Newman points out in his chapter, which links SCP to developing sensible foreign policy (demonstrating that terrorism is political after all), the tactics of terrorists are much enhanced by globalization, and especially by the information technology revolution. The British in Malaya were able, using dreadfully violent and Draconian methods, to wipe out insurgency in Malaya in the 1950s. Today, the portrayal of such violence by a Western democracy against such a small force would make such a strategy politically infeasible.

The U.S. invasion of Iraq was confronted with just such a problem. And it was in response to this problem of asymmetrical warfare that David Kilcullen wrote the "Twenty Eight Articles" paper reproduced (with permission) in this volume. Kilcullen, recipient of a Ph.D. in military science, and at the time adviser to General David H. Petraeus, the commander in Iraq, describes these articles as based on field notes he made while on duty in various operations dealing with insurgency (in Indonesia and other places). They clearly reflect an approach that is strikingly similar to situational crime prevention, among them the necessity of understanding the environment (cultural and physical) within which specific offences occur; identifying stakeholders (often women) and capable guardians (community leaders); reducing rewards of terrorists; understanding and identifying dangerous individuals (sometimes children); giving residents good positive reasons to side against the insurgents; explaining how to protect targets; identifying hotspots; and many more. In sum, these articles show how the collection and analysis of information is fundamental to a successful campaign, providing continuity in use of this information in a systematic way. The articles also demonstrate how difficult it is to convince commanding officers that insurgent activities can be more effectively overcome by the collection and use of information ("intelligence") rather than by setting up a bastion in a walled compound from which patrols emerge briefly and then return. The problem faced in getting military commanders to think in terms of problem solving rather than firepower is not unlike the problem of getting police chiefs to think in terms of problem-oriented policing (which is closely related to SCP) rather than the single solution they commonly use to solve all crime problems – arrest.

Among the great fears of terrorism after 9/11 was the fear of weapons of mass destruction. Politicians cried, "we can't protect everything" – yet in the U.S. particularly, politicians continued to proceed on just that basis, distributing homeland security money according to standard political practices (i.e., to gain political favors) with little regard to identifying what targets really needed to be protected. Building on Clarke and Newman's (2006) "EVIL DONE" diagnosis of the inherent but differential attractiveness of targets to terrorists, Rachel Boba's chapter develops a plan for systematically assessing what targets are most likely to be attacked. It is true that we cannot protect everything – but neither can terrorists attack just any target, since they too have limited resources. They must select the target that suits their operational capacity. So it turns out that we have to protect just those targets that are most likely to be attacked. Boba's paper shows how to do it.

The target risk assessment approach does much to allay the irrational fears of ordinary people and their local community leaders, who harbor fears of suffering an imminent attack (constantly reminded by the terrorist threat levels broadcast by the federal government). However, it does little to allay the overwhelming fear of Armageddon, the death and destruction that could be wrought by a weapon of mass destruction. Even here, the rational approach of problem solving makes clear that these fears could mostly be unfounded, and that an attack by a terrorist group using a weapon of mass destruction is unlikely. And the reason? Terrorists do not have the resources or the operational know-how to do it. William Clark, an immunologist and widely read science writer, reveals in his chapter the specific steps that a terrorist group must take to acquire, manufacture and then disperse a biological weapon. He convincingly demonstrates that using such a weapon is (and has been) certain to result in failure for the terrorists. In fact, we know that the overwhelming preference for conventional weapons – small arms and explosives – by terrorists is the result of their widespread availability. Almost all terrorist attacks have used conventional weapons, and in situations where they have not – Clark's examples center on biological weapons – they have fallen far short of their objective. It might be argued that the 9/11 attacks were unconventional and highly successful. But in fact, these attacks used airplanes as weapons, a technique available and used since World War I. The 9/11 attacks are better described as an innovative use of conventional weapons, in the same way as roadside bombs and suicide bombing are an innovative use of conventional weaponry.

The step-by-step approach to uncovering the steps necessary to carry out a biological attack, as exemplified in Clark's paper, has been advocated by situational crime preventionists for some time. In particular, the seminal paper by Cornish (1994) outlined the "script" approach to understanding how offenders carry out their tasks. The script concept is a logical outcome of the rational choice approach to understanding and explaining crime, and it has been used to explain a variety of crimes, in particular credit card and check fraud (Mativat and Tremblay, 1997; Lacoste and Tremblay, 2003), child sexual abuse (Wortley and Smallbone, 2006), and suicide bombing (Clarke and Newman, 2006). Minwoo Yun's chapter presents a case study of hostage taking in Afghanistan. It convincingly demonstrates that the script approach can help not only in understanding the operational constraints and advantages of hostage taking by terrorists, but also in offering points of intervention and tactical suggestions for negotiation. However, examining the sequence of events that leads up to a terrorist attack can also reveal unexpected links among what might otherwise be considered unrelated events. For example, the Oklahoma City bomber Timothy McVeigh was tracked down, in large part, because of a traffic violation.

The paper by Joshua Freilich and Steven Chermak applies the script method to two case studies that involve far-rightists fatally attacking law enforcement personnel in the United States. The case studies are used heuristically to demonstrate the vitality and effectiveness of both traditional "hard" SCP measures (that prevent an offender from successfully completing a desired illegal act), as well as recently proposed "soft" strategies (that prevent cues or prompts from occurring that might further inflame a suspect's motivation or ideology during a specific incident). Their chapter illustrates that SCP is concerned with analyzing all aspects of a particular incident, including ideological issues. The consistent hallmark of situational crime prevention, though, is to analyze all factors through a "prevention" lens, as opposed to taking a "root causes" approach.

The chapter by Roberta Belli and Joshua Freilich focuses on ideologically motivated tax refusal, a nonviolent crime committed by far-right extremists in the U.S. Recent research has demonstrated that antecedent events, including violent and nonviolent acts, may be important indicators of the path taken by terrorists to an attack – the "pre-phase" as Yun calls it. Similarly, some have speculated that nonviolent offenses, such as the refusal to comply with tax laws as a form of anti-government protest, may act as a gateway to "escalating" illegal behavior that includes violent acts. Belli and Freilich's innovative study expands SCP's counterterrorism reach and applies it to the non-violent – but politically motivated crime of tax refusal (Newman & Clarke, 2006). Their study opens up many opportunities for groundbreaking research, considering that the vast majority of terrorism definitions and research limit its universe of cases to acts that involve force or violence (Freilich, Chermak and Simone, 2009). Their paper also demonstrates that the rational choice model and SCP strategies can be effectively applied not just to the more typical crimes of commission, but to crimes of omission (where non-action is the crime) as well. The chapter thus makes important contributions to both the rational choice/ SCP and terrorism literatures.

What is most remarkable about the collection of papers in this volume is their diversity of style, the contrasting backgrounds of the authors and the different disciplines represented in their approach. Some chapters were written specifically for this volume by seasoned academics whose background in situational crime prevention or crime science is well known. Others were papers that emerged from conferences on terrorism or crime prevention. The chapter by Joseph Clare and Frank Morgan, for example, had its beginnings at a 2007 conference in Perth, Australia on terrorism and torture, where Clarke and Newman presented their ideas on applying situational crime prevention to the problem of terrorism. Clare and Morgan later refined and presented their paper at the 17th Annual Environmental Criminology and Crime Analysis conference in July 2008, and eventually developed it into a more formal chapter for this volume. Of particular interest, though, is its crossing over to another discipline, in this case the epidemiology of disease, to show how recent developments in applying situational crime prevention to terrorism have seemingly broken the "rule of specificity" so ardently promoted by the traditional SCP approach.

The chapter by Nick Ross originated at an international conference sponsored by John Jay College of Criminal Justice in Puerto Rico in June 2008. The presentation made by Ross, a seasoned journalist and television commentator, was so dramatic that we asked for few modifications of it in order to preserve its powerful format. But don't be deceived by the non-academic style of the writing. Ross, a prime mover in the establishment of the Jill Dando Institute for Crime Science at University College London, relentlessly applies the problem-solving logic that is the hallmark of situational crime prevention to uncovering the errors made by politicians and social scientists in responding to terrorism. Interestingly, Ross's chapter takes us full circle as he demonstrates that the SCP measures employed by the British government "bought" it time as it wore the Irish Republican Army down. This in turn increased the willingness of the IRA to negotiate the ceasefire with the British government. In other words, advocates of taking seriously the ideology and grievances of aggrieved parties may have the most to benefit from SCP techniques. Indeed, successfully implemented SCP techniques may be one of the most effective mechanisms that make negotiated settlements possible.

REFERENCES

Clarke, R. V., & Newman, G. R. (2006). *Outsmarting the terrorists*. New York: Praeger Publishers.

Cornish, D. (1994). The procedural analysis of offending and its relevance for situational prevention. *Crime Prevention Studies, 3*, 151–196.

Freilich, J. D., Chermak, S. M., & Simone, Jr., J. (2009). Surveying American state police agencies about terrorism threats, terrorism sources, and terrorism definitions. *Terrorism and Political Violence, 21*(3), 450–475.

Mativat, F., & Tremblay, P. (1997). Counterfeiting credit cards: Displacement effects, suitable offenders, and crime wave patterns. *British Journal of Criminology, 37*(2), 165–183.

Lacoste, J., & Tremblay, P. (2003). Crime innovation: A script analysis of patterns in check forgery. *Crime Prevention Studies, 16*, 171–198.

Wortley, R., & Smallbone, S. (2006). *Situational prevention of child sexual abuse.* Crime Prevention Studies, vol. 19. Monsey, NY: Criminal Justice Press.

SPATIO-TEMPORAL MODELLING OF INSURGENCY IN IRAQ

Shane D. Johnson
University College London

Alex Braithwaite
University College London

Abstract: *In the wake of the 9/11 terrorist attacks, counter-insurgency operations have taken primacy in many states' policy agendas. In this chapter we provide an overview of the Iraq conflict and review existing theory regarding insurgent targeting strategies. In particular, we focus on how attacks might be organized in space and time given the resources available to insurgents, and the spatial and temporal constraints that shape their behavior. Using data for a six month interval of time, we then examine space-time patterns of two types of attack: IED and non-IED. The results indicate that both types, of attack cluster in space and time more than would be expected if their timing and location were independent. Simply put, following an attack at one location others are more likely nearby within a short interval of time, but the risk of attack within the vicinity diminishes with time. Importantly, the precise patterns vary by attack type, suggesting that they are generated by different types of insurgent strategy and that different counter-insurgent tactics will be appropriate for different types of attack.*

Crime Prevention Studies, volume 25 (2009), pp. 9–32.

INTRODUCTION

Counter-insurgency operations have been catapulted to the forefront of many states' policy agendas in the wake of 9/11. While it is not historically unprecedented for major powers to focus their attention upon such operations,[1] there is a general belief that they have now overtaken more conventional forms of conflict in states' security priorities. This represents a relatively recent shift and, accordingly, uncertainty obscures successful identification of the most appropriate application of military force in countering the increased threat from insurgent activities. This uncertainty is manifest most vividly within the membership of the "coalition-of-the-willing" – outside military forces from the U.S. and its allies – where fierce debates rage as to the wisdom and impact of their continued military presence in Iraq. More generally, a great deal of uncertainty surrounds the prospects for security and prosperity in Iraq during and beyond the period of foreign occupation. It is yet to be definitively established whether or not, for instance, the incremental surge in U.S. forces on the ground from the spring of 2007 permanently lowered levels of insurgent violence nor what will be the effect of the U.K. troop withdrawal – planned to begin July 2009. What is certain, however, is that while violence continues there is little chance that credible, stable, consolidated democratic institutions will emerge to facilitate confident citizen participation in government.

These debates are all the more pertinent now that Barack Obama – a strong advocate of setting a timetable for withdrawal – has been elected 44th President of the U.S.A., replacing George W. Bush – himself an advocate of the stay-the-course doctrine. One reason for the prolongation of the "stay-the-course" versus "timetable-for-withdrawal" debate is the lack of accurate empirical evidence identifying factors that exacerbate or mitigate the severity of insurgent activities on the ground. Accordingly, great value ought to be attached to advances in the understanding of ongoing insurgent campaigns against Coalition troops. Of particular interest are details about Improvised Explosive Devices (IEDs), which have, since late 2004, become the greatest threat to the military on the ground in Iraq.

In this chapter we build on previous work (Townsley, Johnson & Ratcliffe, 2008; see also N. F. Johnson, 2006) concerned with the spatio-temporal distribution of insurgent activity. In line with the approach suggested by advocates of situational crime prevention (e.g., Clarke, 1997), and recognizing that different types of insurgent activity may be influenced by different factors and reflect different targeting strategies, we analyse patterns for different types of activity separately. Here, we focus on IED attacks and compare these to patterns of non-IED insurgent attacks.

In what follows, a brief review of the literature identifying insurgent strategies among non-state actors is used to identify a series of consistent expectations. These largely centre upon the claim that insurgents are highly likely to allocate their scarce resources purposefully in periodic and clustered patterns so as to maximise their prospects for taking control of new territories and winning the public relations competition. Accordingly we employ a procedure initially developed within the field of epidemiology (Knox, 1964) – refined by research within the situational crime prevention literature (e.g., Johnson & Bowers, 2004; Johnson et al., 2007; Townsley et al., 2003) – to test the hypothesis that space-time patterns of insurgent activity resemble those of a contagious process – occurring closer in space and time than would be expected assuming that the timing and location of events were independent. The testing of this key hypothesis is designed to provoke the derivation of additional hypotheses regarding operational practices within insurgent campaigns and counterinsurgent responses. Example hypotheses are addressed in the concluding remarks of the paper.

INSURGENT STRATEGY

We employ a simple definition of insurgency that identifies it as the use of force by a non-state actor hoping to coerce a government to affect some policy change in deviation from the status quo.[2] Importantly, we consider the terms terrorism and insurgency largely interchangeable, though we recognise that traditionally they have been dealt with as two distinct forms of non-state actor challenges to the central government; with the former referring to attacks against "innocent" civilians and the latter being associated with attacks against the officials and military assets of the government. For instance, while the United States Department of State specifies in its definition of terrorism that violence is " . . . perpetrated against noncombatant targets . . . " (U.S. Department of State, 2003, p. xiii), the United States Department of Defense (DOD) chooses to define terrorism more generally as "the unlawful use or threatened use of force or violence against individuals or property to coerce or intimidate governments or societies, often to achieve political, religious, or ideological objectives" (White, 2003, p. 12). We choose to treat these two terms as synonyms because we would claim they are both driven by a desire to effect policy change and, in the case of Iraq, there is a growing tendency for campaigns to employ violence against both sets of targets: of the 118,246 insurgent attacks between June 2004 and August 2007, 85,284 targeted Coalition troops, 21,725 targeted Iraqi Security Forces, and 11,237 targeted civilians.[3]

A range of recent studies have detailed rationalist explanations for the employment of insurgent violence that do not rest solely upon the existence of (what is commonly perceived as being irrational) fanaticism (see, e.g., Crenshaw, 1998; Wilkinson, 1986; Hoffman, 2006 Pape 2003, 2005; and Kydd & Walter, 2006). Martha Crenshaw, for instance, characterizes insurgency " . . . as an expression of political strategy . . . " in which the resort to violence is viewed as " . . . a willful choice made by an organization for political and strategic reasons, rather than as the unintended outcome of psychological or social factors" (1998, p. 7). We identify four common themes among these strategic arguments, each of which overlaps significantly, ultimately reiterating the claim that insurgency can be characterised as a struggle between a government and a non-state actor(s) over control of territory and public opinion. Moreover, each implies that attacks should be non-random and at least loosely coordinated so as to maximize impacts.

Exhaustion Strategies

It is commonly recognised that insurgents are militarily and politically weak actors who lack sufficient strength in numbers to enable them to compete against the political leadership through legitimate processes and whose tool-kit for countering politically powerful actors, with whose authority they fundamentally disagree, is, therefore, restricted to violent means (see, also, Lacquer, 1977; Bell, 1978; Crenshaw, 1981, 1998; Carr, 1997). "Generally, small organizations resort to violence to compensate for what they lack in numbers. The imbalance between the resources terrorists are able to mobilize and the power of the incumbent regime is a decisive consideration in their decision-making" (Crenshaw, 1998, p. 11). The reality of this power asymmetry tends to point insurgents toward strategies of exhaustion (see, e.g., Kydd & Walter, 2006, and Lapan & Sandler, 1993). These strategies involve focusing scarce resources upon small, (winnable), isolated, periodic uses of force. In aggregation it is hoped that such a strategy will exhaust the opponent's abilities (money, lives) or (more likely) will/morale. The success of exhaustion strategies depends upon being able to strike the right balance between maneuver (fleeing) and engagement (fighting). In other words, it is suggested that insurgents aim to employ strategies that are likely to optimize the impact of limited resources and the spatial and temporal constraints (Townsley et al., 2007) that limit their activity.

Morale-Building Strategies

Violence can also be employed to prepare the ground for mass revolt, inspiring resistance by example by demonstrating the vulnerability of the government coming under attack (Hewitt, 1993; Marighella, 1969). Metz (2003) argues that insurgents rely upon being able to highlight the inability of the government to guarantee peace and stability for the broader population. Whilst traditional views might characterize the course of insurgency as a steady escalation of violence until the insurgents have built a military force to match and defeat the government, the Iraqi case differs insofar as it resembles the Palestinian struggle where violence can be used to target a potentially weak-willed foreign occupier, increasing tensions between the domestic population and the occupier, ultimately designed to compel withdrawal (see, e.g., Wilkinson, 2000; Pape, 2003, 2005). In particular, this strategy is aimed at demonstrating to sympathetic audiences that the movement stands a chance of victory in its struggle against a status quo power and, therefore, that continued support is not in vein. Accordingly, this logic also implies a strategy in which resources are expended in bursts that maximise exposure but minimise the likelihood of capture.

Public Relations Strategies

Insurgent violence is also identified as having a useful agenda-setting function within a broader population that is not necessarily sympathetic to the movement (see, especially, Thornton, 1964). "By attracting attention it [violence] makes the claims of the resistance a salient issue in the public mind. The government can reject but not ignore an opposition's demands" (Crenshaw, 1998, p. 12). The public relations battle against the government can be thought of as existing at three levels. First, there is a need to draw attention to the goal of the movement with a view toward attracting new recruits. For Bueno De Mesquita (2005) this results in attempts to demonstrate that the insurgency is not futile; to demonstrate that the insurgency can harm its targets and that it has some prospect of success.

Second, there is a broader (not necessarily supportive) population within the state that could help swing the balance in the ongoing struggle between Government and Insurgents – as they could provide implicit support by not opposing the use of violence for broader aims. The dominant discussion in the literature in this respect refers to the strategy of *outbidding*, whereby competing factions utilise isolated violence to muster support (see, e.g., Bloom, 2005; Crenshaw, 1981). Third, there is the population of the state committing forces to counter-insurgency that can also be swayed in opinion, it is argued, if they feel the ongoing costs of the insurgency are too high. As with the *exhaustion* and *morale-building* strategies detailed above, it is expected that insurgent attacks will be non-random and that some effort will be made to optimize limited resources that are subject to spatial and temporal constraints, once again maximising exposure whilst minimising the potential for capture.

Provocation Strategies

Finally, it is claimed that the employment of violence may serve to provoke a harsh government retaliation which would undermine the government's democratic credentials and that could, therefore, serve to alienate the masses, pushing them toward supporting the resistance organization opposing the government (see, e.g., Thornton, 1964, Fromkin, 1975, Crenshaw, 1981; McCauley, 2006; Pridemore & Freilich, 2007; LaFree, Korte, & Dugan, 2009). Most recent discussions of this strategy have identified the vulnerability of liberal democracies, in particular, to violence so designed (see, e.g., Wilkinson 1986; Pape 2003, 2005).

In summary, each of these broad categories of strategies highlight the fact that insurgents face a significant power asymmetry and must, therefore, allocate their scarce resources so as to *exhaust* their opponent's morale by demonstrating their weakness and/or authoritarian tendencies, while building morale among their own supporters. Consequently, it is anticipated that attacks will cluster in time and space, so as to magnify their occurrence.

There is a paucity of research concerned with the spatial[4] distribution of insurgent activity that has used point (rather than regional) level data, let alone that which considers patterns in space *and* time (though Berrebi & Lakdawalla, 2007, and N. F. Johnson, 2006, offer welcome exceptions; see also Cothren, Smith, Roberts & Damphousse, 2008; Rossmo, Harries & McGarrell, 2008). However, the limited research that has examined patterns of insurgent activity using point-level data does provide support for the hypothesis discussed above. For example, using three months of data concerning IED attacks in Iraq, Townsley, Johnson and Ratcliffe (2008) demonstrate that attacks cluster in time and space more than would be expected if the timing and location of events were independent.

The Townsley et al. (2008) paper focused on only one type or attack (IEDs), but raised more questions than it answered. Consequently, in the current study we provide a replication and extension of the Townsley et al. work. Before presenting the analyses, we provide a little more detail about the Iraq conflict and the use of IED and non-IED attacks by insurgent actors.

FREQUENCY AND LOCATION IN THE IRAQI INSURGENCY

The insurgency in Iraq took hold almost immediately after America's successful completion of a conventional campaign against Hussein's military forces. This insurgency grew steadily – both in terms of the numbers of insurgents engaging Coalition forces and the level of violence they executed – for nearly five years after the conclusion of the conventional campaign. The "surge" in Coalition forces in April 2007 had the positive effect of marginally reducing levels of violence; however, at present the insurgency comprises myriad organizations united only by their mutual desire to undermine the transitional government in Iraq and oust the foreign occupying forces of America and her coalition of allies. These groups have employed suicide bombings, IED attacks, kidnappings, murders, sniper techniques, and mortar attacks.

IEDs are booby traps – disguised, victim-triggered devices, often in form of roadside bombs. There is a long tradition to the employment of such weapons by insurgents and terrorists including in Malaya, Vietnam, Northern Ireland, and Sri Lanka. It is likely that they have become so prevalent in Iraq as a result of the expertise gained by fighters in the Iraq-Iran war of the 1980s and the availability of explosives, especially mines from that time.

As of November 17, 2008, IEDs had claimed 1,812 of the 4,197 hostile Coalition troop fatalities in Iraq, having increased year-on-year since the invasion in March 2003, representing, for instance, 70% of monthly casualties (among those killed in action) in 2005, up from 26% in 2004 (Ryu, 2005). IEDs are now, therefore, the single largest cause of America's losses in battles.[5] While it had been hoped that early symbolic victories (e.g., the death of Saddam Hussein's sons and the capture of Hussein himself) would abate the killings, in fact it was soon recognized that insurgents were becoming increasingly well organized – combining ambushes, the employment of rocket-propelled grenades (RPGs), the placement of IEDs, and small arms fire. Accordingly, massive budgetary allocations have been allotted to projects safeguarding troops on the ground and specifically targeting the threat from IEDs (Miles, 2005, 2006) – including $1.2 billion between 2003 and 2006 allotted to reinforce and armour humvees against their deployment (Garamone, 2004).

In March 2006, Bush claimed that terrorists were employing IEDs because they lack strength to tackle America's conventional forces: "After the terrorists were defeated in battles in Fallujah and Tal Afar, they saw they could not confront Iraqi or American forces in pitched battles and survive, and so they turned to IEDs, a weapon that allows them to attack from a safe distance without having to face our forces in battle" (Smith, 2006). At least anecdotally, it appears as if insurgents have, in fact, proven to be very successful in overcoming American countermeasures. For instance, they have built bigger bombs in reaction to America's armoring of humvees; and they have employed remote detonation devices that can be used up to 2 kilometers away in response to the increasing number of captures/killings of bombers by Americans (Ryu, 2005).

INSURGENCY DATA

The advances presented in this study depend upon access to rich data detailing the evolution of the insurgent campaign. Such data is (understandably) hard to come by. In this instance, we have a comprehensive dataset detailing all incidents, representing a variety of acts (committed by insurgent forces against Iraqi and Coalition forces), that were reported to Multi-National Force-Iraq (MNF-I) through daily Significant Activity (SIGACTS) Reports. This "unclassified" data, available for the period January-June 2005, was made available by the Reconstruction Operations Center.[6] These data, treated as "sensitive," have been employed elsewhere within academic communities, such as in articles describing the utility of geographic profiling techniques in the search for Insurgent hideouts.[7]

Our primary focus in this study concerns spatial and temporal patterns in insurgent activity. In future work our aim is to uncover their correlates. There were a total of 7,409 attempted IED attacks in the first six months of 2005, of which 3,882 successfully exploded and 3,527 were deployed but failed to explode and were subsequently found and cleared by Coalition forces. Visual inspection of the data plotted on a map clearly demonstrates that attacks have taken place in many areas of Iraq, but with a heavy concentration around Baghdad, and into the Anbar and Ninewa Governorates to the east and north of the capital, respectively. Considering attacks, there were a total of 5,537 recorded incidents that were not classified as IEDs: these include mortar, rocket, surface-to-air, sniper, and small arms attacks, as well as ambushes and grenades. Intuitively, the most significant distinction between the IED and non-IED categories of attacks is that the latter involve an immediate engagement between insurgents and counterinsurgents, whereas the former are spatially- and temporally- remote activities which, whilst often more capital intensive, are arguably less labour intensive.

The chapter proceeds as follows. First, we describe and employ procedures for identifying space-time clustering patterns in insurgent activities. Second, we present a series of tables and graphs to detail the patterns these procedures uncover. Third, we conclude by discussing the possible policy implications of these findings and offer a series of hypotheses regarding potential correlates of the observed patterns.

METHOD AND RESULTS

Identifying Space-Time Clustering

Analyses were conducted to determine whether (for both event types: IED and non-IED attacks) events occurred close to each other in space *and* time more than would be expected if timing and location were independent. The method used was a variant of that developed in epidemiology to test for disease contagion (see Knox, 1964; Besag and Diggle, 1977). It has been detailed elsewhere (Johnson et al., 2007), so only an overview will be provided here.

For a given data set, each event is compared to every other, and the geographic distance and time elapsed between each pair of events computed. This generates 1/2 n(n-1) comparisons. A contingency table which summarises the results (e.g., how many events occurred within 500 meters and 14 days of each other) is populated. The dimensions (i.e., the spatial and temporal bandwidths used) of the contingency table are selected to provide a sensitive analysis of the hypothesis tested, whilst ensuring that the observed cell frequencies are adequate for reliability. One might select a temporal bandwidth of one day to provide detail, but at this level of resolution, the cell frequencies may be too small. To ensure validity of inferences made, a range of space-time bandwidths was used. Since the same general pattern emerged for each combination, only those using intervals of 7 days and 500 meters are reported.

The contingency table generated to summarise the observed distribution is then compared with what would be expected if the timing and location of events were independent. To do this, the process described is repeated but using permutations of the data set in which the date on which the crimes occurred is randomised (or shuffled) across events.[8] As a full permutation is virtually impossible for even a moderately sized data set, a Monte Carlo (MC) simulation is used to draw a random sample of 99 permutations. The results of the MC simulation are then compared with the observed distribution, and the frequency with which each cell value for the observed distribution exceeds those for the permutation test recorded. The number of times that the observed cell frequency exceeds those generated by the MC simulation provides an estimate of the statistical significance of the results for that cell. For example, if an observed cell frequency exceeds those generated by the MC simulation only 50% of the time, this would indicate that the observed value would be expected roughly 50% of the time even if the location and timing of insurgent activities were independent. However, if the observed frequency for a particular cell exceeds the values generated during the MC simulation 95% of the time, then this would indicate that the observed result would be unlikely to occur under the null hypothesis. Formally, the statistical significance (see North et al., 2002) of an observed value for any particular cell is computed using Eq. (1).

$$p = \frac{rank}{n + 1}$$

Where n is the number of simulations, and $rank$ is the position of the observed value in a rank ordered array for that cell.

An indication of the size of the observed effect (or Knox ratio) can be derived by dividing the cell frequency for any particular cell by the median value generated by the MC simulation. To illustrate, a value of one so derived would indicate that the observed frequency for a cell was that expected under the null hypothesis. A value of two would indicate that twice as many events occurred within a given space-time proximity of each other as would be expected according to the null hypothesis. In the event that attacks (IED and non-IED) are clustered in space *and* time, the Knox ratios for the cells with the shortest space-time intervals will be above one, indicating that relative to expectation according to the null hypothesis, there is an over-representation of events close in space *and* time.

It is important to note that the approach to analysis takes account of the fact that some locations will be more attractive or accessible to insurgents than others, and that activity may be more intense at some points in time than others. The question of central importance is whether attacks cluster in space *and* time above and beyond what would be expected given these assumptions – evidence which would corroborate the expectation that insurgents act purposively to deploy their scarce resources most efficiently: namely, concentrated locally and episodically.

Results of the Knox Analysis

For the six month interval analysed (January-June 2005), there were a total of 3,775 IED attacks across Iraq which resulted in explosions. For unexploded IEDs the intended timing of the attack or the date on which the device was planted will be unknown; only the date on which the IED was uncovered will be available. For this reason, data for events of this type were excluded from analysis.

For each incident, data were available regarding the spatial location – accurate to a resolution of 100 meters – and the date of the attack. The results shown in Table 1 are based on 99 iterations of the MC simulation. In addition to showing the Knox ratios, to ease interpretation, each cell of the table is shaded in grayscale proportionate to the value of Knox ratio (e.g., a Knox ratio of 1.5 (1.1) would be shaded 50% (10%) grayscale). The findings confirm that IED attacks cluster in space *and* time. That is, while there may exist "hotspots" of activity, the patterns are also dynamic. When an IED attack occurs at one location there appears to be elevation in risk at locations within 2 kilometers for a period of around 14-21 days. The pattern generally conforms to one of spatio-temporal decay; decreasing as a function of time and space. It also appears that previously targeted locations are at an elevated risk between 28-35 days after a previous attack. This is not unlike the pattern observed by Berrebi and Lakdawalla (2007) for terrorist attacks in regional and national capital cities in Israel.

In line with the strategies discussed in the introduction, one interpretation of the patterns is that insurgents move and do so with an observable

Table 1: Space-Time Clustering of IED Attacks (statistically significant ratios in bold, p < 0.025)

		Days between events								
		<7	7-14	14-21	21-28	28-35	35-42	42-49	49-56	56-63
	≤500m	**1.49**	1.09	0.99	0.97	**1.13**	0.95	1.08	1.10	0.93
	500m-1km	**1.14**	**1.15**	**1.12**	1.04	1.00	0.99	0.99	1.08	**1.17**
	1-1.5km	**1.13**	**1.08**	1.04	1.03	1.05	1.07	1.10	1.06	0.99
Distance between events	1.5-2km	**1.06**	0.97	1.07	1.04	0.99	1.04	1.03	1.03	1.05
	2-2.5km	1.04	1.01	0.98	0.96	1.02	0.98	1.05	1.10	1.11
	2.5-3km	**1.13**	1.01	1.00	1.07	0.97	0.99	1.05	**1.15**	1.05
	3-3.5km	1.03	0.98	1.01	0.98	1.03	1.06	1.05	1.04	1.05
	3.5-4km	1.05	1.01	1.02	0.99	0.95	0.99	1.06	1.00	0.99
	4-4.5km	1.02	1.03	1.00	1.03	1.00	1.00	1.00	1.00	1.02
	4.5-5km	1.04	0.99	0.95	0.99	1.03	0.96	1.03	1.01	1.02

Note: The data were accurate to a resolution of 100 meters, and so an examination of attacks at the exact same location was not possible.

regularity but – in the short term at least – return to the locations of previous attacks when local defences once again permit. Without the addition of counterinsurgency data it is, of course, impossible to show that the patterns are generated by insurgents adopting such strategies, but the patterns are certainly consistent with this suggestion.

Table 2 shows the same analysis for the range of non-IED attacks. Again, it is evident that events cluster in space and time, but in this case the pattern is more diffused, with the risk of attack appearing to endure for longer and extending over longer distances. In other words, when a non-IED attack occurs at one location there is an elevated risk at proximate locations (interestingly, more distant locations than for IED attacks – up to 5 kilometers in this instance) for a period of 28-35 days. Though more diffuse than the pattern for IED attacks, non-IED attacks then also subsequently also conform to a pattern of spatio-temporal decay. Table 2

Table 2: Space-Time Clustering of Attacks (statistically significant ratios in bold, p < 0.025)

		<7	7-14	14-21	21-28	28-35	35-42	42-49	49-56	56-63
						Days between events				
Distance between events	≤500m	1.73	1.31	1.16	1.11	1.14	1.01	0.93	0.80	0.95
	500-1km	1.34	1.24	1.20	1.14	1.12	1.02	0.92	0.86	0.97
	1-1.5km	1.28	1.22	1.14	1.12	1.06	1.01	0.97	0.98	0.91
	1.5-2km	1.19	1.14	1.13	1.10	1.05	1.01	1.02	0.98	0.97
	2-2.5km	1.20	1.13	1.11	1.09	1.11	1.02	1.02	0.99	0.95
	2.5-3km	1.17	1.09	1.07	1.07	1.09	1.02	1.06	1.04	1.01
	3-3.5km	1.13	1.08	1.07	1.10	1.04	1.04	1.02	1.02	1.00
	3.5-4km	1.13	1.10	1.10	1.08	1.03	1.03	1.00	0.99	1.00
	4-4.5km	1.10	1.06	1.08	1.05	1.06	1.01	1.06	1.07	1.06
	4.5-5km	1.08	1.08	1.09	1.01	1.05	1.03	1.07	1.05	1.06

Note: The data were accurate to a resolution of 100 meters, and so an examination of attacks at the exact same location was not possible.

also demonstrates that at proximate locations, the risk of attack is lower than expected after seven weeks or so have elapsed.

The Duration of Risk Elevation

The general pattern observed – that events (of each type) which occur close to each other in space are more likely to also occur close to each other in time – could be generated by (at least) one of two processes. First, as the analysis so far presented examines only the space-time clustering of pairs of events, it is possible that the observed patterns could be generated by there being many more pairs of events occurring close to each other in space and time, but with there being very few instances where three or more events occur close to each other in space and time (Johnson & Bowers, 2004). Second, it is possible that the results are generated by three or more events clustering in space and time. The two possibilities are shown

Figure 1. Illustrations of different distributions that would generate the same patterns of space-time clustering in the analysis of pairs of events.

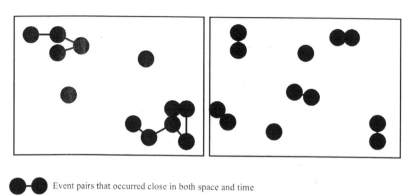

⬤▬⬤ Event pairs that occurred close in both space and time

⬤ Isolated events

in Figure 1. The operational implications of the findings for counter-insurgency practices vary according to what type of process generates the findings. If the latter, this means that once an attack occurs at a location a series of attacks are likely to occur swiftly nearby and hence that the allocation of resources to recent attack sites would be wise. If the former, such an allocation of resources would likely prove sub-optimal, making a different response strategy more appropriate.

An alternative approach to analysis involves the examination of poly-order chains of events that occur close in both space *and* time (Johnson et al., 2007; Townsley, 2007). This would provide an indication of the duration of localized increases in the likelihood of insurgent activity and answer the question "after how many attacks are insurgents likely to target new locations?" For example, if the longest clusters that could be identified generally consisted of only two events, this would suggest that rarely do insurgents sustain their targeting in the same locale for any period of time. To examine this issue, an algorithm was developed to identify series of events that occurred close in both space *and* time, ranging from two events (pairs) onwards. The approach allowed the frequency of different poly-order chains (e.g., pairs, triples, quads and so on) to be enumerated and compared with chance expectation, assuming that the timing and location of events are independent.

The identification and summary of series of events can be done in a variety of ways. Here, for every (reference) event of a given type (again,

IED or non-IED attacks), any antecedent event (of the same type) that occurred within a critical distance and time of it was identified and added to the series. Additionally, any events that occurred within the critical distance and time of one or more events already identified as part of that series were added to the chain. Thus, for every event, the aim of the analysis was to determine how many others had occurred nearby in the recent past.[9]

It is important to note that using this method it is possible that any chain identified could be part of a longer chain identified when considering (reference) events that occur later in the data. For example, if event E occurs on day 100 and four events (A,B,C and D) are identified that recently occurred near to it, this would be recorded as a chain of 5 events. If, on day 101, event G occurs near (in space and time) to events A-E, a chain of 6 events will be identified. For the two chains, there will be considerable overlap (five of the six events) in the members of the two sets. Other approaches to analysis exist, but this method allows us to answer the simple question "for how many events did N events previously occur nearby in space and time?," which is a question that is likely to have tactical implications. The fact that chain membership is likely to overlap is not a problem for interpretation of the analysis as the use of a permutation test allows us to compare the observed values with those expected, assuming the timing and location of events independent.[10]

In what follows the critical thresholds for inclusion in a chain were 500m and one-week, respectively. Other thresholds could, of course, be used and the length of the chains identified will be positively related to the thresholds selected. The selection of the thresholds should be informed by the purpose for which the analysis is undertaken. In an operational context, it may be more useful to employ a longer interval (say 1km). However, the aim of the analyses presented here was to illustrate the method and discuss the possible implications of the results.

For IED attacks, the longest series identified consisted of 10 attacks. Before discussing the differences between what was observed and what would be expected, it is important to note the implication of this finding, which is that it clearly illustrates the flux of attacks. If IED events occurred in the same places all the time, considerably longer series would have been identified. This suggests a need for a dynamic capability in the (re)deployment of resources. Simply defending the same areas over time is unlikely to direct resources to the right places at the right times.

Considering what would be expected if the timing and locations of events were independent, essentially the same approach as described in

Figure 2. Analysis of poly-order chains for IED attacks. (Note: y-axis is on a log scale.)

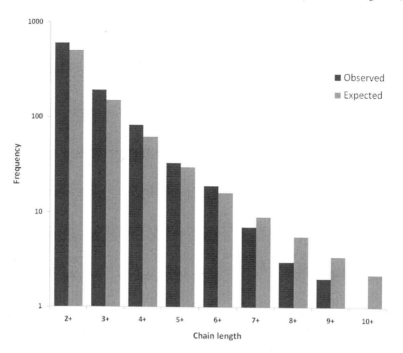

the previous section was used. That is, a permutation test was used such that across iterations of a Monte Carlo simulation, the timing and locations of events were shuffled. To establish p- values, for every iteration the results of the permutation were compared to the observed data. Figure 2 shows the mean frequencies for chains of each order (2, 3, 4 and so on) that would be expected assuming that there is no dependency regarding where *and* when IED attacks occur. There were significantly more chains of 2-4 events than would be expected if the timing and locations of attacks were independent (all ps<0.01). There were few chains of 5 or more events and the numbers observed did not exceed what would be expected on a chance basis, given (for example) the spatial distribution of IED attacks. More generally, the difference between the observed and expected frequencies decreases as a function of the order of chain considered. In a further analysis, a spatial threshold of 1 kilometer was used to identify chains. In this case, the longest chain identified was obviously longer (25 events), but the same general pattern – of the observed and expected frequencies converging at longer chain orders – was observed.

Figure 3. Analysis of poly-order chains for non-IED attacks. (Note: y-axis is on a log scale.)

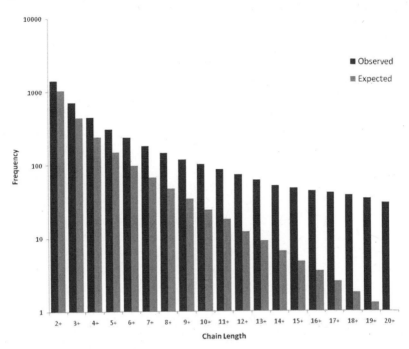

For attacks, the longest chain was 32 events. For the purposes of illustration, Figure 3 shows the observed and expected frequencies for chains up to 20 events or more long. The differences between the expected and observed frequencies were statistically significant for all chain lengths and it is evident that, in contrast to the pattern for IED attacks, the difference between the observed and expected frequencies actually increases for higher chain orders.[11]

Thus, the profile for attacks is very different to that for IED attacks. Simply put, non-IED attacks – including small arms fire and RPG and mortar attacks – appear to be sustained around the same location for longer intervals than do IED attacks. This difference clearly warrants additional investigation. We would suggest that perhaps this can be explained by variance in choices made by insurgents acting strategically to overcome counterinsurgency practices. For instance, IED attacks – having consistently been identified as the greatest threat to Coalition troops – attract greater counterinsurgency resources. Accordingly, rational insurgents looking to optimise their application of scarce resources may be more likely to employ a roving strategy in order to circumvent counterinsurgency forces.

Discussion

Patterns of insurgent activity will be a function of many things. In this chapter we have focused on how recent activity might inform the timing and location of future attacks. It appears that for both types of attack (IED and non-IED), the recent locations of events provide useful markers for where future ones will next occur (see also, Townsley et al., 2007). However, the period of time over which historic events offer predictive value appears to vary across attack types. Of the two types considered, the space-time patterns of IEDs seem to be more abrupt, possibly suggesting (as already argued) a more deliberate strategy on the part of insurgents. It also appears to be the case that for IED attacks, the risk of further incidents within a previously targeted locality quickly subsides but then increases again around one month later. This chimes with the findings of Berrebi and Lakdawalla (2007) who – using a different methodology – found a similar pattern for terrorist attacks in politically sensitive cities of Israel (but not in other areas). Further investigation of the reliability of this finding is warranted. So too is the investigation of any factors that might indicate when further (delayed) attacks are likely and when they are not.

In the research reported, we presented analyses of the patterns for the two types of attack independently. Had we not done so, we would have failed to uncover the differences in the patterns for the two types of attack and the consequent implications they might have for counterinsurgent forces. Separating the types of attack in this way follows the tradition of those who study situational facilitators of crime opportunities. Such researchers (e.g., Clarke, 1997) have long since suggested that where analyses are conducted to uncover preventive solutions to a given crime *problem* (such as burglary) it will be necessary to separate the crime events into more specific sub-types, where possible. For instance, for burglaries where entry is gained via the rear of a property (which amongst other things affords the offender stealth), the preventive solution is likely to be quite different than where it is gained via the front. In the same way it is important to distinguish different types of insurgent attack; after all, the resources required, the organization necessary and the availability of suitable targets, are likely to vary by attack type.

In addition to studying attack types separately, further analyses might be conducted to see if the space-time patterns for one type of attack are independent of those of the others, or if there exist associations between when and where different types of attack occur. Put another way, following a non-IED insurgent attack at a given location, is it the case that the risk of an IED (or other type of) attack is elevated at proximate locations in the near future? An approach to analysis – which has been applied to the analysis of crime data – has been articulated elsewhere (Johnson et al., 2009) so we will not discuss the method further here. However, it is worth saying that this type of analysis might inform approaches to next event prediction. The general finding that insurgent attacks cluster in space and time has predictive value, and the analyses of poly-order chains offer additional insights by showing how many attacks of a given type are likely to occur within a particular space-time interval of previous events. However, it is possible that still further insight may be provided by the analysis of inter-attack type patterns of insurgent activity.

These findings may (for example) be used to refine existing methods of next event predictions, such as *prospective mapping* (Bowers et al., 2004; Johnson et al., 2007; Johnson et al., 2008). Briefly, this approach to hotspot derivation departs from traditional methods by considering the timing of events as well as their location, along with features of the urban backcloth that might affect crime placement. In analyses so far conducted (Bowers et al., 2004; Johnson et al., 2007; Johnson et al., 2008), the approach has been shown to be more accurate than contending alternatives. An obvious next step would be to see how accurate this type of approach is in the forecasting of when and where insurgent attacks are most likely, and how efficient any search strategies based upon such predictions might be.

More generally, further investigation of spatial variation in risk will be useful. As a starting point, enumerating those locations most (least) at risk will be helpful. Clarke and Newman (2006; Newman and Clarke, 2008) have developed the EVIL DONE acronym to describe those types of location that terrorists are most likely to favor in the USA; these being those that are Exposed, Vital, Iconic, Legitimate, Destructible, Occupied, Near, and Easy. Boba (this volume) provides an illustration of how this type of analysis may be implemented using spatially referenced data and a geographical information system. In further work we aim to collate data on features of the urban environment for the Iraq region so that correlates of insurgent activity might be identified. This type of work will require the use of spatial models sensitive to the effects of unmeasured variables (e.g., see Anselin and Kelejian, 1997) so that any patterns so identified do not result from spurious associations.

Counterinsurgent tactics will also be a salient influence on space-time patterns of insurgent activity, either attracting or deflecting it. We are currently in the process of exploring the possibility of modeling the influence of insurgent/counter-insurgent interactions using both real world data and computer simulations (for an example of the application of agent based modeling in the investigation of insurgent activity, see also N. F. Johnson, 2006).

The approach to analysis discussed here is relatively simple, but we believe it provides insight that might otherwise go unnoticed or would be unconfirmed. The findings suggest different strategies are likely to be warranted for different types of attack and that attacks occur with a regularity which is likely to make them predictable.

In closing we speculate on how the results suggest counter-insurgency resources might be allocated. First, it appears, for instance, that rapid and localised allocations may help to protect locales from the spectre of IED attacks, but a more sustained presence at IED hotspots (potentially covert) may prove beneficial, particularly if research identifies those types of location at which the risk of attack is likely to initially decrease only to subsequently rise again.

Second, one interpretation of the above findings – which resemble a slow pattern of spatial diffusion – is that non-IED attacks are not targeted against iconic locations but, rather, against Coalition forces that are locally present. If this is the case, then it may be wise to allocate defences more uniformly so as to minimize the density of targets (in this case clusters of Coalition forces) that might attract insurgent attention. Additional effort focused on proactively stemming the flow of arms and munitions might be more effective than simply reacting to new attacks. Again, each of these hypotheses warrants investigation with more detailed data.

Address correspondence to: Shane D. Johnson, Jill Dando Institute of Crime Science, University College London, Second Floor Brook House, 2-16 Torrington Place, London, WC1E 7HN, UK; e-mail: shane.johnson@ucl.ac.uk

Acknowledgments: The authors would like thank Mike Townsley and the editors of this book for comments on an earlier version of this chapter.

NOTES

1. For instance, the United Kingdom in Malaya and the United States in Vietnam did just this in the mid-twentieth century.
2. For more comprehensive treatment of the variety of definitions offered for "terrorism" and "insurgency" in the broader social science literature, see Schmid & Jongman (1988) and Hoffman (2006).
3. Figures come from the U.S. Department of Defense's "Measuring Stability and Security in Iraq" report to Congress from December 2008.
4. For an excellent example of research which examines changes in patterns of insurgency over time, see N. F. Johnson (2008).
5. Casualty data are available at www.globalsecurity.org and www.defenselink.mil.
6. This Center is run by the Aegis Specialist Risk Management Group on behalf of the MNF-I. Details: https://brief.aegisiraq.com
7. Examples of work on geographic profiling of insurgent activities can be found online at: http://www.nta.org/docs/Geoprofiling.pdf / and http://www.tec.army.mil/publications/GeoProMilCap.pdf
8. As the location of events is preserved, risk heterogeneity – the fact that some places and some periods of time are more risky than others – is accounted for in the analysis.
9. The number of longer chains will be somewhat underestimated as the data are only available for a six month window of time. This creates a temporal edge effect. In some respects this is not problematic as the observed patterns are compared to those expected, given that there is an edge effect.
10. As a permutation test is used, the assumption of independence – a requirement of traditional statistical tests – is not a requirement.
11. Additional analyses that used a 1 kilometer threshold generated the same general patterns. That is, the observed frequencies were always larger than those expected and the ratio of the two increased with chain order. The longest chain identified in this case was 89 events.

REFERENCES

Anselin, L., & Kelejian, H. H. (1997). Testing for spatial error autocorrelation in the presence of endogenous regressors. *International Regional Science Review*, *20*, 153–182.

Bell, J. B. (1978). *A time of terror: How democratic societies respond to revolutionary Violence*. New York: Basic Books.

Berrebi, C., & Lakdawalla, D.. (2007). How hoes terrorism risk vary across space and time? An analysis based upon the Israeli experience. *Defense and Peace Economics, 18*(2), 113.

Besag, J. & Diggle, P. (1977). Simple Monte Carlo tests for spatial pattern. *Applied Statistics, 26*, 327–333

Bloom, M. (2005). *Dying to kill: The allure of suicide terrorism.* New York: Columbia University Press.

Bowers, K. J., Johnson, S. D., & Pease, K. (2004). Prospective hot-spotting: The future of crime mapping? *British Journal of Criminology, 44*, 641–658.

Bueno de Mesquita, E. (2005). The quality of terror. *American Journal of Political Science, 49*(3), 515–530.

Carr, C. (1997). Terrorism as warfare: The lessons of military history. *World Policy Journal, 31*(1), 1–8.

Clarke, R. V. (1997). *Situational crime prevention: Successful case studies* (2nd ed.). Monsey, NY: Criminal Justice Press.

Clarke, R. V., & Newman, G. (2006). *Outsmarting the terrorists.* Westport, Conn: Praeger Security International.

Cothren, J., Smith, B. L., Roberts, P. & Damphousse, K. (2008). Geospatial and temporal patterns of preparatory conduct among American Terrorists. *International Journal of Comparative and Applied Criminal Justice, 32*(1), 23–42.

Crenshaw, M. (1981). The causes of terrorism. *Comparative Politics, 13*(4), 379–399.

Crenshaw, M. (1998). The logic of terrorism: Terrorist behavior as a product of strategic choice. In W. Reich (Ed.), *Origins of Terrorism: Psychologies, Ideologies, Theologies, States of Mind* (pp.7–24. Washington, DC: Woodrow Wilson Center Press.

Fromkin, D. (1975). The strategy of terrorism. *Foreign Affairs* (July), 683–698.

Garamone, J. (2004). Armored humvees, tactics address IED threats. *American Forces Press Service*, December 8th.

Hewitt, C. (1993). *Consequences of political violence.* Aldershot, UK: Dartmouth.

Hoffman, B. (2006). *Inside terrorism* (2nd ed.). New York: Columbia University Press.

Johnson, N. F. (2006). The mother (nature) of all wars? Modern wars, global terrorism, and complexity science. *APS News, 15*(10), 8.

Johnson, N. F. (2008). Complexity in human conflict. In D. Helbing (Ed.), *Managing complexity: Insights, concepts, applications.* Berlin: Springer.

Johnson, S. D., Bernasco, W., Bowers, K. J., Elffers, H., Ratcliffe, J., Rengert, G., & Townsley, M. T. (2007). Space-time patterns of risk: A cross national assessment of residential burglary victimization. *Journal of Quantitative Criminology, 23*, 201–219.

Johnson, S. D., & Bowers, K. J. (2004).The stability of space-time clusters of burglary. *British Journal of Criminology, 44*, 55–65.

Johnson, S. D., Birks, D., McLaughlin, L., Bowers, K. J., & Pease, K. (2007). Prospective mapping in operational context. Home Office online Report 19/ 07. Home Office: London.

Johnson, S. D., Bowers, K. J., Birks, D. & Pease, K. (2008). Predictive mapping of crime by ProMap: Accuracy, units of analysis and the environmental backcloth. In D. Weisburd, W. Bernasco, & G. Bruinsma (Eds.), *Putting crime in its place: Units of analysis in spatial crime research.* New York: Springer.

Johnson, S.D., Summers, L., Pease, K. (2009). Offender as forager? A direct test of the boost account of victimization. *Journal of Quantitative Criminology, 25*, 181–200.

Knox, G. (1964). Epidemiology of childhood leukaemia in Northumberland and Durham. *British Journal of Preventive Social Medicine, 18*, 17–24.

Kydd, A., & Walter, B. (2006). The strategies of terrorism. *International Security, 31*(1), 49–80.

Lacquer, W. (1977). *Terrorism.* London: Weidenfeld & Nicholson.

LaFree, G., & Dugan, L., Korte, R. (2009). The impact of British counter terrorist strategies on political violence in Northern Ireland: Comparing deterrence and backlash models. *Criminology, 47*(1), 17–46.

Lapan, H., & Todd, S. (1993). Terrorism and signaling. *European Journal of Political Economy, 9*(3), 383–397.

Marighella, C. (1969). *Minimanual of the urban guerrilla.* Retrieved online at: http://www.marxists.org/archive/marighella-carlos/1969/06/minimanual-urban-guerrilla/

McCauley, C. (2006). Jujitsu politics: Terrorism and response to terrorism. In P. R. Kimmel & & C. E. Stout (Eds.), *Collateral damage: The psychological consequences of America's war on terrorism* (pp. 45–65). Westport, CT: Praeger.

Metz, S. (2003). Insurgency and counterinsurgency in Iraq. *The Washington Quarterly, 27*(1), 25–36.

Miles, D. (2005). Defeating IEDs demands going after munitions source. *American Forces Press Service*, June 22nd.

Miles, D. (2006). DoD tap industry know-how in ongoing counter-IED efforts. *American Forces Press Service*, January 24th.

Newman, G., & Clarke, R. V. (2008). *Policing terrorism: An executives guide.* US Department of Justice.

North, B. V., Curtis, D., & Sham, P. C. (2002). A note on the calculation of empirical p values from Monte Carlo procedures. *American Journal of Human Genetics, 71*, 439–441.

Pape, R. (2003). The strategic logic of suicide terrorism. *American Political Science Review, 97*, 343–361.

Pape, R. (2005). *Dying to win.* New York: Random House.

Pridemore, W. A., & Freilich, J. D. (2007). The impact of state laws protecting abortion clinics and reproductive rights: Deterrence, backlash, or neither? *Law and Human Behavior, 316*, 611–627.

Rossmo, K., Harries, K., & McGarrell, E. (2008). *Expanding the frontiers of crime prevention: New problems in new environments.* Paper presented to the Environmental Criminology and Crime Analysis meeting, Izmir, Turkey, 17–19 March.

Ryu, A. (2005). Roadside bombs cause increasing concern in Iraq. *Voice of America.* 28th September.

Schmid, A., & Jongman, A. (1988). *Political terrorism: A new guide to actors, Authors, concepts, data bases, theories, and literature.* New Brunswick, NJ: Transaction.

Smith, S. D. (2006). Terrorists can't face our forces in battle, so they use IEDs, Bush says." *Armed Forces Press Service*, March 13th.

Thornton, T. (1964). Terror as a weapon of political agitation. In H. Eckstein (Ed.), *Internal War* (pp. 71–99). New York: Free Press.

Townsley, M. T. (2007). *Near repeat burglary chains: describing the physical and network properties of a network of close burglary pairs.*

Townsley, M., Homel, R. & Chaseling, J. (2003). Infectious burglaries: A test of the near repeat hypothesis. *British Journal of Criminology, 43*, 615–633.

Townsley, M. T. Johnson, S. D., & Ratcliffe, J. R. (2008). Space-Time Dynamics of Insurgent Activity in Iraq. *Security Journal, 21*(3), 139–146.

U.S. Department of State. (2003). *Patterns of global terrorism.* Washington, DC: U.S. Department of State.

White, J. (2003). *Terrorism: 2002 update* (4th ed.). Belmont, CA: Wadsworth/ Thomson Learning.

Wilkinson, P. (1986). *Terrorism and the liberal state.* London: MacMillan.

Wilkinson, P. (2000). The strategic implications of terrorism. In M. L. Sondhi (Ed.), *Terrorism and political violence: A Sourcebook.* Indian Council of Social Sciences: Haranand Publications.

REDUCING TERRORIST OPPORTUNITIES: A FRAMEWORK FOR FOREIGN POLICY

Graeme R. Newman
University at Albany, SUNY

Abstract: *Major counter-terrorism foreign policy of the U.S. and other Western nations has been driven by traditional strategies based on concepts of nation states using economic and military power to exploit and maintain access to natural resources and labor markets. While these policies have contributed to the vibrant global markets of the 21st century and unprecedented economic development in many developing countries, they have also created ample opportunities for terrorists, helping them reach their targets and kill with greater efficiency and lethality. Using an approach adopted from situational crime prevention, it is argued that counter-terrorism foreign policy must focus on reducing opportunities for terrorists in two different ways: (1) by identifying the characteristics of globalization that provide opportunities for terrorists to carry out their attacks successfully, and (2) by understanding the specificity of terrorist attacks at the local level so that opportunity-reducing techniques can be tailored to address each specific kind of terrorist attack. This approach will serve to directly link foreign policy that is traditionally confined to treaties and geopolitical debates, to actual operations on the ground.*

Crime Prevention Studies, volume 25 (2009), pp. 33–59.

Introduction: Situational Crime Prevention and Terrorist Opportunity

Clarke and Newman (2006) demonstrated that terrorist behavior could be understood in the same way that we understand much criminal behavior. If we "think thief" (Ekblom 2002) we can understand and anticipate the decisions and logical steps that thieves must take in order to steal credit cards, cars, jewelry, electronic goods, or identities and convert them into cash. So too with terrorist behavior. We can identify the steps taken by terrorists to carry out specific kinds of terrorist attacks. Suicide bombings of restaurants require different planning than remote detonation of a bomb in a railway carriage. This approach leads logically to identifying the opportunities of which terrorists take advantage. Many of these opportunities occur in the everyday social and economic arrangements that we take for granted, indeed, are a necessary part of normal commerce. Clarke and Newman (2006) classified the opportunities for terrorists into four kinds: (1) targets, (2) weapons, (3) tools, and (4) facilitating conditions.

The Four Pillars of Terrorist Opportunity

1. *Targets.* Eight characteristics of targets make them attractive to terrorists. They may be:

   Exposed (the Twin Towers were sitting ducks)

   Vital (electricity grids, transportation systems, communications)

   Iconic (of symbolic value to the enemy, e.g., Taj Hotel in Bombay)

   Legitimate (terrorists' sympathizers cheered when the Twin Towers collapsed)

   Destructible (Twin Towers were not indestructible)

   Occupied (kill as many people as possible)

   Near (within reach of terrorist group, close to home)

   Easy (a car bomb placed within 8 feet of Murrah Federal Building in Oklahoma City)

2. *Weapons.* Nine characteristics of weapons make them attractive to terrorists:

Multi-purpose: Explosives have more application than a rifle, but can't be reused.

Undetectable: Plastic explosive is used because it is easy to conceal.

Removable: Small arms are light weight and portable.

Destructive: Explosives kill and destroy more than a handgun.

Enjoyable: Terrorists like their weapons and become attached to them.

Reliable: If a weapon doesn't work, a mission may fail.

Obtainable: Can it be bought or stolen easily?

Uncomplicated: Is it easy to use?

Safe: Using IEDs is more dangerous than using guns.

3. *Tools available for conducting the mission.* Tools of terrorism are products that are used in the course of an attack. Among these important and essential (depending on the mission) products for conducting terrorism are: rented or stolen vehicles; mobile phones, cash and credit cards; false or stolen documents such as passports and driving licenses; and information about targets such as maps, timetables and schedules. It will be noted that many of these tools that terrorists use are also tools that ordinary offenders use: stolen cars, stolen mobile phones, false or stolen identities.

4. *Facilitating conditions.* These are the social and physical arrangements of modern society that make specific acts of terrorism possible (Napoleoni, 2005). They make it ESEER for terrorists to carry out their missions:

Easy: Officials susceptible to corruption; traditional non-bank monetary system.

Safe: Few ID requirements for monetary or retail transactions.

Excusable: Family member previously killed by local anti-terrorist action.

Enticing: Local culture/religion endorses heroic acts of violence.

Rewarding: Financial support available from local charities to new immigrants.

These pillars of opportunity operate at both a global and local level. For example, in order for terrorists to carry out a suicide bombing on a routine basis, they must have available a steady supply of appropriate explosives, which is made possible by the global trade in weaponry. They must have adequate resources to buy weapons and pay benefits to families of suicide bombers, money which comes from sources around the world, such as Islamic charities in the case of Al Qaeda. At the local level, however, the terrorists must have a detailed knowledge of the target locations and their accessibility, contact with local suppliers of weapons, ways of obtaining tools that are untraceable, and conditions that make their operations in the locality easier to undertake without detection. The first step in understanding this locality-driven aspect of terrorism is to focus on the specific economic, physical, cultural and social environment on the ground in which terrorists operate. By identifying these, we can then proceed to trace the links between those acts that are essentially local and the global conditions that both enhance and constrain them.

TERRORISM AT THE LOCAL LEVEL

The four pillars of terrorist opportunity identify the opportunities that have, depending on historical circumstances, always been present for terrorists who must, in the first place, be successful in their attacks on the ground. This means that they must choose, above all, the location in which they will operate – whether on a routine basis or as a one-off attack – and within that location, the target they will attack. It should be emphasized that these choices are *entwined* in the local conditions, as Kenney (2006) has so well demonstrated. Knowing how to make a bomb is very different from the experience of knowing how and where to place it at the target. Doing a bombing in the streets of Baghdad is an entirely different undertaking to doing a bombing in Bombay, for example. In fact, in the case of the terrorist attacks in Bombay in December of 2008, terrorists demonstrated their knowledge of the local flaws in security to easily penetrate their targets (entering the Taj hotel through an unsecured back door, for example). So the operational choices will be driven by local conditions and opportunities which will, in turn, be defined by the attractive features of the targets, the availability of weapons and tools of terrorism and the presence of facilitating conditions. These are summarized in Table 1 in the form of a checklist that a police chief of mayor of a town or city may draw up in order to identify places that are more likely to be the focus of terrorist attack, or terrorist activity. This table is schematic, providing only a very limited sample of the opportunities available to terrorists at the

Table 1:   Local Opportunities for Terrorism

TARGETS

How many targets in this locality rate high on EVIL DONE characteristics?	Number
Exposed	
Vital	
Iconic	
Legitimate	
Destructible	
Occupied	
Near	
Easy	
Total	

WEAPONS (Easily available=3, Available=2, Not available=1)	Score
How available are weapons from local sources (legal markets, illegal markets, theft from military facilities, theft from construction sites)?	
Small arms (handguns, single action rifles, shotguns, etc.)	
Machine guns, grenades, rocket powered grenades	
Conventional explosives (e.g., semtex, mines)	
Materials for IEDs (improvised explosive devices: obtained from hardware stores, chemical factories, etc.)	
Materials for WMDs (research facilities, hospitals, nuclear facilities)	
Total	

TOOLS (Very difficult=3, Difficult=2, Easy=1)	Score
How difficult is it to:	
Rent a truck with a false ID	
Steal a car without getting caught	
Obtain a false driving license or other document (birth certificate, passport)	
Rent a house in a neighborhood without being noticed	
Obtain or steal a mobile phone	
Total	

Table 1 *(continued)*

FACILITATING CONDITIONS (Yes=3, Maybe=2, No=1)	Score
Could terrorists take cover in local communities?	
Is there corruption in local government?	
Are there lax ID authentication practices in government and businesses?	
Do local religious or political groups actively support immigrants?	
Have there been local anti-terrorism reprisals?	
Rewarding: Local charities assist immigrants (legal or illegal)	
Total	

local level. For a more detailed account, see Newman and Clarke (2008). It is also confined to examples of opportunity that prevail at the local level. However many local opportunities are conditioned by, or are dependent on, global conditions.

GLOBALIZATION AND TERRORIST OPPORTUNITY

Globalization is the historical process, fueled by technology, that has seen the increased ease of movement of capital, goods, labor and services around the world; the rise of a global media accompanied by an information revolution that has reached into every home, even the homes of those in least developed countries; rapid migration of people from poorer to richer parts of the globe; the rise of global markets and manufacturing; increased wealth of emerging economies; and political instability that typically accompanies rapid historical change. Of these, probably technology is the most important since, as Schneier (2006, p. 87) has argued, "Throughout history technology has changed the power balance between attacker and defender." The ways in which the balance of power has been tipped in favor of the attackers through enhanced opportunities of globalization are summarized in Table 2.

If we take but one example from Table 2, the communication revolution, we can easily see how globalization has created and enhanced opportunities for terrorists.

Table 2: Globalization and the Enhancement of Terrorist Opportunity

Globalization	New or enhanced opportunities
TARGETS More airplanes and ships	• Airplanes easy targets for destruction, hostage taking, ships easy targets for piracy
More attractive buildings and facilities	• More high rise buildings increase number of densely populated targets • Skyscrapers are exposed targets • Security not built into the design of buildings
Global deployment of personnel	Governments and nationally recognized companies easier targets when their personnel and facilities are located close to terrorist base
WEAPONS Political instability	• WMD technology sold or stolen by rogue states
World glut of conventional weapons	• Political instability more easily morphs into violent protest with weapons availability • Organized crime enhances illegal arms market
Improved technology of weaponry	• Conventional weapons made more lethal, efficient, portable, concealable, available, affordable • Increased lethality and efficiency of weapons increases range of targets that are accessible or destructible • New detonation techniques increase range of targets that are accessible or destructible
TOOLS Communications revolution	• Mobile phones make terrorist group operations more efficient • Terrorist groups recruit members on Internet • Internet facilitates communication with terrorist operatives • Terrorists disseminate videos of hostages and killings on Internet to supplement network news coverage

(continued)

Table 2 (*continued*)

	• Information on bomb making, target locations etc. available on the Internet
	• Internet facilitates anonymous communication
Transportation efficiency	• Increased air travel offers many opportunities for attack, hostage taking, use of airplanes as weapons, suicide attacks
	• Technology makes production of false identities easier
	• Car and truck rental made easy by credit cards
	• Mass container shipping offers ready smuggling tool

FACILITATING CONDITIONS

Movement of capital	• International financial markets make money laundering easier
	• Financial markets create conditions in which terrorists and organized criminals have common interests
Movement of goods and services	• World wide proliferation of weapons
	• Weapons trade links organized crime to terrorism
	• Drug trafficking source of money to terrorists
	• Human trafficking makes crossing borders easier
Global media (publicity)	• TV and mass media magnify impact of terrorist attacks
	• Mass media exposes government excesses in responding to terrorism
Movement of people	• Migration, forced and unforced makes crossing borders much easier
	• Terrorists can reach distant targets more easily
	• Immigrant groups may be exploited at site of target

1. *Violent attacks create opportunities for global media.* Terrorist attacks, especially if they occur in a hot spot of international conflict (e.g., Palestine) feed the gluttony of 24 hour news coverage. Many of the global news media networks could not hold their audiences without such attacks.

2. *Terrorist attacks, especially if routine, provide conditions in which new alternative news networks may be created and flourish.* Al Jazeera, the television network, is a prime example. These alternative networks provide imagery of attacks that differ markedly from those offered in the Western media. They now offer a significant source for terrorists to market their propaganda and are routinely used by terrorists to enhance ongoing terrorist attacks, such as in releasing videos of pleading hostages.

3. *Terrorist attacks are magnified by the media that cover them.* Brief, very violent attacks are constantly repeated on news networks. Drawn out terrorist attacks such as those that include hostages, as in the November 2008 Bombay attacks, command constant global media coverage until they are resolved, sometimes over days, even weeks.

4. *Government (over)reactions to terrorist attacks are magnified by global media.* The Western and alternative media news coverage of Guantanamo Bay, Abu Ghraib prison, the trial of Saddam Hussein all served to magnify government excesses and intrusions on human rights – enough to serve as cover for the abuses of human rights that are the obvious immediate result of terrorist attacks. Thus, the distinction between the "good guys" and "bad guys" is blurred considerably.[1]

5. *Terrorist violence broadcasts an intense ideological message.* Al Qaeda found soon after its 9/11 attack that its message was relayed everywhere, but more importantly everywhere there were Muslims. The result was a rash of attacks that echoed their ideology in many parts of the world.

IMPLICATIONS FOR FOREIGN POLICY

All terrorism is local. Terrorism before the 21st century, with some few exceptions, was largely confined to specific locations, usually within particular countries or regions.[2] There are three reasons for this. First, the location of targets is a primary concern for terrorists, so that they are likely to attack those that are close to their base of operations and where conditions facilitate their operations, such as in planning and reconnaissance (Clarke & Newman, 2006; Hamm, 2007; Cothren et al., 2008;

Rossmo et al., 2008; Berrebi & Lakdawalla, 2006). Second, attacking targets that are far from the home base, such as in another country, requires transportation and communications, which bring additional difficulties for planning and logistics for the terrorists. Weapons must be transported, personnel must cross borders secretly, money must be gotten to the terrorists, etc. Even in the 20th century, a period when the movement of money and materiel were facilitated by rapidly increasing globalization in the latter half of that century, the major terrorist undertakings that could be sustained over a substantial period of years were essentially local or regional: in Northern Ireland, Israel and the occupied territories of Palestine, the Shining Path in Peru, the Marxist revolution in Cuba, various other Marxist inspired movements in Latin America and Asia, and the PKK (Kurdish separatists) in Turkey. These terrorist groups were able to sustain their attacks for many years because their activities were confined to specific locations within their country of operation ("domestic terrorism"), or the terrorists were able to operate from a base established just across the border in a neighboring country. When these terrorist operations take hold, they do, of course, threaten the stability of the nations that they attack, which leads to the third reason.[3]

While terrorism of the past has been directed at specific governments, it has also been directed at achieving control over land that defines the boundaries or nationality of the government which terrorists wish to topple, such as in the Balkans. *Terrorism is directed at people not governments.* Terrorism of the 21st century may be directed at specific governments, but it is also directed at changing the hearts and minds of those who globally are able to observe and follow their exploits. Thus, modern terrorists cannot lose a war in the traditional sense, since the fight is not over occupying territory but rather over occupying the minds of people everywhere. Even in locations where occupying territory appears to be the major point of contention, such as in the occupied territories in Palestine, the tenor of terrorist attacks has been primarily addressed to the media. There is no better example than the declaration to the world by Hassan Nasrallah, leader of Hezbollah, of "victory" over the Israelis who invaded Lebanon in 2006, even though in the traditional sense Hezbollah had "given up territory."[4]

Global does not mean networked. If terrorism occurs globally and in regions, does this mean that all these acts are connected in any planned way? Terrorists have traditionally used tactics that magnify their exploits to make them appear more powerful than they are; this is a well known tactic of "asymmetrical" warfare. However, they do not adopt this technique as a new policy of warfare, but because circumstances demand it. Their acts scattered around the world may appear similar in methodology or even in message, but they are similar because of the common opportunities of which they take advantage, not because the methods of attack have been exported by a cunning super-organized terrorist group based somewhere in Pakistan and Afghanistan. Rather, they are confined to exploiting the opportunities afforded them by the conditions (e.g., a friendly local community, easily accessible targets) that prevail in their location or region (Clarke and Newman, 2006; Hamm, 2007). Sageman (2008) has demonstrated that the terrorism of Islamic jihadists has changed from those directed from Al Qaeda central command, to home grown jihadists in immigrant communities who, inspired via the Internet by Al Qaeda, attack their domestic governments.

Toppling governments is of secondary importance to 21st century terrorists. Spheres of influence are still occupied by nations, not terrorist groups, though terrorists may be exploited by nations. It may be that Al Qaeda does occupy a sphere of influence somewhere between the border of Afghanistan and Pakistan, but what *nation* would really care about influence over such inconsequential territory, where there are few natural resources and the labor force is less than useful? It may be argued that Osama Bin Laden, leader of Al Qaeda, would gain considerably if he could expand his influence in this region to take over Pakistan and thus its nuclear technology. But if he did so, the battle would revert to a traditional one that Bin Laden has so far avoided (except in his initial defeat in Afghanistan in the aftermath of 9/11): one nation against many, and a few nuclear weapons against thousands. The battle lines would be drawn in a new cold war, one similar to that won by the U.S. in the 20th century. Thus, spheres of influence in the traditional sense of foreign policy apply less to the acquisition or occupation of territory (or even possession of weapons of mass destruction) and more to the influence over the ideological and religious propaganda that is imparted to people everywhere. Although Al Qaeda has ramped up its attacks on Afghanistan, one doubts that the goal is to take over that nation. Why would Bin Laden want to occupy Afghanistan and thus become a nation, exposing himself to the traditional forms of warfare between nation states, one of which he has already lost? It is far more effective not to win such a war, but like a sore that will not heal, to continue exploiting the global opportunities of terrorist enhancement, constantly feeding the ideological message of Al Qaeda to people everywhere.

Terrorist attacks disaggregate allies. The reportage of government excesses serves to inflame public outrage in democracies which, in turn, puts pressure on politicians. The result is that some members of an allied coalition, such as the Iraq war, are pressured to withdraw their support. The withdrawal of Spanish support of the coalition in Iraq, the result of an election that was directly affected by the terrorist attack on trains in Madrid, is a clear example. Berrebi and Klor (2006, 2008) have demonstrated this effect of terrorist attacks on elections in Israel.

Terrorists are, nevertheless, outsiders. Globalization in the 21st century has increased the opportunities for terrorists to carry out more effective and efficient attacks, but it has not changed the facts of their situation: that is, they remain a minority as they always have been; they must manage their affairs in secret, they must devise ways of getting financial support, they must try to make themselves appear more powerful than they are, they must still make the dangerous trip to their target and they must constantly recruit new members. They are therefore constantly vulnerable and have many points of weakness which a situational crime prevention approach can target. These weaknesses, which essentially reflect their dependence on the four pillars of terrorist opportunity, should inform any foreign policy designed to counter terrorism. Failure to understand terrorism from this point of view has led to several foreign policy blunders.

MISTAKES OF THE PAST

1. Mistaking terrorism for a nation without borders

If terrorist groups like Al Qaeda are beholden to no nation, or represent no nation, foreign policy that is based traditionally on dealing with nations has great difficulty in directing its actions against such an entity. In fact, while foreign policymakers recognize this difficulty, at the same time, they implement policies that link the terrorists to nations, such as the "axis of evil" identified in President Bush's speech soon after the 9/11 attack. This speech did much to transform the idea of terrorism as an ideology that knew no borders into the traditional terms of nation-based foreign policy. One strand of this policy led to the invasion of Iraq as a kind of substitute for the "nation of terrorism." Critics of that war quickly denounced it as "another Vietnam" in which the U.S. would be stuck in a quagmire with no exit plan. In fact, the Vietnam War was a good example of this mistaken foreign policy, buttressed by the "domino theory" that, if not stopped in its tracks, communism would spread to other neighboring countries. This error grew from the view of foreign policy as concerned with the geopolitical positioning of nations, rather than taking note of the ways in which communism spread by infection, not unlike any virus, which does not recognize borders. The same holds true for the spread of the Islamic extremism of Al Qaeda.

However, there is a persuasive argument to direct foreign policy at nations that provide opportunities for terrorists to operate. Such nations are many – those that make crossing borders easier by providing passports with little authentication; those that give safe haven for terrorists by allowing training camps; those that export massive amounts of weaponry without controls to terrorists or to middlemen who sell to terrorists; those that share nuclear technology freely and without sufficient controls; those that allow banks to behave freely without knowing their customers, thus making money laundering easier. In fact, if we made a complete list, there would be few countries that would not be represented as providing or increasing opportunities for terrorists. The U.S. State Department has adopted just this approach in its annual review of all nations' efforts, or lack thereof, to reduce opportunities for human trafficking (U.S. State Department, 2008). It needs to do the same for terrorism. While it is true that the U.S. State Department does publicize a list of states that support terrorism, the criteria for this list are unknown, and the list tends to be used largely for political purposes rather than for identifying systematically those states that facilitate opportunities for terrorism as outlined in this paper.[5]

2. Declaring war on terrorism

The 9/11 attack upset the traditional geopolitical foreign policy view of terrorism. The U.S. immediately reacted by identifying all actions by groups against nation states as terrorist, suddenly grouping the Irish Republican Army, which had benefited from a benign neglect by the U.S., with Al Qaeda. The declaration of war against terrorism everywhere ("if you are not with us you are against us"), eventually led to the Iraq adventure. This policy was misplaced because we know from our experience of the "war against crime" that declaring war on a word introduces a constricting mindset to police, who are then hampered from analyzing logically the variety of crime problems they face.

3. Assuming that terrorism will be prevented by spreading democracy

The spread of democracy was used as one justification for invading Iraq. But we know that with more democracy there is more crime simply because there are more opportunities to commit crime. Countries that are not democracies, such as Singapore and Saudi Arabia, are renowned for their very low crime rates. It is therefore quite possible that democracies make terrorism more likely rather than less likely. Democracies also make countering terrorism more difficult. In the past, one effective technique used by governments was to use very harsh repressive tactics to put down insurgencies and terrorism.[6] This worked in a number of places, such as with the Soviets in Hungary in 1956, or the British in Malaya 1948-52. Today, these tactics are fraught with danger and there is growing evidence that they do not deter terrorism (Freilich & Pridemore, 2007; LaFree et al., 2009; McCauley, 2006; Pridemore & Freilich, 2009). Excesses in fighting against terrorists by governments are dramatically uncovered by a free press, with very serious repercussions in democratic countries whose governments depend on the public discourse for approval of their actions. It is important to recognize, therefore, the limits that democracies place on their governments in conducting foreign exploits, especially wars, whether of the traditional kind or against insurgents.[7] Today, no war or response to terrorist attacks can hide the awful facts of violence, especially in democracies with open media. The reactions of the masses in democracies are therefore difficult to predict or control. In the long run, politicians must do their bidding. There is little doubt that the constant portrayal of terrorist and insurgent violence in Iraq weakened the will of many Americans. And this is the aim of any war: to weaken the will of the enemy. In short, terrorist attacks help destabilize democracies. The constant portrayal of violent attacks spreads fear among ordinary people, which is transferred to their politicians. Democracies must struggle with this problem daily, and understand that strategies must be devised that avoid their exposure to this kind of global outrage by ordinary people who naturally do not like to see the violence of wars where civilians are killed, and must be totally convinced that any such adventures are "worth it." Making this case is increasingly difficult, since the threat of, for example, not having access to foreign oil in 20 years time must be weighed against the carnage of attacks seen live on television. This is a simple example. Consider how impossible it is to argue that "more democracy" at some unspecified time in the future, is worth the violence of today.

4. Spy based foreign policy

Foreign policy is obviously driven by information. During the rise of nation states in Europe during the 17th through 20th centuries, the focus of foreign policy was on the military assessment of foreign countries, their warring designs and capabilities. The collection of secret information concerning government intentions and strategies formed the bedrock on which foreign policy was constructed. Spies were thus the essential part of collecting secret information. In the U.S., the Central Intelligence Agency (CIA) developed its extensive spying system, as other nation states developed theirs. Yet it is well known in foreign intelligence circles (before the advent of the Internet) that some 80% of information collected by "spies" is available from open sources.[8] Even the use of satellites to spy on military facilities is no longer confined to government or military use. Many satellites are now put into orbit by private companies, and it is these that make global communications possible and provide GPS technology. The fact is that keeping information secret is extremely difficult in the 21st century. The historical basis of foreign policy has not prepared it well for dealing with terrorism that operates independent of any nation state.

5. Abandoning the propaganda machinery of foreign policy

After the Cold War, the U.S. dismantled its far reaching propaganda machinery, such as the Voice of America and various information agencies around the world. It is puzzling that the powerful role that the media played in bringing the Vietnam War into people's living rooms was not understood by American foreign policy experts prior to going to war in Iraq. It was undoubtedly the incessant revelations of war scenes every night in network news in the U.S. that fed the widespread disapproval of the Vietnam War and the eventual withdrawal of American troops. It was the clear indication of what was to come: the theater of war is a *real* theater, people everywhere today get to see graphic detail of all violence associated with war, insurgency and terrorism. In this sense, the "war against terrorism" is aptly framed, if we consider that this is a war of words and images. Indeed it might be called a "media war" (Schechter, 2003; Hachten & Scott, 2002, Kellner, 2005). It is puzzling that the U.S., arguably a media giant, has failed miserably to adopt a clear media-based policy for matching terrorists at their own media game. For example, Kilcullen (in Packer, 2006) estimates that the U.S. expenditures in Pakistan from 2002 to 2006 were $6 billion on military, $6 billion on intelligence, and just $1 billion on economic and social development. The media has feasted on the negative effects of military and intelligence expenditure. If an equal amount were spent on economic and social development it would be more difficult for the media to ignore this more positive approach.

Nation centered global policy

The traditional strategies of global influence meant that foreign policy was implemented according to simplified generalizations about nation states, with little understanding of local cultures and politics within those nation states, unless one particular state was seen as a threat to national interests (such as the overthrow of the leftist government of Chile in the early 1970s with covert U.S. support).[9] Though there was recognition of the shortcomings of this approach to foreign policy, and some attempts were made to change it after the Chilean adventure, in fact the efforts to understand the local cultures and even the political arrangements of regions from a foreign policy point of view were seriously limited by the U.S. Congress.[10] At first impression, a foreign policy that is informed by global and national issues should be enough. But terrorism of the 21st century is primarily (if not always) rooted in local cultures and politics, as argued above. It is true that the CIA and National Security Administration (NSA), until the end of the Cold War, extended their tentacles into many nations. However, the mindset that drove their activities on the ground in those countries was not one that sought to identify the characteristics of local cultures that offered opportunities for terrorist activity, the many opportunities described throughout this paper.[11] Rather it was driven by a military objective: find the culprits and their terror cells and destroy them. This is a commonly held mindset in military and policing circles: that terrorism and crime are the result of a finite number of evil people. Get rid of these people and you get rid of terrorism. Unfortunately, one can kill or put in prison an ample number of criminals or terrorists. The effects on terrorism or crime are negligible. Indeed, in the case of terrorism, a strong argument can be made that tracking down and killing terrorists as a sole basis of counter-terrorism policy actually increases terrorism, because it creates resentment and victims (real or perceived) of government injustice, thus providing a ready supply of new recruits to terrorist groups.[12]

In sum, we can see that the assumptions of past foreign policy are a hindrance to developing a coherent foreign policy that acknowledges the opportunities offered by globalization, the local conditions that both constrain and enhance them and the constantly changing conditions that tilt the balance of power back and forth between attackers and defenders.

TOWARD A FOREIGN POLICY THAT IS BOTH GLOBAL AND LOCAL

Intelligence: What information does counter-terrorism foreign policy require?

In so far as terrorism is concerned, the problem that spy agencies have is not so much to obtain secret information about government intentions, but to collect information that is relevant to terrorist activity so that it may be prevented. Thus, any intelligence agency should be structured in such a way that it is ready to collect the relevant information from specific locations and global processes that enhance terrorism, as listed in Tables 1 and 2 respectively. Note that this does not call for the establishment of an extensive spy network that is poised to ferret out terrorist cells, and through interrogation of captured terrorist suspects, obtain the names of others who may be terrorists. While there are probably no globally organized terrorist organizations in existence (though we know that some terrorist groups have the capability to strike globally when their message is echoed by sympathizers), putting all one's spying resources into tracking down members of terrorist groups and eradicating them is mostly fruitless, rather like swatting flies. We know that catching terrorists will generally not prevent future attacks (just as catching criminals does not in itself prevent future crime).[13] Thus, collection of voluminous amounts of information from eavesdropping in the hope of assembling names of accomplices of an imagined terrorist organization can be dispensed with, especially as we know that the major portion of such information is never translated so never used.[14]

Instead we should reassign a major portion of foreign intelligence budget to collection of information that speaks directly to the local situation of preventing terrorist attacks. Furthermore, the interrogation of terror suspects with the view to "breaking them" by giving up names of other suspects, feeds the negative global reportage of "torture" and helps promote the terrorists in the eyes of a sympathetic public. Rather, when suspects are interrogated, the interrogation should focus on collecting information on how they plan their attacks, how they can sustain them, and how they make the best of their opportunities in exploiting the availability of targets, weapons, tools and facilitating conditions as described earlier in this paper. Simply using the lists supplied in Tables 1 and 2 would give much more focus on what information to collect.

"Know your turf" as the basis of foreign policy

While the identification of targets, weapons and tools of terrorism is relatively straightforward, identifying the facilitating conditions at the local level can be difficult. Foreign policy adviser Kilcullen (in Packer 2006) insists that the most important rule in conducting foreign policy in a location frequented by insurgents (a form of routine terrorism) is to know one's turf. This means that one must collect detailed information on the specific locality where terrorism occurs: its economic structure, every street and alley, its culture and familial traditions, its history, especially of previous attacks, whether by insurgents or by opponents of insurgents. While much of this information would be collected in the process of identifying targets, tools and weapons as opportunities, the more complex facilitating conditions, such as local culture, require much more attention and expertise, perhaps even of those specifically trained to collect this kind of information – anthropologists.[15] In this way one can build up a picture of why locals may or may not support terrorist activity, the extent that they will resist terrorist threats or instead support the opponents of the terrorists, usually the local government, or an occupying force. Conditions must be created in which ordinary citizens will have an incentive to side against terrorists, even in the face of serious and often brutal threats of retaliation by terrorist forces.

Use traditional nation-based foreign policy to reduce global opportunities

We saw in Table 2 that there are many global mechanisms in place that enhance the conduct of terrorist attacks. Each nation should work with other nations either bilaterally or multilaterally to:

- Limit the spread of WMD technology. So far, only nations are in possession of this technology. Traditional foreign policy methods should therefore apply.

- Limit the marketing of conventional arms. The U.N. has had some limited success in this area, but much more needs to be done to enlist the cooperation of arms manufacturers and dealers and nations that have liberal policies to arms dealing.[16] The suicide terrorism technique demonstrated in the Bombay attacks of 2008 used mainly small arms with impressive strategic effect. [17]

- Limit the links between terrorism and organized crime: how they come about and how to limit their collaboration. Because the arms trade requires the crossing of national borders, this is an area where traditional foreign policy between nation states is relevant. This is perhaps why most progress has been made in this area in fighting terrorism than in any other.[18] Considerable advance has been made in the area of money laundering, but little progress has been made in the field of terrorist use of the international drug trade to support their activities (e.g., the Taliban in Afghanistan). A prime reason for the failure in Afghanistan is the lack of anthropological and economic knowledge of poppy growing areas, along with the necessary finances to support such activity.[19]

- Develop international agreements among governments and relevant businesses to limit the amount and detail (e.g., beheading of hostages) of terrorist violence (any violence for that matter) portrayed on mass media and on the Internet.[20] Limiting video content on the Internet is not impossible if businesses can be convinced to join with governments to do so. China, for example, managed to make Google block certain sites in its search engines.

- Work with relevant nations to tighten up border crossings, identity authentication, air and sea security (air travel, shipping containers). Much has been accomplished here since 9/11, but there are still many countries whose air travel security is poor and whose shipping procedures are insecure.

Grapple with the global/local nexus of terrorism

As we have seen, the global media magnify local events. The powerful imagery of the global media almost always comes from a specific location somewhere in the world where real victims and real aggressors reside. Governments must:

- Include a media impact assessment of every action taken at the terrorist site either as prevention or in response to a terrorist attack;

- Include in any planning of a counter-insurgency a careful assessment by an expert of the impact of this action on local citizens, whether it will affect their sympathies for or against the terrorists; and,

- Avoid keeping suspects in custody to the extent possible, given the negative media exposure that this will inevitably produce.

As noted above, globalization enhances opportunities; but at the local level these opportunities must be acted upon. Governments must encourage local officials and businesses to introduce the necessary security to protect targets, control the local marketing and possession of weapons, track the availability of tools of terrorism, and assess the facilitating conditions that include economic incentives to join the terrorists, cultural history that matches terrorist values, hidden threats by terrorists, and religious and other organizations that support terrorist causes thus offering justifications for local inhabitants to support them. The aim here is not to repress the activities of these groups, but to outsmart them – whether by offering more to local inhabitants to support their welfare, or by starting organizations that offer a better or more attractive prospect for the future.[21]

Keep a rapid deployment force at the ready

Develop expertise in identifying places that are vulnerable to terrorist influence. These are usually those in extreme poverty as a result of failed states, or communities destroyed by a disaster. Provide incentives for local inhabitants to take the side against terrorists. This approach should be backed up by a rapid response force, not of counterinsurgency operatives, but of aid workers who can move in the event of a local disaster. The U.S. Agency for International Development claims that its use of aid to thwart insecurity and terrorism is one of its prime missions, and cites many examples to support this claim.[22] However, the speed with which aid is delivered to disaster areas and the tardiness of Congress in allocating the necessary resources have been questioned, especially in respect to the aftermath of the Asian tsunami disaster,[23] though in the long run it appears that the U.S. image was greatly improved in Indonesia as a result of its aid.[24]

Expect change

Conditions constantly change because of the movement of people, information and new technologies around the world. Attackers and defenders must adapt to these changes.[25] In many respects, attackers have been better in adapting their strategies and tactics in response to changing conditions (Kenney, 2006). For example, the increased airport and airline security introduced after the hijackings of the 1970s made it difficult for terrorists to hijack airplanes. However, even though suicide bombers had been active for many years, defenders did not anticipate that this technique would be used in the hijacking of airplanes and their subsequent use as guided missiles on 9/11. In contrast, the PKK suffered because it did not change its strategy in response to changes in government strategy after the capture of the Kurdish separatist leader Ocalan in Turkey (Kim and Yun, 2008). Ways to anticipate terrorist adaptation ("thinking out of the box" as the 9/11 Commission urged) must be built into any foreign policy and its implementation (Clarke & Newman, 2006, pp. 218-240).

CONCLUSIONS

It is surely clear that traditional foreign policy has gotten the U.S. and other western nations into one quagmire after the other. The situational crime prevention approach to terrorism forces us to rethink how terrorism is implemented locally and what are its global implications. The reaction toward the end of the last century was to cry out that we were confronted with a "clash of civilizations." It is not the "clash of civilizations" that confronts us, but the "globalization of civilizations" fuelled by the unstoppable march of technology. Civilizations (cultures, ideologies and religions) have never recognized national borders. It is logical that they should flourish with globalization. Foreign policy of the 21st century would do well to acknowledge this historical change. Its understanding requires us to work both at the global level to comprehend and apply the beneficial elements of globalization to preventing terrorism, but also locally to recognize that it is increasingly individuals who live in specific places and cultures whose combined power, thanks to globalization, may one day even surpass that of nation states.

The approach of situational crime prevention would undoubtedly require drastic changes in the way that foreign policy is both formed and implemented. It would require an infrastructure of foreign policy support staff that could provide the kinds of information needed by a global/local approach to terrorism that focuses on reducing opportunities. This would require, at a minimum, building up a substantial number of staff who are trained in anthropological methods, and other social scientists such as media experts and psychologists who understand the role and significance of information and propaganda. Finally, there will be the need for constant assistance by skilled operational researchers to solve specific problems on the ground in the face of terrorist or insurgent attack (Clarke and Newman, 2006 pp. 231-243). None of these changes are possible until foreign policy understands that terrorism is both enhanced and constrained by global and local opportunity.

Address correspondence to: grn92@albany.edu

NOTES

1. Belatedly, the Bush White House recognized this foreign public relations problem and sent its very successful domestic public relations expert, Karen Hughes, to fix the problem. Unfortunately, the techniques used to control U.S. domestic media relations in order to get Bush elected did not transfer to foreign relations. Hughes (a former TV news anchor) imagined that a single media event (getting a few local housewives in Iraq together on a TV talk show) would change everything. Of course, one event could never match the repeated showing of successful terrorist attacks on global news media.
2. The regional patterning of terrorist incidents is, however, complex, requiring more research to identify the factors involved in affecting regional choice of targets and their relationship to terrorist bases of operations. See for example Braithwaite (2006).
3. It has also been shown that terrorist groups will cling to their location driven terrorist strategies even when conditions change that make carrying out their operations more difficult (Yun and Kim, 2008).
4. As Kilcullen has noted: "Traditional diplomacy, with its emphasis on treaties and geopolitical debates, is less relevant than the ability to understand and influence foreign populations—not in their councils of state but in their villages and slums." (Cited in Packer, 2006.)
5. In fact, the list is far too short to be of any significance. As of October 2008, the countries on the list of states that sponsor terrorism included only Cuba, Iran, Sudan and Syria. If one were to take into account the many global and local opportunities for terrorism as described in Tables 1 and 2, the list would comprise many more.

6. The word "insurgent" is used to refer to the most serious or extreme forms of terrorist acts, both in quality and quantity, that occur on a routine basis.

7. The atrocities committed in wars fought in the first half of the 20th century were not public knowledge until some time after the wars were over. The idea that "we," being the allies, would not deliberately target civilians in war has been a long cherished myth. The policy that led to the carpet bombing of Dresden in World War II, for example, was debated by parliaments and in the media of the time, but the abhorrence of this tactic was not really acknowledged in the public consciousness until recently.

8. The 80% rule is a widely shared estimate, but there is no credible source for it. However, perusal of the extensive operations on open source intelligence (OSINT) is enough to suggest that its contribution to intelligence is very substantial. See for example the Wikipedia entry at: http://en.wikipedia.org/wiki/Open_source_intelligence.

9. This foreign policy mistake viewed the spread of communism from a geopolitical point of view that assumed that an ideology could be stopped by toppling a government. It is of interest that the U.S. actually spent considerable resources understanding the local culture and politics and employed anthropologists to help them do this. Unfortunately the information was used for the wrong policy reasons. History demonstrates the error. Communism was defeated when the U.S. won the cold war against the Soviets. But as an ideology it still does not go away, as seen in recent political changes in Brazil and Guatemala. It spreads like a virus, but it also mutates to take advantage of global conditions. This mutation continues at breakneck speed in China.

10. 94th Congress 1st Session, *Covert Action in Chile 1963-1973*. Staff report of the select committee to study governmental operations with respect to intelligence activities. United States Senate. U.S. Government Printing Office. Washington: 1975.

11. It is worth noting that the debacle of Waco was a direct result of the Federal Bureau of Investigation's failure to understand the cultural and local aspects of the Koresh movement (Barkun, 1996). It has since made efforts to correct this by reaching out to academics for their input on local cultures, which also extends to "Christian patriots" and others who may potentially perpetrate domestic terrorism (Barkun, 2007).

12. We know from situational crime prevention that interventions and responses must be tailored to the specific type of offence. Kim and Yun (2008) have shown that depending on the type of terrorist strategies used by the PKK Kurdish separatists in Turkey, for example, some interventions worked and others did not. Tough and immediate responses work for some conditions and not others, a finding also corroborated by LaFree et al. (2009) in regard to Northern Ireland, and Pridemore and Freilich (2007) on abortion crimes.

13. This does not exclude going after some specific terrorist group leaders whose charisma serves to export and inflame terrorism, or when it is known that the specific terrorist group is very limited in membership, such as the Shining Path in Peru (Clarke and Newman 2006, pp. 72-74), or when a specific member with specific skills, such as a bomb maker is eliminated (Hamm, 2007). However the successes in this regard have been limited. Even when a particular terrorist group is broken up, it is often reborn as a number of other terrorist groups (Clarke and Newman, 2006, 72; Smith and Damphousse, 2009; Jones and Libicki, 2008). The popularity of network analysis argues that if we identify the key "nodes" of networks these can be eliminated and thus the network will collapse. However, this presupposes that terrorist networks are organized in a "node" fashion, and that sophisticated networks exist in the first place (Krebs, 2002). The extent to which various organizational structures or patterns of networks exist in terrorist movements is unknown. Much that is organized in drug trafficking, for example, turns out to be very much a cottage industry of family members or friends (Clarke and Newman, 2006).

14. Concerning the FBI, not considering the many other intelligence collecting agencies, the Office of the Inspector General (*The Federal Bureau of Investigation's Foreign Language Program* . . . , 2004) found that a significant (though impossible to determine) amount of intelligence collected was not translated, or if translated was too late to be of any use. More importantly, the FBI has failed to prioritize the types of information given the translators. This indicates that it has no clear idea of what kinds of information are more important or relevant – a problem solved by approaching intelligence from the point of view of opportunities as described in this paper.

15. Anthropologists were influential on foreign policy and even planning of battles in World War II. They have had little input since the scandal

of the CIA's Project Camelot (advised by anthropologists), helped topple Chile's President Allende in 1973. Montgomery McFate (in Packer, 2006) argues that they are urgently needed now to help refocus U.S. foreign policy on specific locations where terrorism occurs.

16. See for example The Small Arms Survey that collects information on weapons, their dissemination and control, working with many international NGOs: http://www.smallarmssurvey.org/index.html.

17. Unlike suicide bombing attacks in Israel and elsewhere, which require extensive networks of suppliers and skilled bomb makers, small automatic arms are more easily available. Countries with liberal gun ownership and sales policies, such as the United States, should be very concerned at this latest terrorist adaptation.

18. Sageman (2008) has argued that one of the main contributors to the containment of Al Qaeda activities since 9/11 has been increased border security.

19. The problem seems intractable without substantial government attention and perseverance, and of course money. See for a brief overview: The Economist (2008), "Afghanistan's great purple hope: Bring on the pomegranate," Nov 27.

20. Or, if certain imagery of terrorist violence cannot be eliminated, perhaps it could be limited to a certain number of repetitions over a certain period of time. Repetition is perhaps the most effective method of propaganda. Hence the constant repetition of advertisements on TV.

21. See for example, Moisés Naím (2003), Five Wars of Globalization, Foreign Policy, January/February: http://www.foreignpolicy.com/story/cms.php?story_id=2&page=0.

22. USAID: Testimony of James Kunder, Assistant Administrator for Asia and the Near East before the Senate Foreign Relations Committee, United States Senate, Washington, D.C., March 2, 2005.

23. "Irate Over 'Stingy' Remark, U.S. Adds $20 Million to Disaster Aid," by Steven R. Weisman, New York Times, December 29, 2004.

24. "US Tsunami Aid Boosts American Image in Indonesia," by Nancy-Amelia Collins, Jakarta, 28 July 2005: http://www.voanews.com/english/archive/2005-07/2005-07-28-voa2.cfm.

25. Offender adaptation has been recognized in the field of situational crime prevention for some time. See for example Ekblom (1997, 2002).

REFERENCES

Barkun, M. (2007). Purifying the law: The legal world of "Christian patriots" *Journal for the Study of Radicalism, 1.1,* 57–70.

Barkun, M. (Ed.) (1996). *Millennialism and violence.* London and New York: Routledge.

Berrebi, C., & Klor, E. F. (2008). Are voters sensitive to terrorism? Direct evidence from the Israeli electorate. *American Political Science Review, 102,* No. 3 (August), 279–301

Berrebi, C., & Klor, E. F. (2006, December). On terrorism and electoral outcomes: Theory and evidence from the Israeli-Palestinian conflict. *Journal of Conflict Resolution, 50*(6), 899–925.

Berrebi, C., & Lakdawalla, D. (2006). *How does terrorism risk vary across space and time? An analysis based on the Israeli Experience.* Santa Monica, CA: RAND.

Braithwaite, A. (2006). The geographic spread of militarized disputes. *Journal of Peace Research, 43*(5), 507–522.

Clarke, R. V., & Newman, G. R. (2006). *Outsmarting the terrorists.* Westport, CT: Greenwood PSI.

Cothren, J., Smith, B. L., Roberts, P. & Damphousse, K. (2008). Geospatial and temporal patterns of preparatory conduct among American Terrorists. *International Journal of Comparative and Applied Criminal Justice, 32*(1), 23–42.

Ekblom, P. (1997) Gearing up against Crime: A dynamic framework to help designers keep up with the adaptive criminal in a changing world. *International Journal of Risk, Security and Crime Prevention, 2,* 249–265.

Ekblom, P. (2002). From the source to the mainstream is uphill: The challenge of transferring knowledge of crime prevention through replication, innovation and anticipation. In N. Tilley (Ed.), *Analysis for crime prevention.* Crime Prevention Studies, vol. 13. Monsey, NY: Criminal Justice Press.

Ekblom, P. (2002). Future Imperfect: Preparing for the crimes to come. *Criminal Justice Matters, 46,* Winter 2001/02, 38–40. London: Centre for Crime and Justice Studies, Kings College.

Freilich, J. D., & Pridemore, W. A. (2007). Politics, culture and political crime: Covariates of abortion clinic attacks in the United States. *Journal of Criminal Justice, 35*(3), 323–336.

Hachten, W. A. & Scott, J. F. (2002). *The world news prism: Global media in an era of terrorism.* Iowa: Iowa State University Press

Hamm, M. S. (2007). *Terrorism as crime: From Oklahoma city to Al-Qaeda and beyond.* New York: NYU Press.

Jones, S. G., & Libicki, M. C. (2008). *How terrorist groups end: Lessons for countering al Qa'ida,* Rand Monograph. Doc. No. MG-741-RC.

Kellner, D. (2005). *Terrorism, war and election battles.* Boulder, CO: Paradigm Publishers.

Kenney, M. (2006). *From Pablo to Osama: Trafficking and terrorist networks, government bureaucracies, and competitive adaptation.* University Park: Pennsylvania State University Press.

Kim, E. & Yun, M. (2008). What works? Countermeasures to terrorism: A case study of PKK. *International Journal of Comparative and Applied Criminal Justice, 32*(1), 65–88.

Krebs, V. E. (2002). Mapping networks of terrorist cells. *Connections, 24*(3), 43–52.

LaFree, G., Dugan, L., & Fahey LaFree, S. (2007). Global terrorism and failed states. In J. J. Hewitt, J. Wilkenfeld & T. R. Gurr (Eds.), *Peace and Conflict* (pp. 39–54). Boulder: Paradigm Publishers.

LaFree, G., Korte R. & Dugan, L. (2009). The impact of British counter terrorist strategies on political violence in Northern Ireland: Comparing deterrence and backlash models. *Criminology, 47,* 501–530.

McCauley, C. (2006). Jujitsu politics: Terrorism and response to terrorism. In P. R. Kimmel & C. E. Stout (Eds.), *Collateral damage: The psychological consequences of america's war on terrorism* (pp. 45–65). Westport, CT: Praeger.

Napoleoni, L. (2005). *Terror incorporated: Tracing the dollars behind the terror networks.* New York: Seven Stories Press.

Newman, G. R., & Clarke, R. V. (2008). *Policing terrorism: A police chief's guide.* COPS. U.S. Department of Justice

Packer, G. (2006). *Knowing the enemy: Can social scientists redefine "the war on terror"? The New Yorker,* Dec. 18, 2006: Retrieved from: www.newyorker/archive.

Pridemore, W. A., & Freilich, J. D. (2007). The impact of state laws protecting abortion clinics and reproductive rights: Deterrence, backlash, or neither? *Law and Human Behavior, 31*(6), 611–627.

Rossmo, K., Harries, K., & McGarrell, E. (2008). Paper presented to the Environmental Criminology and Crime Analysis meeting, *Expanding the frontiers of crime prevention: New problems in new environments.* Izmir, Turkey, 17-19 March.

Sageman, M. (2008). *Leaderless jihad: Terror networks in the twenty-first century.* Philadelphia: University of Pennsylvania Press.

Schechter, D. (2003). *Media wars: News at a time of terror.* NJ: Rowman and Littlefield.

Schneir, B. (2006). *Beyond fear: Thinking sensibly about security in an uncertain world.* New York: Springer.

Smith, B. L., & Damphousse, K. R. (in press). Patterns of precursor behavior in the life span of a U.S. environmental group. *Criminology and Public Policy.*

U.S. Office of the Inspector General, Federal Bureau of Investigation (2004). *The Federal Bureau of Investigation's Foreign Language Program–Translation of counterterrorism and counterintelligence foreign language material.* Report no. 04-25, Redacted and Unclassified. Washington, DC

U.S. State Department (2008). *Human Trafficking Report 2007.* Washington DC: U.S. State Department.

TWENTY-EIGHT ARTICLES: FUNDAMENTALS OF COMPANY-LEVEL COUNTERINSURGENCY[1]

David Kilcullen[2]

Introduction[3]

There are no universal answers, and insurgents are among the most adaptive opponents you will ever face. Countering them will demand every ounce of your intellect. But be comforted: you are not the first to feel this way. There are tactical fundamentals you can apply, to link the theory with the techniques and procedures you already know.

What is counterinsurgency?

If you have not studied counterinsurgency theory, here it is in a nutshell: this is a competition with the insurgent for the right and the ability to win the hearts, minds and acquiescence of the population. You are being sent in because the insurgents, at their strongest, can defeat anything weaker than you. But you have more combat power than you can or should use in most situations. Injudicious use of firepower creates blood feuds, homeless people and societal disruption that fuels and perpetuates the insurgency. The most beneficial actions are often local politics, civic action, and beat-cop behaviors. For your side to win, the people do not have to like you but they must respect you, accept that your actions benefit them,

Crime Prevention Studies, volume 25 (2009), pp. 61–70.

and trust your integrity and ability to deliver on promises, particularly regarding their security. In this battlefield popular perceptions and rumor are more influential than the facts and more powerful than a hundred tanks.

Within this context, what follows are observations from collective experience: the distilled essence of what those who went before you learned. They are expressed as commandments, for clarity but are really more like folklore. Apply them judiciously and skeptically.

PREPARATION

Time is short during pre-deployment, but you will never have more time to think than you have now. Now is your chance to prepare yourself and your command.

1. **Know your turf.** Know the people, the topography, economy, history, religion and culture. Know every village, road, field, population group, tribal leader and ancient grievance. Your task is to become the world expert on your district. If you don't know precisely where you will be operating, study the general area. Read the map like a book: study it every night before sleep, and re-draw it from memory every morning, until you understand its patterns intuitively . . .

2. **Diagnose the problem.** Once you know your area and its people, you can begin to diagnose the problem. Who are the insurgents? What drives them? What makes local leaders tick? Counterinsurgency is fundamentally a competition between many groups, each seeking to mobilize the population in support of their agenda — counterinsurgency is always more than two-sided. So you must understand what motivates the people and how to mobilize them. You need to know why and how the insurgents are getting followers. This means you need to know your real enemy, not a cardboard cut-out. The enemy is adaptive, resourceful and probably grew up in the region where you will operate. The locals have known him since he was a boy – how long have they known you? Your worst opponent is not the psychopathic terrorist of Hollywood, it is the charismatic follow-me warrior who would make your best platoon leader. His followers are not misled or naïve: much of his success is due to bad government policies or security forces that alienate the population . . .

3. **Organize for intelligence.** In counterinsurgency, killing the enemy is easy. Finding him is often nearly impossible. Intelligence and opera-

tions are complementary. Your operations will be intelligence driven, but intelligence will come mostly from your own operations, not as a "product" prepared and served up by higher headquarters. So you must organize for intelligence. You will need a company S2 and intelligence section including analysts. You may need platoon S2s and S3s, and you will need a reconnaissance and surveillance element. You will not have enough linguists — you never do — but consider carefully where best to employ them. Linguists are a battle-winning asset: but like any other scarce resource you must have a prioritized "bump plan" in case you lose them. . .

4. **Organize for inter-agency operations.** Almost everything in counterinsurgency is interagency. And everything important — from policing to intelligence to civil-military operations to trash collection — will involve your company working with civilian actors and local indigenous partners you cannot control, but whose success is essential for yours. Train the company in inter-agency operations — get a briefing from the State Department, aid agencies and the local Police or Fire Brigade. Train point-men in each squad to deal with the inter-agency. Realize that civilians find rifles, helmets and body armor intimidating. Learn how not to scare them. Ask others who come from that country or culture about your ideas. See it through the eyes of a civilian who knows nothing about the military. How would you react if foreigners came to your neighborhood and conducted the operations you planned? What if somebody came to your mother's house and did that? Most importantly, know that your operations will create temporary breathing space, but long-term development and stabilization by civilian agencies will ultimately win the war.

5. **Travel light and harden your CSS (Combat Service Support).** You will be weighed down with body armor, rations, extra ammunition, communications gear, and a thousand other things. The enemy will carry a rifle or RPG, a shemagh and a water bottle if he is lucky. Unless you ruthlessly lighten your load and enforce a culture of speed and mobility, the insurgents will consistently out-run and out-maneuver you. . . . Also, remember to harden your CSS. The enemy will attack your weakest points. Most attacks on coalition forces in Iraq in 2004 and 2005, outside pre-planned combat actions like the two battles of Fallujah or Operation Iron Horse, were against CSS installations and convoys. You do the math. Ensure your CSS assets are hardened, have

communications, and are trained in combat operations. They may do more fighting than your rifle squads.

6. **Find a political/cultural adviser.** In a force optimized for counterinsurgency, you might receive a political/cultural adviser at company level: a diplomat or military foreign area officer, able to speak the language and navigate the intricacies of local politics. Back on planet Earth, the Corps and Division commander will get a POLAD: you will not, so you must improvise. Find a political/cultural adviser from among your people or perhaps an officer, perhaps not ... Someone with people skills and a "feel" for the environment will do better than a political science graduate. Don't try to be your own cultural adviser: you must be fully aware of the political and cultural dimension, but this is a different task. Also, don't give one of your intelligence people this role. They can help, but their task is to understand the environment – the political adviser's job is to help shape it.

* * *

* * *

9. **Have a game plan.** The final preparation task is to develop a game plan: a mental picture of how you see the operation developing. You will be tempted to try and do this too early. But wait: as your knowledge improves, you will get a better idea of what needs to be done, and of your own limitations. Like any plan, this plan will change once you hit the ground, and may need to be scrapped if there is a major shift in the environment. But you still need a plan, and the process of planning will give you a simple robust idea of what to achieve, even if the methods change. This is sometimes called "operational design." One approach is to identify basic stages in your operation: e.g. "establish dominance, build local networks, marginalize the enemy." Make sure you can easily transition between phases, both forward and backward in case of setbacks. Just as the insurgent can adapt his activity to yours, you must have a simple enough plan to survive setbacks without collapsing. This plan is the "solution" that matches the shared "diagnosis" you developed earlier it must be simple, and known to everyone ...

10. **Be there.** The first rule of deployment in counterinsurgency is to be there. You can almost never outrun the enemy. If you are not present when an incident happens, there is usually little you can do about it. So your first order of business is to establish presence. If you cannot

do this throughout your sector, then do it wherever you can. This demands a residential approach of living in your sector, in close proximity to the population, rather than raiding into the area from remote, secure bases. Movement on foot, sleeping in local villages, night patrolling: all these seem more dangerous than they are. They establish links with the locals, who see you as real people they can trust and do business with, not as aliens who descend from an armored box. Driving around in an armored convoy – day-tripping like a tourist in hell – degrades situational awareness, makes you a target and is ultimately more dangerous.

11. **Avoid knee jerk responses to first impressions.** Don't act rashly, get the facts first. The violence you see may be part of the insurgent strategy, it may be various interest groups fighting it out, or it may be people settling personal vendettas. Or, it may just be daily life: "normality" in Kandahar is not the same as in Kansas. So you need time to learn what normality looks like. . . . Of course, you cannot avoid making judgments. But if possible, check them with an older hand or a trusted local. If you can, keep one or two officers from your predecessor unit for the first part of the tour . . .

* * *

13. **Build trusted networks.** Once you have settled into your sector, your next task is to build trusted networks. This is the true meaning of the phrase "hearts and minds," which comprises two separate components. "Hearts" means persuading people their best interests are served by your success; "Minds" means convincing them that you can protect them, and that resisting you is pointless. Note that neither concept has to do with whether people like you. Calculated self-interest, not emotion, is what counts. . . . Actions that help build trusted networks serve your cause. Actions or even killing high-profile targets or that undermine trust or disrupt your networks help the enemy.

* * *

* * *

16. **Practice deterrent patrolling.** Establish patrolling methods that deter the enemy from attacking you. Often our patrolling approach seems designed to provoke, then defeat, enemy attacks. This is counter-productive: it leads to a raiding, day-tripping mindset or,

worse, a bunker mentality. Instead, practice deterrent patrolling. There are many methods for this, including "multiple" patrolling where you flood an area with numerous small patrols working together. Each is too small to be a worthwhile target, and the insurgents never know where all the patrols are – making an attack on any one patrol extremely risky. Other methods include so-called "blue-green" patrolling, where you mount daylight overt humanitarian patrols, which go covert at night and hunt specific targets. Again, the aim is to keep the enemy off balance, and the population reassured, through constant and unpredictable activity – which, over time, deters attacks and creates a more permissive environment. A reasonable rule of thumb is that one to two thirds of your force should be on patrol at any time, day or night.

* * *

18. **Remember the global audience.** One of the biggest differences between the counterinsurgencies our fathers fought and those we face today is the omnipresence of globalized media. Most houses in Iraq have one or more satellite dishes. Web bloggers, print, radio and television reporters and others are monitoring and commenting on your every move. . . . Beware the "scripted enemy," who plays to a global audience and seeks to defeat you in the court of global public opinion. . . . Get the press on-side: help them get their story, and trade information with them. Good relationships with non-embedded media, especially indigenous media, dramatically increase your situational awareness, and help get your message across to the global and local audience.

19. **Engage the women, beware the children.** Most insurgent fighters are men. But in traditional societies, women are hugely influential in forming the social networks that insurgents use for support. Co-opting neutral or friendly women, through targeted social and economic programs, builds networks of enlightened self-interest that eventually undermine the insurgents. You need your own female counterinsurgents, including interagency people, to do this effectively. Win the women, and you own the family unit. Own the family, and you take a big step forward in mobilizing the population. Conversely, though, stop your people fraternizing with local children. Your troops are homesick; they want to drop their guard with the kids. But children are sharp- eyed, lacking in empathy, and willing to commit atrocities

their elders would shrink from. The insurgents are watching: they will notice a growing friendship between one of your people and a local child, and either harm the child as punishment, or use them against you. Similarly, stop people throwing candies or presents to children. It attracts them to our vehicles, creates crowds the enemy can exploit, and leads to children being run over. Harden your heart and keep the children at arm's length.

20. **Take stock regularly.** You probably already know that a "body count" tells you little, because you usually cannot know how many insurgents there were to start with, how many moved into the area, transferred from supporter to combatant status or how many new fighters the conflict has created. But you still need to develop metrics early in the tour and refine them as the operation progresses. They should cover a range of social, informational, military and economic issues. Use metrics intelligently to form an overall impression of progress, not in a mechanistic "traffic light" fashion. Typical metrics include: percentage of engagements initiated by our forces versus those initiated by insurgents; longevity of friendly local leaders in positions of authority; number and quality of tip-offs on insurgent activity that originate spontaneously from the population; economic activity at markets and shops. These mean virtually nothing as a snapshot – trends over time are the true indicators of progress in your sector.

* * *

* * *

21. **Exploit a single narrative.** Since counterinsurgency is a competition to mobilize popular support, it pays to know how people are mobilized. In most societies there are opinion-makers: local leaders, pillars of the community, religious figures, media personalities, and others who set trends and influence public perceptions. This influence – including the pernicious influence of the insurgents – often takes the form of a "single narrative": a simple, unifying, easily-expressed story or explanation that organizes people's experience and provides a framework for understanding events. Nationalist and ethnic historical myths, or sectarian creeds, provide such a narrative. The Iraqi insurgents have one, as do al-Qa'ida and the Taliban. To undercut their influence you must exploit an alternative narrative: or better yet, tap into an existing narrative that excludes the insurgents. This narrative is often worked out for you by higher headquarters – but only you

have the detailed knowledge to tailor the narrative to local conditions and generate leverage from it. For example, you might use a nationalist narrative to marginalize foreign fighters in your area, or a narrative of national redemption to undermine former regime elements that have been terrorizing the population. . . .

* * *

* * *

24. **Small is beautiful.** Another natural tendency is to go for large-scale, mass programs. In particular, we have a tendency to template ideas that succeed in one area and transplant them into another, and we tend to take small programs that work and try to replicate them on a larger scale. Again, this is usually a mistake – often programs succeed because of specific local conditions of which we are unaware, or because their very smallness kept them below the enemy's radar and helped them flourish unmolested. . . . .

25. **Fight the enemy's strategy, not his forces.** At this stage, if things are proceeding well, the insurgents will go over to the offensive. Yes, the offensive – because you have created a situation so dangerous to the insurgents, by threatening to displace them from the environment, that they have to attack you and the population to get back into the game. Thus it is normal, even in the most successful operations, to have spikes of offensive insurgent activity late in the campaign. This does not necessarily mean you have done something wrong (though it may: it depends on whether you have successfully mobilized the population). At this point the tendency is to go for the jugular and seek to destroy the enemy's forces in open battle. This is rarely the best choice at company level, because provoking major combat usually plays into the enemy's hands by undermining the population's confidence. Instead, attack the enemy's strategy: if he is seeking to recapture the allegiance of a segment of the local population, then co-opt them against him. If he is trying to provoke a sectarian conflict, go over to "peace enforcement mode." The permutations are endless but the principle is the same – fight the enemy's strategy, not his forces.

26. **Build your own solution – only attack the enemy when he gets in the way.** Try not to be distracted, or forced into a series of reactive moves, by a desire to kill or capture the insurgents. Your aim should be to implement your own solution the "game plan" you developed

early in the campaign, and then refined through interaction with local partners. Your approach must be environment-centric (based on dominating the whole district and implementing a solution to its systemic problems) rather than enemy-centric. This means that, particularly late in the campaign, you may need to learn to negotiate with the enemy. Members of the population that supports you also know the enemy's leaders – they may have grown up together in the small district that is now your company sector – and valid negotiating partners sometimes emerge as the campaign progresses. At this stage, a defection is better than a surrender, a surrender is better than a capture, and a capture is better than a kill.

* * *

27. **Keep your extraction plan secret.** The temptation to talk about home becomes almost unbearable toward the end of a tour. The locals know you are leaving, and probably have a better idea than you of the generic extraction plan – remember, they have seen units come and go. But you must protect the specific details of the extraction plan, or the enemy will use this as an opportunity to score a high-profile hit, re-capture the population's allegiance by scare tactics that convince them they will not be protected once you leave, or persuade them that your successor unit will be oppressive or incompetent. Keep the details secret, within a tightly controlled compartment in your headquarters.

* * *

✦

Acknowledgments: Although any errors or omissions in this paper are mine alone, many people contributed directly or indirectly to it. They included Caleb Carr, Eliot Cohen, Audrey Cronin, Hank Crumpton, Janine Davidson, Jeff Davis, T.X. Hammes, John Hillen, Frank Hoffman, Scott Kofmehl, Christopher Langton, Tom Mahnken, Tim Mulholland, John Nagl, Tom Ricks and Mike Vlahos. Rob Greenway, Bruce Hoffman, Olivier Roy and Marc Sageman influenced my thinking over several months. A current serving officer of the Central Intelligence Agency, and two other members of the intelligence community, also made major contributions but cannot be named. Finally, the many company commanders, platoon leaders and others I worked with in Iraq and elsewhere inspired this effort. You carry the burden of counterinsurgency today, and into the future.

NOTES

1. These excerpts are reproduced with the permission of the publishers of *Military Review*, The Professional Journal of the U.S. Army. This paper reflects the author's personal judgments and does not represent the views of any department or agency of the U.S. Government or any other government (Washington, D.C., 29 March, 2006). Written from fieldnotes compiled in Baghdad, Tajji and Kuwait City, 2006.
2. The author, who holds a doctoral degree in military science, was an adviser to General David H. Petraeus when the latter was commander of the multinational forces deployed in Iraq.
3. Ellipsis points and asterisks are inserted to show where text in the original article has been omitted in this reprint.

EVIL DONE

Rachel Boba
Florida Atlantic University

Abstract: *Resources of local communities are often not spent on pre-paring for a specific terrorist attack, but more generally on actions that seek to reduce the success of attempted attacks as well as damage if an attack is successful. To assist with this process, this chapter presents a fairly specific, but general, approach for individual target assessment as well as several analysis strategies for assessment of groups of targets in a particular jurisdiction. The unique contribution of this chapter is the breakdown of Clarke and Newman's (2006) "EVIL DONE" factors into a set of items that that can be easily scored consistently across targets and among individual analysts. For local authorities, the chapter's goal is to analyze target risk long before a threat is posed or a terrorist attempt is made, as well as to analyze all the potential targets within a community to prioritize prevention strategies and allocation of resources. For researchers, the chapter's goal is to present a methodology that can be used to evaluate targets of different types and across jurisdictions to provide practitioners with context and com-parison for their own analyses as well as test the validity and reliability of the methodology itself.*

Introduction, Purpose, and Goals of this Chapter

Since September 11, 2001, the development of counterterrorism strategies for prevention and response has become a principal concern for state and local governments in the U.S. The Department of Homeland Security has provided millions of dollars over the last several years to fund equipment and programs in local jurisdictions to strengthen prevention, protection, response, and recovery capabilities (Office of Homeland Security, 2008). However, it is a challenge for local law enforcement and city officials to identify the best way to examine their risk and prepare their local communities for the possibility of terrorist attacks. Law enforcement and other government officials at the federal level focus on specific threats, timing, and intelligence information, but it is the responsibility of local authorities to protect themselves as best they can from any type of terrorist threat, whether foreign or domestic. Consequently, resources of local communities are often not spent on preparing for a specific terrorist attack, but more generally on increasing surveillance and detection, hardening targets, or other actions that seek to reduce the success of attempted attacks as well as damage if an attack is successful (Willis, Morral, Kelly, & Medby, 2005).

The purposes of this chapter are: (1) to provide local officials and researchers with a methodology for evaluating risk of terrorist attacks for individual targets, and (2) to provide strategies for aggregate analysis of groups of targets within local jurisdictions by focusing on both the vulnerability of a physical target and the expected loss that could result from a terrorist attack. The risk assessment methodology presented here offers a way that potential targets or groups of targets can be analyzed and prioritized for protection in the absence of a specific threat. For local authorities, the goal is to use the methodology to analyze target risk in order to target-harden and adjust place management practices long before a threat is posed or a terrorist attempt is made, as well as to analyze all the potential targets within a community to prioritize prevention strategies and allocation of resources. For researchers, the chapter's goal is to present a methodology that can be used to evaluate targets of different types and across jurisdictions. The results of such studies would establish ranges of normal and high risk to provide practitioners with context and comparison for their own analyses as well as test the validity and reliability of the methodology itself.

In their recent book, *Outsmarting the Terrorists* (2006), Ron Clarke and Graeme Newman lay out the framework for applying situational crime prevention to terrorist activity at the local level. The authors assert that we "must identify vulnerable targets, prioritize them for protection, analyze their specific weaknesses, and provide them with protection appropriate to their risks" (p. 4). In order to do this, Clarke and Newman identify four key pillars of situational opportunities that terrorists exploit in order to commit terrorist acts. They relate to targets, weapons, tools, and facilitating conditions. Targets are physical structures, either static or moving, where the terrorist attack occurs (e.g., buildings, monuments, transportation hubs, and vehicles). Weapons are the means used to destroy or damage a target (e.g., explosives, guns, chemicals, missiles). Tools are everyday objects that are used in the commission of an attack (e.g., vehicles, identity cards). Finally, facilitating conditions are circumstances or processes that assist the terrorists in their attacks (e.g., loopholes in services or access to buildings, money laundering) (Clarke & Newman, 2006).

To guide this chapter, it is helpful to break down the analysis of situational opportunities of terrorism into three levels or units of analysis. They are: (1) a specific target under a specific threat, (2) a general threat to a target, and (3) a general threat to areas within a community. The first level is the most specific and consists of using the most current intelligence information on terrorist activity to identify an immediate and impending attack on a specific target. This level requires consideration of all four pillars presented by Clarke and Newman (2006), ongoing collection of intelligence data, and the most immediate, tactical responses. Typically, the analysis of these specific threats is the responsibility of federal counterterrorism agencies. Local authorities may assist in collecting information for these specific threats, but are more often tasked with preparing and protecting themselves against more general threats. Consequently, this first level of analysis is not covered in this chapter.

Alternatively, the second and third levels are the focus of this chapter. The second level of analysis concerns assessing individual targets that are not under a specific threat but may be at a general risk for a terrorist attack. In the terrorist risk assessment literature, risk is defined as being a combination of two factors: vulnerability and expected loss (Clarke & Newman, 2006; Newman & Clarke, 2008; Willis et al., 2005). Vulnerability of a particular target refers to "the inherent features of targets that make them susceptible or attractive to attack by terrorists" (Clarke & Newman, 2006, p. 90). Consequence refers to the magnitude and type of damage that results from successful terrorist attacks (Willis et al., 2005), and it can be defined in terms of fatalities, injuries, economic losses, or other types of damage, such as isolation (e.g., transportation) or lack of necessities (e.g., electricity, food, and water). However, because the issue here is examining potential, not actual consequences in the local context, consequences are referred to as "expected losses" (Newman & Clarke, 2008). Thus, the goal at the second level is to provide general assessments of vulnerability and expected loss for individual targets.

More specifically, the second level of analysis centers on Clarke and Newman's "target" pillar of opportunity. In the analysis and problem solving of crime, problem locations (Boba, 2008a) or "risky places" (Clarke & Eck, 2005) are individual addresses (e.g., one convenience store) or a type of place (e.g., all convenience stores) at which there is a concentration of crime or problematic activity. The nature of the activity at the location, the people within it, and its surrounding environment create more opportunities for crime than other non-problematic locations. Analysis focuses on identifying these places and prioritizing them for response (Center for Problem Oriented Policing, 2008). Clarke and Newman (2006) argue the same is true for potential terrorist targets: "in theory, there are an unlimited number of targets for terrorist attack (subway systems, buses, trains, airliners, power plants, reservoirs, embassies, public buildings, prominent individuals, etc.), but they do not all offer the same opportunity. Terrorists must choose among the various distinguishing characteristics of targets" (p. 9). They assert that it is not reasonable to protect every target equally, but by analyzing the risk of targets and prioritizing prevention based on the analysis, the opportunities for attack can be lessened and the potential harm reduced.

In order to assess terrorist targets and subsequently prioritize them, Clarke and Newman (2006) have developed a series of factors based on situational crime prevention concepts. These factors are concerned with the vulnerability of a potential terrorist target, and address whether it is exposed, vital, iconic, legitimate, destructible, occupied, near, or easy (discussed in detail later). These factors are combined to compose the acronym EVIL DONE. According to Clarke and Newman (2006), the attractiveness of a location for terrorists is a combination of these factors, with more vulnerable targets containing more of these factors. The aim of using EVIL DONE to assess the vulnerability of a potential target is not to predict a specific attack, but to evaluate risk more generally and assist local authorities in prioritizing their prevention activities.

The second consideration in assessing a target's risk is the expected loss if the target is attacked. This second level of analysis seeks to evaluate targets generally, so specific losses are often difficult to determine. Thus, the objective of a general assessment of expected loss focuses on the potential loss of life and serious injury since it is the most serious consequence of a terrorist attack and the highest priority for prevention. In a recent publication, Newman and Clarke (2008) provide a method for evaluating the expected loss that includes the consideration of loss of life and injury that could occur in and around a potential target. This and the EVIL DONE approach are combined here to create a methodology for an overall assessment of risk of individual targets at the local level.

The third level of analysis is the aggregate examination of individual target risk assessments within a set geographic area (e.g., city, county, police jurisdiction). The results of the individual target risk assessments within a jurisdiction are combined, along with consideration of the area affected by each target, to produce hotspots of risk. The aim of this aggregate analysis is to assist local agencies in prioritizing their resources and prevention efforts in the most affected areas of their communities (i.e., places where targets cluster and the risk is greatest).

To reiterate, this chapter focuses on the second and third levels of analysis – individual target risk assessment and aggregate analysis of target risk. Most notably, the chapter seeks to refine the EVIL DONE factors by developing a system for evaluating each one of its factors in more detail than currently exists in the literature. There is some research being conducted that evaluates the vulnerability of individual targets using EVIL DONE (Ekici, Ozkan, Celik, & Maxfield, 2008); however, the EVIL DONE strategy is still somewhat vague and requires more specificity if it is to be used consistently and effectively.

INDIVIDUAL TARGET RISK ASSESSMENT

Before a particular target or group of targets can be evaluated, they must be selected from a group of locations within the local community that is under examination. Even though the final risk assessments of targets will vary, not all locations may even need to be evaluated. Generally, the types of targets that are selected for terrorist risk assessment include, but are not limited to: nuclear power plants, ammonium nitrate repositories, airports, railroad tracks, mass transit lines, amusement parks, shopping malls, landmarks, research laboratories, dams, petroleum refineries, ports, government buildings, motorways, rivers, and major utility lines (Newman & Clarke, 2008; Ronczkowski, 2004). More specific examples that consider both the type of target and the local environment include: a suburban shopping mall, a downtown shopping district, a railway station located downtown, a bus station in front of a market, a paint factory near a residential suburb, and a toxic waste dump near a school (Newman & Clarke, 2008). It is difficult to provide specific advice for selecting potential targets since the selection is based on the local community context. For instance, a small town may not have targets that would be selected if they were located in a larger urban area. However, in order to prioritize response, officials would thoughtfully select targets relative to the other locations in their community.

Once the targets are selected, evaluating the risk of a specific type or timing of an attack can be very difficult. In fact, it is for this reason that Clarke and Newman developed the EVIL DONE factors. Before these factors are evaluated, it is recommended that those individuals assigned to the analysis be familiar with not only the specific characteristics and nature of the local targets, but also the research literature on each type of target. For example, there are comprehensive research and evaluation reports on types of targets such as railroads (Wilson, Jackson, Eisman, Steinberg, & Riley, 2007), airplanes (Dugan, LaFree, & Piquero, 2005), and shopping malls (LaTourrette, Howell, Mosher, & MacDonald, 2006). Even though these reports may not speak to factors existing in a particular community, they can be helpful in evaluating the vulnerability and expected losses generally.

Importantly, there are inordinate amounts of research literature and variables that could be considered in a risk analysis, but in a general assessment at the local level, these must be pared down to ensure the analysis is realistic and timely. In this vein, this chapter provides a break down the EVIL DONE factors into a set of items that that can be easily scored consistently across targets and among individual analysts. The results are then combined with Newman and Clarke's methodology for assessing expected loss of human life (Newman & Clarke, 2008) to generate an individual target risk assessment. The following sections describe the methodology for assessing vulnerability using EVIL DONE and expected loss.

Vulnerability: EVIL DONE

Each factor of EVIL DONE is described here and adapted from Clarke and Newman (2006, pp. 92-96) and Newman and Clarke (2008, Brief 29). The EVIL DONE factor items have been created specifically for this chapter and have been developed after consideration of the CARVER schema (Criticality, Accessibility, Recuperability, Vulnerability, Effect and Recognizability), a protocol used by the U.S. Special Operations Forces to provide a systematic way to assess targets from the point of view of the owners of the target rather than from the point of view of the terrorists, which is primarily the viewpoint of EVIL DONE (Newman & Clarke, 2008, Brief 30). Yet, many of the new EVIL DONE factor items are based on common sense knowledge of targets and situational crime prevention concepts. By no means do the items proposed here represent a definitive scoring system, but they are another step closer to quantifying and standardizing assessment of vulnerability based on the EVIL DONE approach.

The scoring items for first six factors (exposed, vital, iconic, legitimate, destructible, and occupied) are scaled (i.e., items are ordinal and mutually exclusive). The scoring items for the last two factors (near and easy) are indexed (i.e., relevant items are summed). For each factor, five is the highest score and represents the value exhibiting the most vulnerability. Zero is the lowest score for each factor. For the six scaled factors, a zero value is warranted when the target does not meet the lowest level of vulnerability listed. For the two indexed factors, a zero value is warranted when the target contains none of the items listed. Thus, the highest total score for the EVIL DONE factors is 40 and the lowest 0. What follows is a description of each factor, the rationalization for the development of its items, and the items themselves denoting their values and examples. When specific circumstances are not covered by the items, it is recommended to make a logical, thoughtful choice as to what is the most relevant item since this is a general approach to the assessment of vulnerability.

Exposed

More visible targets attract more attention than hidden targets or those that are similar to others in the immediate area (e.g., a high rise building). Thus, the Exposed factor of EVIL DONE evaluates the level at which a target is out in the open, visible, and/or attracts attention. The items for scoring a target's exposure consider both the physical shape of the target as well as the type of local environment where the target is located (e.g., urban vs. rural). The type of environment is distinguished because generally urban areas may be considered more exposed than rural areas because they are more populated, located on rivers, boarders, coasts, or may be more recognizable through media, tourism, etc. However, targets that may be relatively small and located in a rural area are likely to stand out because of the types of places around them (e.g., residences and small retail outlets). The items account for both these characteristics and are ranked according to their influence on a target's vulnerability.

The following are the scoring items and examples for the Exposed scale:

Large high rise structure in an urban area 5
    Examples: World Trade Center, Sears Tower, Washington Monument
Large identifiable structure in an urban or rural area 4
    Examples: Golden Gate Bridge, nuclear power plant, Pentagon
Large building or complex in a suburb 3
    (Suburb is considered primarily a residential and retail environment.)
    Examples: shopping mall, high school
Large building or structure in a rural area or small town 2
    Examples: multi-story courthouse, water tower
Cluster of buildings in an urban area 1
    Examples: retail shopping district, university campus

Vital

Terrorists often seek targets that, if damaged, deny a community access to its necessities and will wreak havoc. The Vital factor of EVIL DONE evaluates the level at which a target is critical to a community's day-to-day functioning, possibly its survival. The purpose of attacking these targets is not necessarily to harm people (i.e., poisoning water), but to paralyze and demoralize a community by taking away its necessities. The scoring items consider the type of (e.g., transportation, water, electricity, fuel) and the purpose of (e.g., makes products or distributes products) the target. The items are ranked according to how critical a particular type of target is to a community.

The following are the scoring items and examples for the Vital scale:

Major transportation overcoming a major barrier 5
    Examples: bridge, tunnel
Major transportation paralysis point 4
    Examples: freeway interchange (stack), railroad/subway hub
Power, water, and fuel plants 3
    Examples: power plant, refinery, water treatment plant
Power, water, and fuel conduits 2
    Examples: pipelines, electricity grids, canals
Food distribution 1

Iconic

By destroying a symbol of a country's identity and strength, terrorists hope to weaken the resolve and dishearten its citizens. The Iconic factor of EVIL DONE evaluates the level at which a target has symbolic value. The scoring items consider what a target represents to the terrorist group and how important they believe it is to the country. Thus, those political and national symbols, such as the White House and the Statue of Liberty, are more attractive to terrorists because they represent the entire United States. Commercial, government, and religious targets are important symbols as well but are not as vulnerable because they represent segments of the United States and its culture. Although it may be difficult to anticipate all potential terrorist groups, it is also important to consider how different groups view the iconic nature of a target in different ways. For example, Al Qaeda may see government and political symbols as most iconic, but animal rights extremists and anti-abortion extremists may view research laboratories and abortion clinics/doctors' offices as iconic, respectively.

The following are the scoring items and examples for the Iconic scale:

Major political symbol   5
    Examples: White House, Capitol
Major national symbol 4
    Examples: Statue of Liberty, Mt. Rushmore, Washington Monument
Federal and state government building 3
    Examples: FBI building, State capitol
Major commercial symbol 2
    Examples: Disney, Microsoft
Major city, town, religious building 1
    Examples: city hall, large church or synagogue

Legitimate

The Legitimate factor of EVIL DONE evaluates the level at which a target that terrorists believe, if attacked, will bring them a positive reaction of their sympathizers or would-be sympathizers and not moral condemnation. If the attack is viewed as illegitimate, the terrorist group may lose considerable public support. The scoring items consider what function the target serves and what type of people are typically housed within it. The most legitimate targets are those that house the military or government personnel since these groups dictate the policies and carry out the practices of the government. The least legitimate targets are those that house everyday people doing recreational or everyday things and are seemingly defenseless. For example, a target primarily housing children would be the least legitimate target. For those targets that house a combination of the groups below, select the highest number.

The following are the scoring items and examples for the Legitimate scale:

Houses military personnel or politicians 5
    Examples: Pentagon, Capitol
Houses federal government employees or federal law enforcement
    personnel 4
    Examples: State Department, Treasury Building, FBI headquarters
Houses state or local government or police 3
    Examples: state capitol building, city hall, NYPD Headquarters
Houses civilian workers 2
    Examples: World Trade Center, Microsoft, Ford auto making plant
Houses general citizenry 1
    Examples: shopping mall, amusement park, house of worship

Destructible

Every target is destructible in some way, but some are easier than others and require less effort to destroy. The Destructible factor of EVIL DONE evaluates the amount and accessibility of weapons required to destroy a target. For a terrorist attack to succeed, it must destroy or seriously disable its target. As with concepts of situational crime prevention, perception of a target's destructibility is often as important as its actual destructibility. Thus, when evaluating this factor, perception is just as important to consider. The scoring items consider the amount of and nature of the weapon needed to destroy the target. A target that can be destroyed by a relatively small, more easily accessible weapon is assigned a higher score. Another consideration for this factor is whether the target itself contains materials that enhance its own or another target's destructibility (e.g., airliner filled with jet fuel).

The following are the scoring items and examples for the Destructible scale:

Destructible with an IED 5
    (Improvised explosive device)
Contains chemicals or other materials that would hasten its own
    or another other target's destruction 4
    Examples: Chemical plant, oil refinery, train carrying radioactive
    materials
Destructible with small conventional weapons[1] 3
Destructible with heavy conventional weapons[2] 2
Destructible with a combination of the weapons listed in items 2
    through 5 1

Occupied

The Occupied factor of EVIL DONE evaluates the level at which a target houses people. Many, but not all, terrorist groups seek to kill or injure as many people as possible to cause the most fear. For example, an exception is animal rights extremist groups who typically attack at night when targets are not occupied. However, places with a high density of people (i.e., a relatively large number of people in close proximity) provide the most opportunity for terrorists and present the highest risk of harm. Timing is also an important consideration here because people gather at different time intervals (e.g., daily, weekly, seasonally). The more often a target brings people together, the more opportunity a terrorist has for a successful attack. Thus, the scoring items consider both the amount of people and how often they come together.

The following are the scoring items and examples for the Occupied scale:

Houses many people 24 hours per day, 7 days per week 5
    Examples: military base, hospital
Houses many people 8 – 12 hours daily 4
    Examples: schools, large office buildings
Crowded space at specific times of the day and days of the week 3
    Examples: subway terminals, buses, houses of worship.
Crowded space at specific dates and times 2
    Examples: concert hall, political speech/rally, sports stadium
Crowded spaces at specific times of the year; seasonal 1
    Examples: shopping mall at holiday season, water park, outdoor park
    on holidays

Near

The Near factor of EVIL DONE evaluates the level at which a target is close to the home base of terrorist operations. Criminological studies show that offenders will select targets near where they live and/or work because like everyone else they want to expend the minimum effort and be familiar with their surroundings (Brantingham & Brantingham, 1990). A target that requires less travel by and is more familiar to terrorists provides more opportunity for attack. This is often a major challenge for foreign terrorists, and they may, for example, adapt by entering the target country and living in an immigrant community nearby. Because this method is used for general assessment, it is not likely that there would be information about specific terrorist bases in the area. Thus, the items also consider general factors of proximity – nearness to the country's land or sea borders, ease of travel to the target, and number of similar targets (i.e., more targets allow the terrorist to pick nearer ones). As noted above, the items for this and the next factor are indexes, so instead of a selecting one item to represent the target's vulnerability, each item has a value of 1, and a target's score is determined by adding the values of all the relevant items.

The following are the scoring items and some examples for the Near index:

Close to known/suspected domestic/foreign terrorist base .... ❐
Close to country's border, land or sea (coast) .... ❐
Close to domestic immigrant community .... ❐
Close to major transportation hub .... ❐
    Examples: airport, train station, port
Many similar targets .... ❐
    Examples: bus stops, open markets, subway stations
    Total Score .... ___

Easy

The Easy factor of EVIL DONE assesses the level at which a target is accessible to the public or not well protected. For example, it was easy for domestic terrorist Timothy McVeigh to park the truck bomb just eight feet from the federal building in Oklahoma City, but it was difficult for Al Qaeda to access the World Trade Center on 9/11 because security had been increased after the earlier attack. The scoring items consider accessibility and nature of a target's security. A target with more access and less security requires less effort by terrorists and an increased opportunity for a terrorist attack.

The following are the scoring items for the Easy index:

Public access to building/no security check .... ☐
Parking near the building and/or unrestricted .... ☐
Some entry points unsecured or not monitored .... ☐
Inadequate security personnel .... ☐
Inadequate security cameras and monitoring .... ☐
    Total Score .... —

Table 1 provides a summary of the EVIL DONE factor items and their scores.

Expected Loss: Death and Injury

The second consideration in assessing risk is the expected loss if a target is attacked. There are actual damages that result from successful terrorist attacks that can include the number of people injured or killed, the cost of rebuilding the target, and the collateral damage caused if the target affects other things such as transportation networks, or power, fuel or food distribution. Because this methodology assesses targets generally and does not speculate on the exact type of attack, it is difficult to estimate the wide range of damages that could occur. To facilitate a straightforward and realistic analysis for a local community, expected loss is the assessment of potential loss of life and serious injury, as it is the most serious consequence of a terrorist attack and the highest priority for prevention.

Newman and Clarke (2008, Brief 31) provide a method for evaluating the expected loss of life or injury in and around a particular target. It is more involved than using general population estimates and square area ratios of areas around a target (i.e., residential population density) since many targets do not have residential populations (e.g., government buildings, monuments, retail). They present Table 2, which can be completed for each target to estimate a score for fatalities and injuries of people.

The injury score considers both the seriousness of the injuries as well as the length of time of injuries. Albeit, these are merely estimates as the type of attack can dictate the amount and type of injuries (e.g., gunfire vs. IED). One recommendation is to use a target's corresponding ranking of

Table 1: EVIL DONE Scoring System

EVIL DONE Factor	EVIL DONE Factor
EXPOSED (scale) Large high-rise structure; urban area ... 5 Large identifiable structure; urban/rural ... 4 Large building or complex; suburbs ... 3 Large building; rural/small town ... 2 Cluster of buildings; urban ... 1	**DESTRUCTIBLE (scale)** Destructible with IED ... 5 Contains chemicals or materials that would hasten destruction ... 4 Destructible with small conventional weapons ... 3 Destructible with large conventional weapons ... 2 Destructible with combination of weapons listed in items 2 - 5 .. 1
VITAL (scale) Major transportation overcoming major obstacle ... 5 Major transportation paralysis point ... 4 Power, water, fuel plants ... 3 Power, water, fuel conduits ... 2 Food distribution ... 1	**OCCUPIED (scale)** Houses many people 24/7 ... 5 Houses many people 8-12 hours daily ... 4 Crowded space at specific times of day/day of week ... 3 Crowded space at specific dates and times ... 2 Crowded space at specific times of year; seasonal ... 1
ICONIC (scale) Major political symbol ... 5 Major national symbol ... 4 Federal or state building ... 3 Major commercial symbol ... 2 Major city, town, or religious building ... 1	**NEAR (index)** Close to known/suspected terrorist base ... ❐ Close to own country's border or coast ... ❐ Close to domestic immigrant community ... ❐ Near major transportation hub ... ❐ Many similar targets ... ❐ Total ... _____
LEGITIMATE (scale) Houses military personnel or politicians ... 5 Houses federal government or federal law enforcement ... 4 Houses local government or local police employees ... 3 Houses civilian workers ... 2 Houses general citizenry ... 1	**EASY (index)** Public access to building/no ID check ... ❐ Parking near and/or unrestricted ❐ Some entry points unsecured ... ❐ Inadequate security personnel ... ❐ Inadequate surveillance cameras .. ❐ Total ... _____

Table 2: Injury and Fatality Scoring System

Time frame	Deaths Score=3 per death	Major injuries (emergency hospital care; score=2 per case)	Serious injuries (Long term care; score=1 per case)	TOTAL INJURY SCORE
Immediate				
Next day or week				
Several months				
Several years				
TOTAL				

the "destructible" factor in EVIL DONE to base the expected loss assessment. For example, if a bus is assessed in EVIL DONE as being destructible with an IED, fatalities and injuries would be evaluated based on what would happen if that bus was attacked using an IED. Whatever the approach, it is important to be consistent across targets in the expected loss assessment so that targets within the same community are rated in the same manner.

Once the EVIL DONE vulnerability and the expected loss assessments are complete for selected targets in a community, the final risk score for each target is the product of the two scores. These scores can then be used in a number of ways to prioritize prevention response.

Aggregate Analysis of Targets

To date, no research using this methodology has been used to determine average scores across a variety of targets and communities to provide comparison for individual target scores. One goal for this author is that this chapter will encourage and guide this type of research. But to begin here, local communities would use the results of the aggregate analysis to provide the context for individual target comparison as well as examine their entire community as a whole.

Figure 1. Example of mean and standard deviation of risk scores.

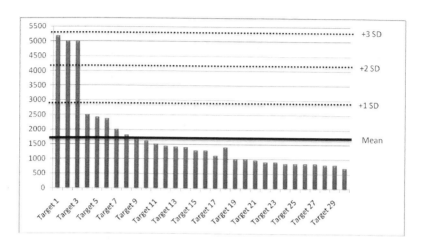

Simple Statistical Analysis

Targets can be ranked from highest to lowest based on their risk assessment score. Local officials would begin terrorism prevention strategies with those ranked highest. This method would be most useful with a small number of targets in a community (under 25). Mean and standard deviation can also be used to compare and prioritize targets for prevention activities. The mean and standard deviation for the distribution of risk scores are determined and then placed on a chart, as in Figure 1, for a straightforward interpretation. In Figure 1, Targets 1, 2, and 3 would be prioritized for prevention since their scores are notably higher than the rest (i.e., over two standard deviations above the mean). How each community uses these analysis results will vary by practical considerations. For example, if a community has resources to only address one or two targets, they might select those furthest from and higher than the mean. Another community may have more resources and may select those above both the first and second standard deviation. In either case, the chart can be used to justify the allocation of resources to particular targets.

Aggregate Geographic Analysis

The previous two strategies examine targets regardless of their locations in a community. But it is also important to examine targets in terms

Figure 2. Example of graduated size point map.

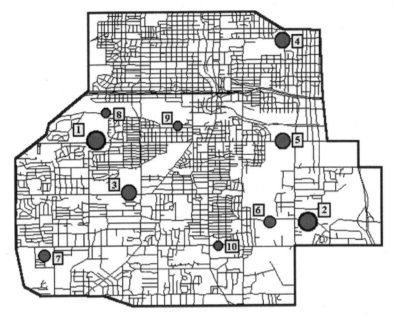

of their relative proximity to one another and their potential effect on surrounding areas. Several methods are presented here that can be used to accomplish this goal.

In the first method, the target locations can be displayed on a map as graduated symbols that are sized based on each target's risk score. Prioritization would occur by simply examining the map for clusters of targets and the sizes of the symbols to determine areas that have higher risk. The size of the symbols can be based on natural breaks of the distribution of scores, in equal intervals, by quantiles (top 25% are the largest size), or using mean and standard deviation. One disadvantage of this method is that if there are a large number of targets in a concentrated area, they may overlap one another, making a visual analysis difficult. However, for smaller communities with fewer targets, this approach is applicable. Figure 2 is an example of a graduated size point map of targets by their risk score (note: the numbers represent their scores' rankings).

In the second method of geographic analysis, the target locations are weighted by their scores and depicted in a density hotspot map. Most simply, a density map calculates the distance between each location and

Figure 3. Example of density hotspot map with target locations.

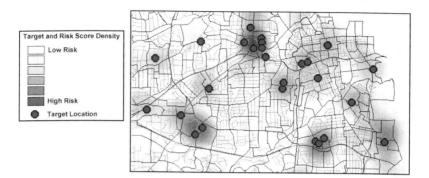

depicts the concentration of targets. Each target location can be weighted by its risk score to provide an analysis of both location concentration and relative risk. One disadvantage of this method is that each target is represented by single or multiple points based on address, but not by the total amount of land coverage (e.g., university campus, retail area with multiple buildings). It is recommended that if a single target consists of multiple addresses, either use the most central address and the total risk score or divide the risk score by the number of addresses and assign each address the result (i.e., a proportion of the risk score).

Figure 3 is an example of what a resulting density hotspot map would look like. Note that the shaded areas are not limited to the examination of predetermined areas, but mimic the flow and location of the target locations themselves. It is recommended to place either points or polygons (depending on their size and land coverage) representing the actual location of each target. This is important because density maps shade areas without targets because they are showing concentration.

Instead of mapping the exact target locations with their risk scores, the third method for geographic analysis requires that all the targets' risk scores be assigned to predetermined areas (e.g., beat, census tracks, census blocks) and totaled to create a graduated area hotspot map. This author has previously outlined this method in detail. It is summarized here, but for a more detailed description, see Boba (2008b).

This analysis strategy is straightforward as well. If there are multiple targets in an area, all the target risk scores are summed for that area. In order to do this analysis, two factors must be determined based on the nature of the community and the nature of each target under examination. First, the size of the geographic unit (i.e., predetermined areas to which the scores are attributed) is selected based on knowledge of the specific jurisdiction, its topography, and proximity to other features. For example, in a jurisdiction with less square mileage, the areas used should be relatively small. Second, the selection of an area at risk based on a target's location might vary by the type of target. For example, the bombing of a mall may only affect the immediate area of the mall since malls are typically surrounded by large parking lots and ring roads; however, bombing of a nuclear or chemical plant may affect a larger area since the bombing would release radiation or chemicals into the air in the surrounding neighborhoods. The risk scores of targets, such as nuclear or chemical plants, may be assigned to the area in which it is actually located as well as to surrounding areas it may effect if attacked (e.g., 1/2 mile radius). Also, a particular target may extend across the boundaries of several predetermined areas (e.g., university campus, canals, railroad tracks). In this case, all the areas the target falls into would be assigned the risk assessment score of that target.

Once the sizes of the geographic areas are assigned and each target is evaluated to determine the areas it could potentially affect, the risk assessment score of each target is placed in the appropriate area(s). Multiple scores are totaled for each area and the result is a graduated area map that shows the hotspots of risk within the community. Hotspots can be determined, depending on the purpose of the analysis, by the natural breaks of the area scores, using mean and standard deviation, or quantiles (e.g., top 25% of the areas). Figure 4 is a general example of a graduated color hotspot map (from Boba, 2008b). The cluster of darkest areas comprises those that are at highest risk and would be prioritized for prevention and resource allocation.

CONCLUSION

The purpose of this chapter has been to provide a method for individual target assessment of terrorism risk and strategies for aggregate analysis of targets within a local community with the goal of prioritizing prevention and resource allocation. In particular, this chapter has provided a new system for evaluating vulnerability of a target based on the EVIL DONE factors. It is the hope of this author that practitioners and researchers test

Figure 4: Example of graduated color hotspot map.

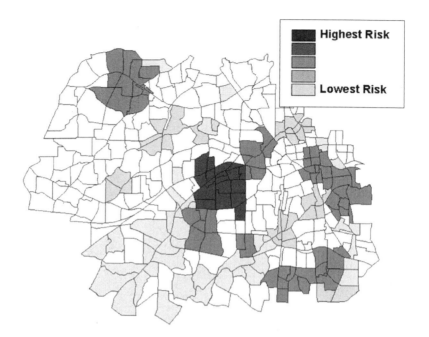

these methodologies and strategies and they are refined even further to offer assistance in the evaluation of risk for terrorism at the local level.

Address correspondence to: Rboba@fau.edu

NOTES

1. Small conventional weapons can be defined as infantry weapons that an individual soldier is able to carry on his own. These weapons include pistols, revolvers, submachine guns, shotguns, rifles, assault rifles, light machine guns and hand grenades. Light weapons, which require two or more soldiers to operate, consist of medium and heavy machine guns, smaller mortars, with caliber of less than 100mm, recoilless rifles,

anti-tank and anti-aircraft guns and some rocket launchers (http://disarm.igc.org/sa_def.php).

2. Heavy weapons would then be anything that fits into the following seven categories: 1. battle tanks, 2. armored combat vehicles, 3. large caliber artillery systems, 4. combat aircraft, 5. attack helicopters, 6. warships, 7. missiles or missile systems. (For more detail see: http://disarm.igc.org/oc-def.php/.)

REFERENCES

Boba, R. (2008a). *Crime analysis with crime mapping.* Thousand Oaks, CA: Sage Publications.

Boba, R. (2008b). A crime mapping technique for assessing vulnerable targets for terrorism in local communities. In S. Chainey & L. Tompson (Eds.), *Crime mapping case studies: Practice and research* (pp. 143–151). West Sussex, England: John Wiley & Sons Ltd.

Brantingham, P. J., & Brantingham, P. L. (1981). *Environmental criminology.* Beverly Hills, CA: Sage Publications.

Brantingham, P. L., & Brantingham, P. J. (1990). Situational crime prevention in practice. *Canadian Journal of Criminology, 32,* 17–40.

Center for Problem Oriented Policing. (2008). *The SARA model.* Retrieved December 29, 2008 from: www.popcenter.org/about/p=sara

Clarke, R. V., & Newman, G. (2006). *Outsmarting the terrorists.* Portsmouth, NH: Greenwood Publishing Group.

Clarke, R. V., & Eck, J. (2005). *Crime analysis for problem solvers: In 60 small steps.* Washington DC: Office of Community Oriented Policing Services.

Dugan, L., LaFree, G. & Piquero, A. (2005). Testing a rational choice model of airline hijackings. *Criminology, 43*(4), 1031–1065.

Ekici, N., Ozkan, M., Celik, A., & Maxfield, M. (2008). Outsmarting the terrorists in Turkey. *Crime Prevention and Community Safety, 10,* 126–139.

LaTourrette, T., Howell, D., Mosher, D., & MacDonald J. (2006). *Reducing terrorism risk at shopping centers: An analysis of potential security options.* Santa Monica, CA: Rand.

Newman, G., & Clarke, R. (2008). *Policing terrorism: An executive's guide.* Washington DC: Office of Community Oriented Policing Services.

Office of Homeland Security. (2008). Retrieved December 29, 2008 from http://www.ojp.usdoj.gov/odp/welcome.html

Ronczkowski, R. (2004). *Terrorism and organized hate crime: Intelligence gathering, analysis, and investigations.* Boca Raton, FL: CRC Press.

Willis, H., Morral, A., Kelly, T., & Medby, J. (2005). *Estimating terrorism risk.* Santa Monica, CA: Rand.

Wilson, J., Jackson, B., Eisman, M., Steinberg, P., & Riley, J. (2007). *Securing America's passenger-rail systems.* Santa Monica, CA: Rand.

BIOTERRORISM: A SITUATIONAL CRIME PREVENTION APPROACH

William R. Clark[1]
University of California at Los Angeles

Abstract: *By the end of 2009, the U.S. will have spent over $60 billion preparing to defend Americans against a bioterrorist attack and its consequences, in spite of the fact that there has never been a single verified instance of the loss of human life to bioterrorism. Many, both within and outside of government, have proposed that we must reassess our approach to defending against a bioterrorism threat. In this chapter, I propose that the principles of situational crime prevention could be extended to include a detailed analysis of not just the potential targets of bioterrorism, but also of the bioterrorists themselves: their capabilities and, especially, their weapons. This may lead to a much more realistic estimate of the magnitude of the bioterrorist threat, and a more effective distribution of resources in the overall war on ter-rorism.*

Introduction

Situational crime prevention, as an approach to dealing with the threat of terrorism proposes, first, identification and prioritization of potential terror targets, and then rational, detailed analyses of ways to make each target less attractive to would-be terrorists (Clarke & Newman, 2006; Newman &

Clarke, 2008). This is clearly a more efficient (and economical) approach to defending against terrorist attacks than more diffuse campaigns to "root out terrorism at its source." Terrorists must think long and hard about how to allocate their resources – human and otherwise – to achieve their aims, and will seek weapons and targets that give them maximal "bang for the buck" (Boba, 2008).

But any nation's resources – human and otherwise – for defending against terrorism are also not infinite, and defenders, too, must seek to maximize the return on their investment (Boba, 2008; Clarke & Newman, 2006). I propose that the principles of situational crime prevention could profitably be extended to include a detailed analysis of not just the potential *targets* of terrorism, but also of *the terrorists themselves*: their capabilities and, especially, their weapons. As a case in point, I will discuss the assessment of the bioterrorist threat in the United States.

As we can see in Figure 1, the United States government, by the end of 2009, will have spent over $60 billion preparing to defend Americans against a bioterrorist attack and its consequences. Table 1 helps put this in context. We spend more annually on bioterror preparation than on the operation of many branches of the federal government. And yet there has never, in the entire history of modern terrorism, been a single verified instance of the loss of human life to bioterrorism.[2]

The political decisions leading up to this unprecedented expenditure have been discussed in numerous books (see for e.g., Clark, 2008), and need not be detailed here. Rather we will focus on the magnitude of the threat posed specifically by terrorist attacks using biological weapons. This will be useful in determining how to distribute our own resources, including mechanisms like situational crime prevention, in defending ourselves against terrorism generally. Should we continue to spend upwards of $7 billion per year (and the trend shows no signs of abating) to defend ourselves against the possibility of a bioterrorist attack? How likely is it that those individuals or groups who might wish to use biological weapons to sow terror in the United States are actually capable of doing so?

What would it take to make a bioweapon capable of causing mass casualties? The lesson of Aum Shinrikyo.

Aum Shinrikyo was a messianic cult based in Japan in the 1980s and '90s. It is known mostly for its release of sarin nerve gas in the Tokyo subway system in March, 1995, killing 12 people and injuring hundreds more,

Figure 1. Biodefense spending by fiscal year (*=estimated; **=requested).

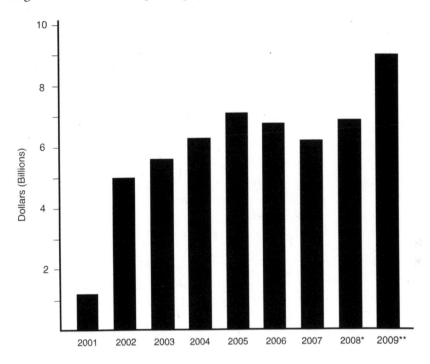

Table 1: Bioterrorism Spending in Context

Agency/Function	Billions Spent
Social Security	7.9
EPA	7.3
Bioterrorism	6.4
Commerce Dept.	6.1
NSF	6.0
Judicial Branch	5.9
Legislative Branch	4.3

some seriously. In a preliminary run-up to this attack, cult members had carried out a previous gassing in the provincial town of Matsumoto that killed seven. Political terrorism for quasi-religious purposes was a clearly defined aim of Aum Shinrikyo. Their major goal was destabilization of the Japanese government to clear the way for the ascendancy of its leader, Shoku Asahara, to political leadership of the country, which would be reformed along cult lines (Kaplan & Marshall, 1996).

Aum cult members were drawn largely from the middle and upper-middle classes of Japanese society. Laborers and service workers had too few assets to be of interest to Aum's leadership. Most were young, and a large portion were college-educated. When interviewed after the cult's collapse, many confessed to a sense of alienation from what they perceived as Japan's materialistic, work-oriented culture, which left them little time to explore themselves and other ways of looking at the world. Most also craved a sense of community and belonging which they found lacking in their daily lives.

But the use of sarin gas in a Tokyo subway by Aum operatives in 1995 was an instance of chemical, not biological, terrorism. A subsequent detailed investigation into cult activities in the years preceding the subway attack revealed, however, that cult scientists had also endeavored to develop lethal biological weapons of terror as early as 1990, well before their work with sarin. The cult was completely broken up and eliminated soon after the subway attacks, and it never did manage to produce an effective weapon based on biological agents. But in trying, they mounted what is still considered the largest, most expensive attempt in history by a non-state entity to develop biological weapons for the express purpose of mass murder.

The research facilities built by Aum Shinrikyo for developing biological weapons were located in their main compound near the village of Kamikuishiki at the base of Mt. Fuji; in a building on the east side of Tokyo; and at Mt. Aso, in Kyushu province. No expense was spared in ordering the most up-to-date scientific equipment for working with viruses, and with bacteria and bacterial toxins.

One of the first biological agents they tried to weaponize was botulinum toxin, one of the deadliest human poisons known: three-billionths of an ounce may be fatal in humans. This nerve toxin is produced by a common soil bacterium, *Clostridium botulinum*, and cult scientists attempted to isolate the toxin from bacteria gathered nearby and grown in culture flasks in their own laboratory. Following established protocols they attempted to harvest and concentrate the toxin from bacterial growth medium, and convert it to a form that could be sprayed from a high-pressure nozzle. This material was actually used in attacks against the Japanese parliament, portions of the Tokyo airport, and even the headquarters of the American Seventh Fleet in Yokohama. None of these attacks produced any casualties. A second generation of botulinum toxin was used in an attempt to kill the royal family during the wedding of the crown prince, again without results.

The cult's scientists subsequently turned their attention to production of weapons-grade anthrax. Anthrax is particularly deadly in its spore form: dry, hard, dust-like particles which, if properly prepared, can be carried great distances by even light winds, and when inhaled produce the most lethal form of the disease of the same name.

The cult used large fans to disseminate what they believed was a highly purified preparation of anthrax spores from the top of a building adjoining their laboratory in Tokyo. Aside from a transient sickening stench, and a few cases of mild illness in people and pets close to the building, there were no effects of the attack. No cases of anthrax were reported or clinically detected. Had they prepared a fully potent batch of infectious anthrax spores, and disseminated it properly, it is likely that thousands – possibly tens of thousands – of people could have been killed. Obviously that was their intent. A second attempt to spread anthrax, this time around the Imperial Palace, was carried out a few months later, again with no effect. Subsequent investigations suggested they had cultured a relatively harmless anthrax strain normally used for animal vaccinations (and thus by definition unlikely to cause disease), and in addition had likely failed to convert it to the more deadly spore form of anthrax.

Why did Aum Shinrikyo fail to achieve its goals?

To prepare and execute successfully the kinds of bioterrorist attacks Aum Shinrikyo was aiming for requires solving an equation in three variables: state-of-the-art laboratory facilities; enough money for equipment and supplies; and people with the knowledge, experience and technical skills to carry out the program.

The cult clearly had the required facilities and more than enough money available to undertake bioweapons production. And it is true that Aum Shinrikyo had an impressive staff of highly trained scientists and physicians in the inner circle (Table 2). But were they up to the task? With all of their impressive credentials, what kind of preparation did they

Table 2: Some Aum Shinrikyo Scientists

Masumai Uchiya	Trained in organic chemistry at Tsukuba University
Toro Toyoda	Graduate studies in particle physics at Tokyo University
Ikuo Hayashi	Cardiovascular surgeon, trained at Keio University in Japan and Mt. Sinai Hospital in New York City
Seiichi Endo	PhD in Molecular Biology; researcher at Kyoto University before joining Aum
Hideo Murai	Graduate degree in astrophysics from Osaka University

really have to develop and deploy weapons-grade anthrax and botulinum toxin (see also Newman & Clarke, 2006)?

University and government laboratories that undertake isolation of pure materials from microorganisms harvested from nature know that it requires a broad range of skilled scientists who are experienced in each of the many phases required for isolation and purification of microbial products. For example, in the case of botulinum toxin, it is not enough to know that it is made by a bacterium (*C. botulinum*) that lives in soil. There is not just one *C. botulinum*; there are at least seven different strains of this bacterium, each producing a different neurotoxin. Only three of these are toxic in humans. There are even regional substrains of these strains, each differing from the others in small but possibly important ways. It takes a real expert to properly identify the right germ to even begin working with.

A specialized microbiology research laboratory will also have skilled protein biochemists, who can take a crude extract of bacterial toxin and put it through the many rigorously controlled steps needed to bring the toxin to a purity hopefully approaching 100%. Preparations of toxin contaminated with left-over bacterial cell-wall products, for example, may trigger a violent immune response which, while not directed specifically at the toxin, may in fact promote a generalized elevated state of non-specific immunity in affected individuals that could destroy the toxin. This is a persistent (but well-understood and controlled) problem in vaccine production.

It is also necessary to know something about the stability of the toxin in various degrees of purity so that it can be stored without losing potency.

In the case of botulinum toxin, highly purified preparations are actually less stable than more crude preparations. Sometimes chemical preservatives may be added, but attaining just the right formulation of preservatives is tricky, and the formulas are among the best-guarded secrets of most bioweapons programs. Various methods of storage must also be tested, and the exact conditions for maintaining stability over time must be rigorously observed. But even under the best conditions, at ambient temperatures and humidity most biological preparations cannot be maintained beyond a month or two.

Then there is the problem of choosing a method of delivery that assures widespread dissemination of the toxin without damaging it. Here it is crucial to consult with a biotechnologist, a combination of biologist and engineer. Should the material be spread from a low-flying aircraft? Wafted by fan from the back of a moving truck or the roof of a building? Pushed through a high-pressure spray nozzle? This requires a knowledge both of the material being disseminated, and the mechanics of various disseminating devices. The effect of dissemination on potency of the toxin must be precisely determined.

And finally, one needs a knowledgeable meteorologist as part of the team. Wind strength and direction, temperature, moisture, and U.V. radiation from the sun, as well as many components of automobile and industrial air pollution, can have a profound effect on botulinum toxin. Wind must be considered not only in terms of lateral direction, but in terms of temperature-driven updrafts as well. U.V. radiation from the sun can greatly reduce the viability of many biological reagents. Failure to take all of these variables carefully into account can decrease many-fold the effectiveness of aerosolized bioweapons.

Aum scientists also encountered serious problems when they tried to produce weaponized anthrax. It appears that in this case, they chose an alternate method for acquiring dangerous pathogens: they probably stole them. Investigations by the Tokyo police suggested that they had most likely obtained their anthrax seed cultures through a lower-level cult member with ties to a local university.

But getting anthrax bacteria (however acquired) to grow in the laboratory requires considerable knowledge of the requirements of different strains. This usually comes from years of experience, judging when cultures must be subdivided, recognizing from the appearance of the cells themselves what more may be needed, or perhaps what is present in excess, for optimum growth. These are not things necessarily picked up in a university-level microbiology lab course.

Even more skill is required to convert expanding cultures to conditions that encourage a high degree of spore formation, without killing off huge amounts of bacteria. The conditions that trigger spore formation are often lethal for the bacteria if not managed properly. But even under the best of conditions, there will be more bacteria (living or dead) than actual spores, and both living and dead bacterial cells must be gotten rid of in order to end up with the highest possible degree of pure spores that will germinate upon settling into human lungs.

Conversion of even high-grade anthrax spores to a form that can be efficiently disseminated is another tricky task. Ideally, the spores should be released as a cloud of very dry, individual spore particles that stay aloft in the air as long as possible. This is an important finishing step, which can be accomplished in a variety of ways, including coating the spores with electrostatic agents that cause them to repel one another and not form clumps. Single spores, and small clumps of a few spores will stay aloft for some time upon dispersal, increasing the possibility of inhalation. But larger clumps will settle too quickly to the ground or other surfaces.

So first of all the spores must be dried, which if not done properly can easily damage them. And once dried they must be stirred gently to break up any large aggregates, which can lead to loss of even more spores. Finally, truly weaponized spores would have to be coated with an electrostatic agent. But the Aum scientists chose instead to spray a liquid slurry of what they hoped was a lethal batch of anthrax spores from the roof of the cult's eight-story laboratory in the Kameido region of Tokyo. This was almost certainly doomed to failure. As Jonathan Tucker has pointed out:

> The capability to disperse microbes and toxins over a wide area as an inhalable aerosol . . . requires a delivery system whose development would outstrip the technical capabilities of all but the most sophisticated terrorists. Not only is the dissemination process for biological agents inherently complex, requiring specialized equipment and expertise, but effective dispersal is easily disrupted by environmental and meteorological conditions. (Tucker & Sands, 1999, p. 46)

A sample of the material sprayed that day was collected by police, and was finally analyzed at an American university in 1999.[3] It was found to contain a low level of anthrax spores and anthrax bacteria, plus many other types of bacteria that may or may not have been part of the material sprayed from the cult's building. A DNA analysis of the anthrax material showed that it was from the Sterne 34F2 strain, used to vaccinate farm animals against anthrax It is essentially completely harmless in humans.

But even had they managed to steal a highly lethal strain of anthrax, given the form of their preparation (liquid slurry), its poor quality, the means used to disseminate it, and lack of attention given to weather conditions, the amount of damage done to humans even in the immediate vicinity of the building would have been minimal at best. Delivery of weaponized biological agents presents a formidable challenge that remains a serious barrier to the use of biological weapons to this day. As even William Patrick, a staunch advocate of a vigorous bioterrorism defense program, admits:

> dry [anthrax] product with the desired properties requires serious development with skilled personnel and sophisticated equipment . . . [While] Iraq successfully produced high quality liquids of anthrax and botulinum A toxin in quantity, their efforts to weaponize their agents were crude and far from successful. . . . By analogy, if a dedicated nation such as Iraq had problems with agent delivery and dissemination, it follows that terrorists would also experience these problems, and at a higher level of intensity. (Patrick, 1996, pp. 208-210)

So the reason for failure of Aum's attempts to produce a functional bioweapon can be summed up in three words: people, people, people. It wasn't a lack of facilities, and it wasn't a lack of money. It wasn't for lack of access to information on how to make a bioweapon. It was a lack of people with years of experience in a dozen different scientific and engineering disciplines essential to the task. While there were a number of individuals among the Aum leadership with advanced training in various scientific and medical fields, none had in-depth backgrounds in microbiology or other biological sciences directly impinging on bioweapons development. None had the biotechnology background for large-scale pathogen production. None had the engineering skills to produce an efficient weapons delivery system (see also Hamm, 2007; Kenney, 2007).

Some in the U.S. government saw the evidence of Aum's dabbling in production of bioweapons as trumpeting a dangerous new escalation in the global threat of bioterrorism. Others saw it as evidence that producing effective bioweapons was not trivial, and likely beyond the capabilities of even the most technically sophisticated terrorists. The latter view did not prevail.

The lessons of "Amerithrax," 2001.

The dissemination of anthrax spores using the U.S. Postal Service in September and October, 2001, is the most serious attempt to carry out an attack on U.S. soil using a bioweapon. The FBI code name for the probe into these attacks was Amerithrax. The Amerithrax attacks provide our first real glimpse into what might happen when determined terrorists produce, or otherwise acquire, high-grade human pathogens and use them effectively. These attacks killed five people, and seriously injured at least sixteen others.

Letters containing anthrax spores were mailed in two batches from New Jersey. The first batch, probably containing five letters, was post-marked September 18, 2001 and sent to news organizations in Florida (American Media, Inc.) and New York (ABC, CBS, NBC and the New York Post). Only the letters to the New York Post and NBC were recovered for forensic analysis. A second batch of at least two letters was mailed on October 9. One was received in the office of Senator Tom Daschle (SD), and a second addressed to Senator Patrick Leahy (VT) was found a few weeks later among undelivered Senate mail.

No harm was done to the individuals to whom the letters were ad-dressed. The targeted individuals rarely opened their own mail. With one or two possible exceptions, the victims of these attacks were office personnel or other associates of the primary targets, or people working in postal facilities through which the contaminated letters had been processed. Whether this "collateral damage" was intended or even envisioned by the terrorist or terrorists is unknown.

Because of their proximity in time to the World Trade Center and Pentagon attacks of September 11, initial focus was on foreign terrorists. It seemed a reasonable assumption that the two incidents could be related.[4] But within a year or two after the attacks, nearly all experts agreed that one or more highly skilled American scientists were responsible, directly or indirectly, for at least the production of the anthrax used, and probably for its dissemination. The FBI leaked the name of one government scientist who was the subject of an intense but inconclusive investigation that lasted six years. More recently, a second scientist was implicated, but has since committed suicide.

The anthrax spores used in the Amerithrax attacks distinguish these incidents from all others we have experienced. Unlike the harmless vaccine strain used by Aum Shinrikyo scientists, at least some of these spores were from a highly virulent form of anthrax, and milled into a fine powder ideal for dissemination by a number of means. FBI tests showed that the spores had been generated in the previous two years, but the initial investigations did not indicate where they had been produced.

The experts are also nearly unanimous that the spores could only have been produced in a very high-tech, fully equipped laboratory, by a person or persons themselves expert in every aspect of growing anthrax bacilli and converting them to spores. The spores may have been stolen from one of these facilities and disseminated through the mails by an unskilled person, but they were very unlikely to have been made by a non-scientist in a garage laboratory, and certainly not by terrorists in a cave in Afghanistan.

So who could mount a bioterrorist attack in the U.S., and how would they go about it?

Individuals – When we think of individuals and bioterrorism, we are really talking about domestic terrorism. It is difficult to imagine an individual foreign terrorist producing and weaponizing a pathogen, and bringing it to the U.S. to mount a deadly attack with no other help. But we are already reasonably certain that an individual *per se* is capable of mounting a bioterrorist attack (or at least of committing a biocrime) against us, because all evidence suggests the Amerithrax perpetrator(s) acted alone.

America has a history of lone avengers, individuals who believe they have a quasi-divine mandate to right some perceived wrong done in the world, usually to them. If some people die in the process, well, so be it. Collateral damage. In recent years, we have the examples of Theodore Kaczynski and Timothy McVeigh to remind us what determined loners can do in their quest for "justice." And it is almost impossible to stop the actions of single individuals. Most have never committed a crime before, never came onto the radar screen of those looking out for the public's security. We may have to live with them as the price of a free and open society.

To the extent that creation and deployment of a bioweapon is an extraordinarily difficult task for even the most determined organized groups, we can feel reasonably assured that an individual, acting alone, is unlikely to be able to mount a major biological attack against America anytime soon. But Amerithrax did happen, and that will rightly never be far from the minds of biosecurity analysts and our political leaders. Steps have been taken to assure that commercial access to pathogens of the quality used in that attack are placed beyond the reach of even the relatively few who know where to look for them in the first place.

And Amerithrax did happen. We will have to leave it at that.

Groups – When it comes to the possibility of bioterrorism by groups in America, there are groups, and there are groups. Domestic groups like the Minnesota Patriot's Council or the Aryan Nations; like the Identity Christians (an inspiration to Timothy McVeigh); and the innumerable so-called "militias" of overweight, middle-aged men that tramp through the woods on weekends – all remind us that the disaffected do not always act alone. Like those who do, these groups generally believe they are acting to right some sort of wrong.

But when we speak of groups and the possibility of bioterrorism, of course, the large pink elephant in the room is Al Qaeda and its various cells, offshoots and copycats. Much has been made of the fact that materials relating to biological weapons were recovered from Al Qaeda training camps near Kandahar, Afghanistan in December, 2001. Milton Leitenberg has described these findings in detail in a recent analysis (Leitenberg, 2005). Among the items found were books on biological warfare and on microbiology, dating mostly from the 1950s and '60s. These would have provided some information relevant to bioterrorism, but that information would have been far from cutting edge. There were also articles from scientific journals, some fairly recent at the time, on pathogens such as *B. anthracis, Y. pestis* and *C. botulinum*, and hepatitis viruses. Among the papers found were clear indications that Al Qaeda had recruited at least one PhD-level scientist to help them, although apparently mostly for procuring additional scientific information.

Also found were letters indicating Al Qaeda may have sent someone to the U.K., with an unspecified amount of money for purchasing vaccines. This might have been for immunization of anticipated laboratory workers. There were also letters containing crude diagrams showing the general layout of a laboratory, a list of some equipment, and references to the need to train people to work in laboratory work. The writer was probably a Pakistani scientist; the intended recipient may have been an Egyptian. The writer says he had visited a laboratory in the UK where research on pathogens was carried out, and had attended scientific conferences on pathogens.

While all this shows that Al Qaeda was seriously investigating the possibility of building bioweapons, nothing among the recovered materials or any other subsequent intelligence gathered suggests it had ever gone beyond the planning stages, or that any pathogenic strains had been obtained or established in an Al Qaeda-associated laboratory. There is certainly no indication they had put together a scientific team of the caliber necessary to assemble and deliver a bioweapon capable of inflicting mass casualties. They had not come even close to achieving what Aum Shinrikyo achieved, which was something less than impressive.

In the end, what is likely to stop groups like Al Qaeda from using bioweapons to achieve their aims against us is that it is just too much trouble. Not only are biological weapons exceedingly difficult to build and operate, the U.S. has now developed vaccines or drugs to counter most known conventional pathogens. Countermeasures for the rest should be available over the next few years. These are being placed into the Strategic National Stockpile, and we have the ability to deliver these materials and more to an attack site within a matter of hours. We would suffer casualties, yes. But not mass casualties. Conventional bombs and chemicals are much easier to obtain and use, and can achieve much the same ends, with much less risk. Sophisticated terrorist groups may well agree with virtually all professional military establishments around the world, who actually had effective bioweapons in hand: they are simply not worth the bother. For Al Qaeda and its ilk, at least the foreseeable future, generating such weapons for terrorist use is very likely a non-starter.

States – What about so-called "rogue" states? Might they undertake the development of biological weapons, and use them themselves in covert operations against the U.S., or give them to terrorists to use (see Table 3)?[5] Many universities in some of these countries have impressive levels of expertise in microbiology, molecular biology, and recombinant DNA technology. A number of their scientists were trained in the U.S., Europe and Japan or Korea, or even Cuba. There may exist, within some of these states, sufficient animosity toward the U.S. that pulling together the necessary experts and convincing them to attempt to develop bioweapons and appropriate delivery systems could be possible. This would take years, and huge amounts of money, for an uncertain outcome. It is not clear that even Iraq, which had an extensive, state-supported bioweapons program through the 1990s, had developed an effective delivery system for the most deadly conventional pathogenic agents.

Would such states have the political will to underwrite such a program, in the face of certain massive retaliation by the U.S. if they were discovered as the authors or facilitators of an attack against us? But perhaps more to the point, could political leaders in these states, which are rarely free and open democracies, live with the uncertainty that one day their terrorist proxies might very well turn these same weapons against them, in order to bring down what the terrorists consider a corrupt or "infidel" government?

Table 3: Some Potential State Suppliers of Bioweapons

Country	Comments
China	Despite denials, suspected of having transferred bioweapons technology to Iran and other countries
Cuba	Has sophisticated biotechnology industry, is suspected of having well-developed bioweapons program
Egypt	Strong university microbiology programs. Allegation by Israel of bioweapons program
Iran	Strong biotechnology base; believed to be pursuing bioweapons program
Kazakhstan	Home to many former Soviet bioweapons facilities, status of which is uncertain. Has never formally renounced bioweapons research
N. Korea	Presumed to have strong bioweapons program, but no reliable intelligence.
Pakistan	Strong biotechnology base. Status of weapons program uncertain
Russia	Very strong background in bioweapons. Current status uncertain, particularly with respect to plague
Syria	Good pharmaceutical infrastructure. Status of bioweapons programs uncertain
Uzbekhistan	Houses several former Soviet bioweapons facilities. Presumed to still hold stockpiles of many Select List pathogens

That would give almost all of these countries pause. The consensus among almost all terrorism experts is that the likelihood of rogue states placing high-grade bioweapons in the hands of terrorist groups is also just about zero.

So, who would do it? To the extent that bioterrorism would ever be used against the United States, all bets are that it would come from organized terrorist groups such as, yes, Al Qaeda. But it is very clear there is a huge, multi-faceted barrier between us and a successful bioterrorist attack by any group. That barrier consists of the extreme difficulty of any such group building an effective bioweapon on its own; the improbability of any organized state providing them with such a weapon; the greatly strengthened array of drug and vaccine countermeasures. It is conceivable that eventually, as some of the technologies involved are simplified, the difficulties in producing a bioweapon could be overcome to some extent. But there is still the problem our own and other militaries had with state-of-the-art bioweapons provided to them ready-made by their own governments: they are difficult to transport and store, as well as to use and control, and have less impact than chemical or nuclear weapons. Or crashing a plane into a building. So why bother?

A FRESH LOOK AT THE BIOTERRORISM THREAT IN THE U.S.

Applying the rigorous analytical techniques of situational crime prevention to the perpetrators of bioterrorism and their weapons, as well as to the targets of bioterrorism, suggests a number of conclusions that can aid policy planners in allocating our scarce national terrorism defense resources in the years ahead.

The likelihood that individual terrorists or terror groups could produce an effective bioweapon capable of causing mass casualties is about as close to zero as one can get. Production of such weapons can only be achieved by a handful of scientific centers in the world. Statements that anyone with a few science courses under their belt could fabricate such weapons are simply nonsense. To the extent such arguments drive the spending of billions of dollars each year for biodefense, it becomes malicious nonsense at best.

Similarly, the notion that any of the small number of laboratories worldwide with the capability of producing a high-grade bioweapon would use it in a direct attack on the U.S. is also close to zero. Even a casual reading of recent history would suggest the response to such an attack would be immediate and devastating. And the likelihood that this subset of capable countries would place such weapons in the hands of terrorists, whose political allegiances are impossible to predict or control, begs enormous scepticism.

The targets of bioterrorism are exclusively people. We can't "harden" people as targets, but we can mitigate the damage that might be done in a bioterror attack. One of the things increased biodefense spending has bought us is an improved public health system, and increased stockpiles of drugs and vaccines to greatly limit the consequences of such an attack. That was appropriate and good, but it does not require the continued spending of billions of dollars to maintain.

The U.S. faces a long and uncertain future in which terror by subnational groups with a wide range of political, social and religious aims will be an ongoing threat. We must focus whatever resources are necessary on defending ourselves against terrorists and the weapons they would use against us. But a close and rational analysis strongly suggests that bioweapons are an extremely unlikely weapon of choice for terrorists, and certainly do not justify the continued spending of tens of billions of dollars to defend against into an indefinite future. A reevaluation of how our precious national resources dedicated to the unfortunately real and necessary war on terrorism are being allocated should be a top priority of government planners.

Address correspondence to: wclark222@ca.rr.com

NOTES

1. William R. Clark is professor emeritus of immunology at the University of California at Los Angeles.
2. The five lives lost in the so-called postal anthrax attacks following the World Trade Center attacks of 2001 may have been the result of bioterrorism. But the presumed perpetrator of these attacks is now dead, and we may never know his true motives. Was it to instill terror, or was it to stimulate government support of an anthrax vaccine he was heavily involved in promoting? In other words, was this an instance of *bioterror*, or of a *biocrime*?
3. See *Bacillus anthracis incident, Kameido, Tokyo, 1993.* In, *Emerging Infectious Diseases* 10:117, 2004.
4. This connection may have been suggested by the belief (later largely discounted) that the terrorists who bombed the World Trade Center in 1993 had included potassium cyanide in the explosive device they used.
5. For a detailed discussion of state biological weapons programs, see www.nti.org.

REFERENCES

Boba, R. (2008). A crime mapping technique for assessing vulnerable targets for terrorism in local communities. In S. Chainey & L. Tompson (Eds.), *Crime mapping case studies: Practice and research* (pp. 143–151). West Sussex, England: John Wiley & Sons Ltd.

Clark, W. R. (2008). *Preparing for armageddon: The science and politics of bioterrorism in America*. New York: Oxford University Press.

Clarke, R. V., & Newman, G. R. (2006). *Outsmarting the terrorists*. Westport, CT: Greenwood PSI.

Hamm, M. S. (2007). *Terrorism as crime: From Oklahoma City to Al-Qaeda and beyond*. New York: NYU Press.

Kaplan, D., & Marshall, A. (1996).. *The cult at the end of the world*. New York: Crown Publishing.

Kenney, M. (2007). *From Pablo to Osama: Trafficking and terrorist networks, government bureaucracies, and competitive adaptation*. University Park, PA: Pennsylvania State University Press.

Leitenberg, M. (2005). *Assessing the biological weapons and bioterrorism threat*. Available free at: www.strategicstudiesinstitute.army.mil

Newman, G. R. & Clarke, R. V. (2008). *Policing terrorism: A police chief's guide*. Washington, DC: COPS Office, U.S. Department of Justice.

Patrick, W. (1996). Biological terrorism and aerosol dissemination. *Politics and the Life Sciences, 15*, 208–210.

Tucker, J. & Sands, A. (1999). The experience of the use of biological weapons by non-state groups: An Unlikely Threat. *Bulletin of the Atomic Scientists, 55*, 46–52.

AN APPLICATION OF SITUATIONAL CRIME PREVENTION TO TERRORIST HOSTAGE TAKING AND KIDNAPPING: A CASE STUDY OF 23 KOREAN HOSTAGES IN AFGHANISTAN

Minwoo Yun
Wheeling Jesuit University

Abstract: *This study examines the applicability of Situational Crime Prevention (SCP) to terrorist hostage taking and kidnapping. In doing so, the current study integrates the SCP model with script theory to explain the temporal mental map of the terrorist hostage takers and provide a theoretical guide to developing SCP measures. The study specifically focuses on the 23 Korean hostages in Afghanistan to examine the feasibility of the application of the SCP model. Qualitative content analysis on newspapers and media reports was used to conduct the case study. Situational factors which significantly influenced the Taliban hostage takers' decision making in each temporal stage of the event were identified and various SCP measures were suggested. The limitations of the study are also discussed.*

Crime Prevention Studies, volume 25 (2009), pp. 111–139.

INTRODUCTION

Conventionally, countermeasures to terrorism are primarily based on two dominant paradigms: the elimination of terrorists or terrorist organizations and the improvement of socio-economic conditions. While both approaches are, in themselves, attractive solutions to terrorism, Clarke and Newman (2006) argue that on only some few occasions has the elimination of particular terrorists or terrorist organizations solved the problem of terrorism, and Kilcullen (this volume) argues that socio-economic aid is only likely to succeed if targeted in specific ways in regions where it can be used to make the lives of local communities more attractive in contrast to what insurgents can offer them. Situational Crime Prevention (SCP) may propose a breakthrough to this deadlocked situation of counter-terrorism (Clarke & Newman, 2006). SCP emphasizes the importance of "criminal opportunity structure" as the immediate cause of an offender's criminal decision making, and thus, by manipulating this criminal opportunity, one can reduce crime. Also, SCP proposes that crime prevention should be crime-specific. A generic prevention that is designed to fit all crimes is ineffective because situational factors differ in each specific type of crime.

Several cases of empirical evidence in the area of counter-terrorism seem to support the validity of the SCP approach. Tightening security measures at airports and on airplanes substantially reduced airline hijackings (Dugan et al., 2005). By following security guidelines, one can reduce the chance of being kidnapped and increase the chance of survival during captivity (Capotorto, 1985). The Turkish government successfully reduced terrorism by the Kurdish separatist group known as PKK during the 1990s because it suppressed the facilitating factors: specifically, by depopulating the rural areas of the southeastern Turkey that provided PKK terrorists with intelligence, logistic supports, and hiding places (Kim & Yun, 2008). And in a final example, there is evidence that hiring private security guards equipped with MAD (Magnetic Acoustic Devices) reduced the chance of Somali pirate attacks (Joe, 2008).

In short, counter-terrorism may require a new paradigm which adopts SCP to counter-terrorism measures. Based on this new paradigm, specific terrorist acts should be thoroughly studied to build prevention measures which disrupt the terrorist opportunity structure and reduce terrorism. Detailed decision-making steps made by terrorists should be uncovered so that prevention and intervention measures can be implemented. When a prevention measure is built and implemented, an evaluation should follow to repair any defects of the prevention measures or to repeal any ineffective measures. For this purpose, scholars, researchers, and governmental and private practitioners should actively cooperate and share vital information. Research and policy measures based on SCP should be the centerpiece of counter-terrorism to improve global security (Clarke & Newman, 2006).

Since SCP requires a "crime-specific" approach, this essay offers an example detailing how SCP can be applied to terrorist hostage taking and kidnapping. Since the mid-1990s, this terrorist tactic has been a significant security concern for the global community and has become one of the favored tactical choices of many terrorist groups. According to police statistics, nearly 2,000 people worldwide have been taken hostage during the past decade (Poland, 2005). In Iraq alone, 1,500 foreign hostages and many times more Iraqis have been taken hostage as of 2007 (Hess, 2008).

This case study specifically focuses on the 23 Korean hostages' case in Afghanistan to study application of SCP to terrorist hostage taking and kidnapping. Since the term "crime- specific" requires detailed information of specific location, time, and circumstance, a study on overall terrorist hostage taking and kidnapping may not fulfill this rigorous standard of "crime-specific." Thus, after briefly examining overall terrorist hostage taking and kidnapping this study will thoroughly analyze the specific case and propose SCP-based counter-measures.

The Korean hostage case in Afghanistan was selected due to the availability of detailed information. The author collected daily newspaper and other media reports for the two month period which covered the entire duration of the hostage incident.[1] Additionally, the author gained inside knowledge and experience as a participant observer, although unintended. During the incident, several media personnel and government officials contacted the author for expert interviews or consultation. Thus, the Korean hostage case is ideal for this study.

CONCEPTUAL CLARIFICATION

The expression "terrorist hostage taking and kidnapping" may be somewhat misleading. Terrorist hostage taking and kidnapping include various heterogeneous terrorist acts in different contexts. Many similar terms are often arbitrarily used by different writers; thus, conceptual clarification is necessary to avoid confusion or misunderstandings.

Hostage taking and kidnapping are two distinctive acts. *Hostage taking* is used to describe the barricade situation. Here, hostage takers are surrounded by the government forces, the military or the police. Their escape route is blocked and thus they are exposed to the constant threat of a government's tactical assault of attempted rescue. This situation significantly favors the government, the crisis responder, and disfavors hostage takers in negotiation. *Kidnapping* is the situation where the government does not know the location of hostage takers and the hostages. Hostage takers seize hostages and disappear – then enjoy great freedom of movement without the feasible threat of a government's tactical assault. Thus, hostage takers enjoy substantial advantages in negotiation (Bolz, 1987; McMains & Mullins, 2001).

Hostage taking and kidnapping can be classified by the identity of hostage takers: (1) those of terrorist cases, and (2) those of criminal cases. Terrorist hostage taking and kidnapping involve hostage takers who are terrorists or terrorist groups. Terrorist hostage takers may take hostages for achieving their strategic or tactical goals. Thus, hostage taking and kidnapping is their weapon of choice for realizing higher objectives. In contrast, criminal hostage taking and kidnapping are committed by common criminals. Hostage taking and kidnapping serve criminals' immediate personal needs. Extorting ransom money is the most common objective. Money gained from negotiations is used for immediate personal spending or invested for further profits. In other cases, hostage taking and kidnapping may be used for criminal hostage takers to realize other personal goals or needs such as escape, sexual pleasure, punishment, or emotional outbursts (Bolz, 1987; McMains & Mullins, 2001).

In hostage taking and kidnapping, three parties play key roles: hostage takers, hostages, and crisis responders. Hostage takers are offenders who take hostages, hold hostages, and conduct negotiations for realizing their goals in exchange for hostages. Also, hostage takers have crucial decision-making power over hostages' fates. Hostages are victims taken and held by hostage takers. During negotiations, these hostages become human trading goods that hostage takers try to sell or exchange to gain something from crisis responders. Crisis responders include the government, hostages' families or employers, or a private corporation for conducting negotiations. Crisis responders are responsible for resolving hostage taking and kidnapping incidents. In negotiation cases, crisis responders serve as buyers or trading partners for hostage takers. In tactical assault cases, crisis responders, usually the government, are rescuers who conduct an operation (Bolz, 1987; Griffiths, 2003).

THEORETICAL PERSPECTIVES

SCP (Situational Crime Prevention)

According to SCP, a criminal event happens with the right conjunction of an offender and criminal opportunity. SCP considers an offender as a rational calculator, whose existence is taken for granted (Clarke & Newman, 2006). The offender who is criminally predisposed, motivated, and adequately resourced for crime decides on a crime commission or crime non-commission in interaction with the following criminal opportunities: (1) a vulnerable and attractive target of crime in a vulnerable target enclosure, (2) the absence of willing and able crime preventers, (3) the presence of unwitting, careless or deliberate crime promoters, and (4) a wider environment logistically favorable for the offender and crime promoters and unfavorable for crime preventers (Ekblom & Tilley, 2000). After a rational calculation, a potential offender is more likely to commit a crime when he or she thinks that criminal opportunity provides an attractive target, a low risk of being caught or punished, and a more favorable or encouraging environment. In this context, a criminal opportunity is the immediate cause of crime (Ekblom & Tilley, 2000).

For crime prevention, SCP attempts to shape, influence, or intervene in the offender's decision-making process by manipulating criminal opportunity structures. SCP proposes five strategic sets of techniques for crime-prevention consideration: (1) techniques that increase the effort required to commit a crime, (2) techniques that increase the risks of committing a crime, (3) techniques that reduce the reward derived from crime, (4) techniques that reduce provocation, and (5) techniques that remove excuses for committing a crime. The increased effort strategy is based on the assumption that increasing the effort needed to commit a crime will deflect many offenders into non-criminal actions instead. Efforts can be increased by target hardening, controlling access to locations, screening exits, deflecting offenders, and controlling tools or weapons. Increased risk strategy may include extending guardianship, natural surveillance through neighborhood watch and artificial surveillance such as closed-circuit television (CCTV). By increasing the risk to offenders of being caught, this strategy attempts to influence many potential offenders to refrain from crime commission. Reduction of rewards is the technique making crime targets or crime commission less attractive. It is based on the assumption that when a potential offender thinks that he or she cannot gain much pleasure or benefit from a crime commission he or she is less likely to commit the crime. Reduced provocation emphasizes the importance of the immediate triggers for criminal events, such as road rage, abrupt conflicts in pubs at closing time, and unmonitored Internet chat rooms. This strategy permits the adoption of techniques that reduce the provocative elements in situations below trigger thresholds and thereby prevent crimes from happening. The removal of excuses strategy makes it difficult for someone to use excuses for criminal behavior, while simultaneously making it very easy to comply with laws, regulations, and by-laws so that the law-compliant action is the least-effort action as well (Brantingham, Brantingham, & Taylor, 2005).

Regarding SCP, one often-raised issue by critics is *displacement*. Displacement is the idea that crime prevention methods that increase the difficulty of crime will result in that crime being "displaced" or moved to another location, time, target, or type of crime. Thus, critics argue that without treating the social or psychological root causes of crime, the total amount of crime will not be reduced. They assert that SCP only displaces the crime and does not affect the total amount of crime (Fanno, 1997). By contrast, SCP proponents argue that although displacement does exist, it is *not* inevitable. SCP indeed reduces crime and even diffuses benefits (meaning that crime-prevention benefits drawn from situational measures diffuse into neighboring areas, time, target, or type of crime where no measures were implemented). Furthermore, SCP is cost-effective and thus a practical approach to prevent or reduce crime (O'Neill & McGloin, 2007).

A variety of empirical evidence supports the SCP argument and finds net crime prevention or reduction effects (Fanno, 1997; Webb, 1997; Guerette & Clarke, 2003; Welsh & Farrington, 2004). For example, research shows that school crime, residential burglary, child sexual abuse, and neighborhood crime were all reduced by the implementation of SCP measures aimed at manipulating situational criminal opportunity (Painter and Farrington, 2001; Bowers, Johnson, & Hirschfield, 2005; O'Neill & McGloin, 2007; Terry & Ackerman, 2008). Further, studies find that often the diffusion of benefits outweighs displacement (Fanno, 1997; Painter & Farrington, 2001; Bowers et al., 2005).

Clarke and Newman (2006) applied SCP to terrorism. According to them, SCP is a cost-effective measure to prevent terrorism and therefore emphasis on reducing terrorist opportunity structures should be given priority for counter-terrorism. Just like common criminals, terrorists are also conditioned by opportunity structures. Clarke and Newman (2006) called this opportunity structure the "the four pillars of opportunity," including targets, weapons, tools, and facilitating conditions. For example, the main features of the targets that terrorists are more likely to choose are exposed, vital, iconic, legitimate, destructible, occupied, near and easy. Terrorists are more likely to choose weapons which are multipurpose, undetectable, removable, destructive, enjoyable, reliable, obtainable, uncomplicated and safe. The availability of terrorist tools such as cars and trucks, credit cards and cash, cell phones, and intelligence also significantly affect terrorists' terrorism commission. Certain facilitating conditions that make terrorism easy, safe, excusable, enticing and rewarding become the social and physical arrangements of society that make specific acts of terrorism possible.

Clarke and Newman (2006) proposed the concepts of "think terrorist" and "outsmarting the terrorists" to design and implement SCP counter-terrorism measures. Unlike conventional crimes, the development of SCP measures cannot rely on traditional methodology for counter-terrorism. There are simply not enough past cases to conduct a thorough statistical analysis. Furthermore, terrorists are constantly adopting and evolving via rigorous and continuous learning. When a terrorist attack occurs, substantial damage may have already been done. Terrorists are less likely to repeat the same type of attack in the future. Thus, collecting sufficient numbers of existing cases and performing an analysis to develop SCP measures are impractical and often meaningless. Instead, the "think terrorist" method can be used to understand the terrorists' decision-making process. We can think in the terrorists' shoes based on an assumption of rational thinking by the terrorists. Although based on an empirical analysis of insufficient past cases, by using our own rational and intellectual imagination we may analyze the terrorists' rational decision-making process. After the outcome drawn from "think terrorist," we may develop counter-terrorism measures by outsmarting the terrorists. Here, we may anticipate the future course of the terrorists' rational decision making. By preparing future counter-terrorism measures based on our anticipation of the future course of terrorists' evolution or adaptation, we can exert extreme pressure on the terrorist opportunity structure and force them to relinquish terrorist acts.

Script Theory

SCP involves the development of techniques to prevent, constrain or disrupt criminal acts. In doing so, SCP uses a variety of opportunity structure manipulations to alter the risks, efforts, and rewards of offending. Naturally, SCP intervention relies upon two important requirements: (1) the need to be crime-specific, and (2) a familiarity with the procedural details of crime commission in relation to specific crimes. In this context, script theory can be well integrated with SCP in order to provide the procedural details of offenders' cognitive decision making in crime commission and thus supplement the aforementioned requirements for SCP (Cornish, 1994).

Like SCP, script theory is also based on a rational choice model. Conditioned by scripts, an individual makes a rational calculation to choose an act in the temporal process of an event. According to script theory, the rational thinking process is a constant cycle of decision making and routinization. When one faces an unfamiliar or crucial situation, he or she may conduct careful decision making. However, when the same person repeats the same act under similar conditions, he or she is less likely to conduct a careful calculation but automatically acts without careful consideration. This habitual practice is called routinization. This cycle of calculation and successive routinization explains that even seemingly irrational and impulsive behaviors – such as driving while intoxicated, assault from a sudden emotional outburst, or habitual gambling are also outcomes of rational choice because these seemingly irrational acts may be the routinized outcome of a rational calculations that had been previously made (Cornish, 1994).

Script theory explains a patterned human behavior based on the concept of scripts. Scripts, also known as event schemata, are memory structures that are procedural knowledge structures for understanding and enacting behaviors (Lord & Kernan, 1987; Erasmus, Boshoff & Rousseau, 2002). Scripts can originate as a result of personal experience, perhaps the most obvious facet of which is hands-on experience. For instance, a criminal offender can learn the sequence of behaviors or actions needed to perform an illegal task by trial and error. This learned sequence of actions then can be represented in memory as a script for illegal task performance. On the other hand, scripts also can originate through the processes of interpersonal and media communication. Simply conversing with other criminals about criminal task performance or watching crime films or crime stories on mass media provides the basis for construction of a script for its specific criminal actions (Gioia & Manz, 1985).

Cornish (1994) applied this script theory to explaining criminal offending. He argued that script theory is relevant for SCP and provides the procedural details of criminal offending. According to Cornish, the script concept consists of different levels of abstraction such as the universal script, metascript, protoscript, script, and track. This different terminology indicates the various levels of generality at which the script concept can operate. These families of conceptually related scripts can be linked hierarchically, from the most specific instances to more inclusive and more abstract categories of script. Universal scripts are the highest level of abstraction, and they consist of several meta-scripts. In this hierarchical order, track is the most concrete level of script (and thus the lowest level of abstraction). For example, crime can be a universal script, crime for financial gain can be a metascript, robbery can be a protoscript, robbery from a person can be a script, and subway mugging can be a track, the lowest level of abstraction or the most concrete level of episode. Also, these tracks are temporally connected along a series of logistical steps. Cornish (1994, p. 174) proposed a simple three-dimensional model of "script permutator" to describe the details of these tracks which are temporally connected along rational decision making steps and also allow alternative options at each temporal step.

AN APPLICATION OF SCP MODEL TO TERRORIST HOSTAGE TAKING AND KIDNAPPING

A theoretical model can be constructed by integrating SCP with a script analysis of the procedural steps of terrorist hostage taking and kidnapping. In this model, SCP can highlight the opportunity structure that influences the terrorists to take hostages and thus employ rational decision making in successive steps. Also, SCP can help design prevention measures for manipulation of this opportunity structure. Script analysis can provide the required details of temporal steps of the event.

Terrorist hostage taking and kidnapping can be one of various different script concepts operating at different levels of abstraction linked hierarchically from the most specific instances (tracks) to the more inclusive and more abstract categories of script. Different levels here include track, script, protoscript, metascript, and universal script. Levels are made up of five different levels of abstraction and generality. For example, terrorist hostage taking and kidnapping would be considered a protoscript. On the higher levels of abstraction and generality, crime can be a universal script, and a terrorist attack – such as a bombing, armed assault, or hostage taking – can be a metascript. On the lower levels of abstraction – and thus more concrete – a script can be a kidnapping for ransom. At the lowest level, a track can be a maritime kidnapping in the case of Somali pirates or kidnapping foreigners traveling on land in the case of Afghanistan.

Terrorist hostage taking and kidnapping are patterned behaviors, and thus outcomes can be predicted (Reber, Singer, & Watson, 1978; Bolz, 1987; Yun, 2008a). The existence of a pattern is due to the fact that the terrorist hostage takers are rational calculators whose decisions are affected or conditioned by situational factors. For example, hostage taking and kidnapping show distinctively different patterns. This difference is because the hostage takers are greatly conditioned by the barricade factor (Bolz, Jr., 1987). Typical hostage takers usually target victims near their operational base because the hostage takers are conditioned by geographical proximity relating to the convenient availability of victims (Ghosh, 2006). Geographically, terrorist kidnapping is concentrated in regions such as Somalia, Afghanistan, and Iraq because terrorists' decisions are conditioned by the effectiveness of government control (Yun, 2008b).

Figure 1 shows the procedural details of terrorist hostage taking and kidnapping. This figure describes how situational conditions or criminal opportunity influences the hostage takers' decision making in each stage of the event. It also shows how SCP measures can be developed to respond to each stage. Each stage of tracks is linked temporally based on script analysis.

As shown in Figure 1, a terrorist hostage taker carries a pre-existing script before the entry of a particular hostage taking and kidnapping episode. The pre-existing script is a generalized script carried by the hostage taker. This pre-existing script can be conditioned by pre-existing opportunity structure. This generalized script can be made of the hostage taker's general experience or skills on hostage taking, family history, religion, or cultural backgrounds. When the hostage taker faces a particular episode of hostage taking and kidnapping, he or she retrieves this generalized pre-existing script to make a decision.

There are several examples of important situational factors forming the pre-existing script. Since the Iraq War began in 2003, the country observed an unusually higher execution rate of hostages. This was due to the impact of Al Zarkawi's beheading tactics ("Zarkawi 'not leading Iraq unrest,'" 2006; Hess, 2008). Since 2005, Afghanistan also observed an increase of hostage execution – seemingly the outcome of the spread of Iraqi kidnapping tactics (Robichaud, 2005). The hostage takers' level of experience or logistical capacity also matters. When the hostage takers are

Figure 1. Temporal steps of terrorism kidnapping.

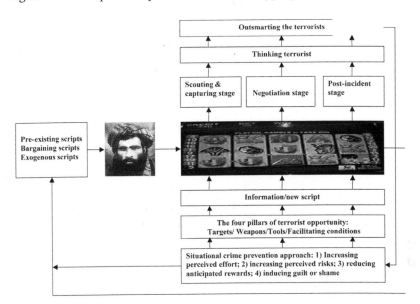

more experienced with hostage taking and kidnapping or have a greater logistical capacity such as weapons, tools, manpower, long-term hostage holding capacity, foods, and availability of competent negotiators, they tend to target high profile hostages, a great number of hostages, or huge ships, airplanes, or vehicles (Dunlop, 2005; Ghosh, 2006; Watkins, 2008). Other important factors may include religion and the nationality of the hostages (Hess, 2008; Yun, 2008a). Al Qaeda even published a "Kidnapping Guide" describing goals and circumstances for kidnapping and how to treat a hostage (Musharbash, 2005). These ample examples suggest that the hostage takers are conditioned by pre-existing scripts formed by situational conditions.

After the beginning of an event, each temporal step is linked with the successive temporal steps of the event. These procedural steps can be represented by the "slot machine" model. Each section of the slot machine represents each temporal stage. Like a slot machine, many different alternative options exist. After the search for the best possible option, the hostage taker makes a decision and moves to the next stage and continues the search of best possible option. Over all, these stages of hostage taking and kidnapping can be divided into three distinctive stages: "scouting and capturing stage," "negotiation stage," and "post-incident stage." Yet, in the real world, these stages can be further divided into additional important stages along the development of a critical situation such as killing a hostage, changing demands, an abrupt incident and the intervention of an influential figure.

In each step of the event, the four pillars of terrorist opportunity (targets, weapons, tools and facilitating conditions) influence the hostage taker's decision making as conditioning immediate causes. These opportunity structures become information and thus form new episodic scripts. This newly acquired script influenced the hostage taker's decision in each temporal step. The hostage taker makes the best possible option in a given stage by integrating this newly acquired script with the pre-existing scripts carried from the event before and previous stages.

There are several examples of situational conditions which form the newly acquired scripts in each stage. In the phase of scouting, the hostage takers' capacity of manpower and other resources can influence the hostage takers' decision making. Usually, each scouting team – which consists of less than five people – looks for a suitable target. Thus, most hostage taking groups cannot cover three or more spots for scouting at the same time (Scotti, 1985). The availability of tools such as a GPS is critical for the maritime hostage takers, since these hostage takers search for a passing ship in open water where spotting a target with unaided vision is difficult (Yun & Gho, 2008). Also, the potential victims' level of vulnerability can influence the hostage takers' decision making. Some potential hostages are careless. They may travel using only a single route instead of randomly choosing three or more different routes. They may dress distinctively or drive a distinctive vehicle and thus can be easily spotted in the local surroundings. The hostage takers need less effort to spot these reckless potential hostages.

In the phase of capturing hostages, the absence or incapacity of security guards may be an important situational condition in the hostage takers' calculation. Usually, the number in each scouting team is limited and their firepower is limited also due to the mobility issue. Thus, a large enough number of security guards with sufficient firepower can effectively deter the hostage takers' launching an attack. Also, because the capturing stage is a very volatile situation, the hostages' acts can critically influence the hostage takers' decision to kill the hostages on the spot or take them as prisoners (Reber et al., 1978).

In the phase of negotiation, several situational factors influence the hostage taker's decision in each critical step of negotiation. Time is a well-known critical conditional factor for successful negotiation. Generally, as time passes, the hostage takers are more likely to feel fatigue, boredom, and anxiety. Thus, they cannot maintain their initial high and firm demands. Rather, they are more likely to surrender or negotiate for less desirable demands (McMains & Mullins, 2001). The hostage takers' own demands also condition their decision making. Some demands are more negotiable than others for crisis responders (McMains & Mullins, 2001). Thus, the reaction of crisis responders to demands certainly conditions the hostage takers' calculation. Psychological aspects such as the Stockholm or London syndrome are also situational conditions affecting the hostage takers' decision. The Stockholm syndrome builds a friendly relationship between the hostage takers and hostages, while the London syndrome builds a hostile relationship between them. Thus, these psychological factors can affect the hostage takers' decision on the fate of the hostages (Poland, 2005). Hostage takers' holding capacity for their hostages is also another critical situational condition. Some hostage takers may have better logistical supplies, safer hiding places, better firepower to deter rescue operations and more local support than others. Thus, they may hold hostages for a longer time (Sater, 1985). In the case of FARC, a Colombian group, hostage takers hold their hostages for several years ("Colombian hostage freed after eight years," 2008). This condition certainly influences the hostage takers' decision in the phase of negotiation. Other situational conditions significantly affecting the hostage takers during this phase may include the level of media/government/public attention, the nationality of hostages, response from the government or families of hostages, the level of pressure from the foreign government or influential figures friendly to the hostage takers and geographical/local/cultural conditions.

The post-incident period is the last phase and it occurs after the conclusion of the event. The event may end when the hostage takers execute their hostages and walk away or when the hostages are released as an outcome of a successful negotiation or rescued by a tactical assault team. After the incident is over, the hostage takers make a report of the post-incident and provide a debrief. At this time, situational factors also influence the hostage takers' calculation. Such factors may include the hostage takers' self-evaluation of the whole event and reactions from released hostages, the government, or the public.

After termination of the event, the outcome can serve as feedback for pre-existing scripts for future hostage takers in future events. The lessons or experience which the hostage taker learned become sources of new pre-existing scripts and stored as general scripts and carried by future hostage takers. In this context, the outcome becomes a situational condition form-ing the future pre-existing script. Also of note here is that a situational crime prevention approach can intervene and affect the formation of new, pre-existing scripts for future hostage taking and kidnapping prevention or reduction. For this purpose, SCP measures can be designed to punish or eliminate the hostage takers after the event or to devalue the hostage takers' gains from the negotiation.

CASE ANALYSIS:
23 KOREAN HOSTAGES IN AFGHANISTAN

In July 19, 2007, 23 Korean Christian missionaries were kidnapped by members of the Taliban while passing through Ghazni Province of Afghan-istan. This incident lasted approximately 40 days. Two male hostages were executed in the initial stage of the negotiation: the first hostage was killed on July 25th and the other on July 30th. The remaining hostages were eventually released after long negotiations between the Afghan government and the Taliban and later between the Korean government and the Taliban. Two female hostages were early released on August 13th, and the remaining 19 hostages on August 29th and August 30th.

Pre-Phase: Pre-existing Scripts

"Abdullah group" was responsible for kidnapping the 23 Korean hostages. This group is referred to as the Taliban Ghazni group and is a subgroup operating in the Ghazni area. Mullah Abdullah was the leader of the group and previously the second-in-command after Daro Khan until Khan's arrest. One report noted that the Ghazni group was composed of 45-50 members and another reported estimated membership at 150; thus, the total number of members is between 40 and 150 (Choi, 2007, August 19; Moreau & Yousafzai, 2007, August 15).

There were several pre-existing scripts which significantly influenced the hostage takers' decision to kidnap the Koreans. First, the arrest of Daro Khan was a direct factor in forming pre-existing scripts leading to the decision of kidnapping. In June 2007, Khan was arrested by the U.S. Army. In response to this incident, the Abdullah group planned to kidnap foreigners to exchange for Khan and other Taliban leaders imprisoned at the U.S. Army base (Moreau & Yousafzai, 2007, August 15).

Second, the success of previous kidnappings for prisoner swaps was another influential factor of forming pre-existing scripts favorable to the kidnapping (Won, 2007, July 23; Kim, 2007, August 19). On March 5, 2007, Daniele Mastrogiacomo, an Italian journalist, was kidnapped along with two Afghan nationals by Mullah Dadullah's men. The Taliban eventually freed Mastrogiacomo in exchange for the release of five Taliban prisoners (including Dadullah's brother Mullah Shah Mansoor and other Taliban commanders). This one-to-five prisoner swap was very successful for the Taliban and later significantly encouraged the Abdullah group to kidnap the Koreans (Kim, 2007, August 19).

Third, the spread of Iraqi-style kidnapping tactics is another important situational condition forming the pre-existing scripts. Afghanistan had few kidnapping incidents before 2005 despite its long years of civil wars, insurgencies, and terrorism. Afghan fighters traditionally preferred more warrior-like direct confrontation in combat. However, the spread of Iraqi-style tactics seemed to turn the tide of terrorism in Afghanistan (In, 2007). Also, the entry of a new stream of fighters in the Taliban seemed to change the culture of the group (called Neo-Taliban) and changed the group to follow more Al Qaeda-style tactics such as kidnappings and beheadings (Lee, 2007; In, 2007). As evidence of this change of group culture and tactics, the world has seen a significant increase of kidnappings and kidnapping for execution in Afghanistan in the last four years (Kim, 2007).

Additionally, existing regional characteristics may have contributed to the formation of pre-existing scripts. For example, Afghanistan has a long tradition of trade and natives customarily practice long and exhaustive bargaining and negotiations in trade. They may cast several options for bargaining and exhaustively test their trade opponents. This cultural practice is widespread in daily trading life of Afghanistan. This age-old custom also shapes the hostage negotiations among Afghan hostage takers (Seo, 2007, July 26; Seo, 2007, August 6). Local and geographical conditions of Afghanistan are other important situational factors as well. Afghanistan has extremely rugged terrain and inhospitable land. Also, the U.S., ISAF (International Security Assistance Force), and Afghan government forces actively conduct search and combat operations there. Under these conditions, it is very difficult for the Taliban to hold hostages and continue negotiations for a long time (unlike Colombia or the Philippines). Although Afghan incidents are kidnapping cases, they seem to resemble a "half-baked" hostage-taking case, because the hostage takers could be easily spotted by strenuous reconnaissance and their escape routes and logistic supplies may be denied in large scale encirclement. Thus, the hostage takers may not enjoy great leverage in negotiation, unlike those in Colombia or the Philippines.

Responding to the aforementioned situational conditions, the following SCP measures could be considered to prevent a repetition of the Korean hostage incident:

- It could be anticipated that the Abdullah group kidnapped foreigners for the release of Daro Khan. Thus, the authorities could monitor this group to prevent possible kidnapping by patrolling possible kidnapping spots, identifying possible holding places for potential hostages, and anticipating potential negotiation processes and potential negotiators for the hostage taking group. Also, the authorities could analyze available resources of this group for kidnapping operations. The number of fighters and logistic supplies could be analyzed beforehand to anticipate this group's capacity of scouting, capturing, and negotiation. Also, the authorities could identify influential figures or groups to the hostage taking group which may play key roles in the potential negotiation.

- Kidnapping foreigners could be anticipated, especially those foreigners who travel by land through Ghazni province. The authority could warn those foreigners and arrange for security guards.

- The authorities could conduct anti-kidnapping campaigns demonizing kidnapping among the local population and thus generate anti-kidnapping sentiment among locals. This campaign may specifically target people in Ghazni province and such increased sentiment may give the authorities a significant advantage in the potential negotiation by inducing guilt or shame to the hostage takers through local opinion.

Phase I: Scouting

Three important situational factors conditioned the hostage takers' decision making in this stage: the three dimensions of offender, victim, and location. Concerning the offender, the Abdullah group might have limited resources available for scouting operations. The group sent two fighters on motorbikes armed with AK-47s and RPGs and equipped with cell phones (Moreau & Yousafzai, 2007, August 15). Although there may be some variation, roughly two to four fighters with similar levels of firepower and telecommunication could be afforded for the hostage taking group at best. Regarding the victims, foreigners traveling by land through the Ghazni province were highly vulnerable. In the location dimension, the highway between Kabul and Kandahar was specifically targeted for identifying foreigners by hostage-taking groups (Hankyoreh, 2007; Moreau & Yousafzai, 2007). This was the hostage takers' logical decision because foreigners are most likely to travel on the highway.

Considering the aforementioned situational conditions, the following SCP measures could be considered to prevent a repetition of the kidnapping incident:

- The authorities could conduct active patrols on the highway, especially within the Ghazni province. This active patrolling could deter the potential scouting operations by the hostage takers or eliminate the fighters scouting for potential hostages.

- The authorities might construct high noise walls along the potentially high-risk section of the highway. This noise walls may interrupt the Taliban scouting team in spotting foreigners traveling along the highway. To reduce the construction cost and to boost the local economy and support, solar panels may be installed along the noise walls. Thus, this construction not only interrupts the scouting operation for potential kidnapping but also generates electricity for the local population ("Melbourne freeway lights go solar," 2007).

- The authority might recommend that foreign travelers use vehicles which are blacked out from the outside and also not so distinctively different from those vehicles used by the local population and thus easily intermingled with local traffic. This measure might interrupt the scouting team from identifying foreign travelers.

- The authority could recommend "no stop" policy for foreign travelers. The authority could advise foreigners not to stop on the highway while traveling. The Koreans stopped in a local village in Ghazni area on the way and spent some time for rest and a tour. This may have given ample opportunity for the Abdullah group to identify potential hostages either via a report by the scouting team or local population (Kim, 2007, August 3).

- The authorities could monitor and intercept radio/cell- phone transmissions. The scouting team needs to continuously communicate with its headquarters in the scouting operation – usually by cell phone or radio. Thus, the constant monitoring and interception of these transmissions may help the authorities to spot the possible locations of the headquarters and the scouting team. By using this information, the authorities may surgically eliminate potential hostage takers.

Phase II: Capturing

The hostage takers' decision was conditioned by two significant situational factors at this stage. There was no armed security guard presence and thus no resistance was expected. Thus, only two poorly armed fighters could capture 23 hostages with ease (Moreau & Yousafzai, 2007). Also, the number of hostages influenced the hostage takers to divide the hostages into five groups and to take them away separately. This grouping was a reasonable decision for the hostage takers (Moreau & Yousafzai, 2007). Usually the hostage takers decide how to divide hostages when they capture a large number of hostages: the hostage takers need to divide hostages into as many groups as possible to prevent a potential rescue operation. Conversely, the hostage takers need to have as few hostage groups as possible since a greater number of divided hostage groups may bring many challenges for the hostage takers regarding negotiation management, the available number of fighters guarding hostages, and the supplies of logistics caring for both captors and hostages. Thus, 23 hostages divided into 5 groups (4 or 5-to-1 ratio) seems a logical decision of the hostage takers.

With respect to the aforementioned situational conditions, the following SCP measures may be considered for this stage:

- The authorities may consider assigning two to four armed security guards. Considering the available number of fighters and the availability of their vehicle and weapons, two to four properly armed security guards could successfully prevent or deter potential or actual attacks of the hostage takers.

- When the hostage takers capture hostages, it is recommended that hostages obey and follow their captors' instructions. This is one of the most volatile stages in a kidnapping incident. The hostage takers are usually very anxious and feel the great necessity to subdue their hostages in any way possible, especially when the hostage takers are far outnumbered by the hostages. Thus, any sign of resistance could result in hostage death. Following the hostage takers' instructions may save the hostages' lives considering the fact that a majority of kidnapping cases end with the hostages' safe return after negotiation (Reber et al., 1978).

- The authorities could anticipate that the hostage takers might divide 23 hostages into 4 or 5 different groups. Considering the hostage takers' necessity to divide a large number of hostages into proper and manageable size groups, the authority might expect this group division and later use this anticipation for the negotiation or rescue operation.

Phase III: Negotiation

Kidnapping incidents may be divided into "negotiation cases" and "no-negotiation cases." The first three days are important criteria for this division as the hostage takers kidnap for negotiation or for non-negotiation purposes (scare tactics or punishment). Usually the hostage takers' purpose can be indirectly uncovered within the first three days. If they do not kill the hostages within the first three days, it is a crucial sign indicating that the hostage takers want to negotiate for something in return (Reber et al., 1978; Jeong & Won, 2007, July, 25). Thus, the negotiation stage begins. In the Korean hostage case, 22 of 23 hostages survived the first three days; thus, it was clear that the hostage takers wanted to negotiate and had a reason to preserve the hostages' lives. The execution of one hostage shortly after the kidnapping could be understood as leverage for the following negotiations.

In the negotiation stage, the hostage takers' decision was influenced by several crucial situational factors (although those factors cannot be an exhaustive list). Conditioned by these factors, the Taliban could not extend negotiations more than two months and also could not simply execute their hostages to resolve the incident; thus, the event was resolved after approximately 40 days with the release of most hostages as the result of negotiations.

Some situational factors forced the Taliban to settle the negotiations within two months. First, the overall "time" factor played a significant role. The Abdullah group initially took a very strong stance in the first two weeks by stubbornly demanding the release of Daro Khan and other Taliban commanders via a 1 hostage to 5 Taliban prisoner exchange (Won, 2007; Choi, 2007, July 31; You, 2007; Moreau & Yousafzai, 2007; Choi, 2007, August 18). However, as time passed, the hostage takers became exhausted and stressed by the deadlocked situation. They were also pressed by the shortage of logistic supplies for themselves and their hostages. The longer they held hostages meant the more money they had to pay for food, water, and other logistics for captors and hostages. Second, the lengthening time period also threatened the hostage takers due to the increasing chances of detection by the Afghan or international authorities. Thus, the hostage takers lowered their demands to the release of low-profile Taliban fighters and a one-to-one Taliban prisoner exchange (Moreau & Yousafzai, 2007; Choi, 2007, August 16; Choi, 2007, August 18; Park, 2007, August 21).

The hostage takers' capacity for holding hostages also significantly pressed the hostage takers to settle the negotiations. The Taliban could not extend the incident more than two months. Ramadan – a very important, month-long Muslim religious observance – was approaching and observant Muslims must stay with their families and refrain from contact with the opposite sex and also participate in a huge dinner for celebration after sunset. Thus, the Taliban fighters guarding the hostages expressed several grievances: they wanted to go home and stay with their families for Ramadan; also, staying in the same space with foreign, unrelated women was religiously unacceptable for the Taliban fighters. Finally, before Ramadan market prices usually rise for food as people buy necessities to prepare for the observance. Thus, the hostage takers had to spend more money to buy food and other necessities for their hostages and those guarding the hostages. The Taliban were pressed, then, to negotiate before Ramadan (Shin, 2007, August 29; Seo, 2007, August 30). In addition to the above reasons, inhospitable Afghan geographical conditions and the constant threat of the U.S., ISAF, and Afghan forces also limited the capacity of holding hostages. Afghanistan's geographical conditions are not suitable for holding a large number of hostages for a long time or traveling with them. Also, inhospitable terrain poses a great challenge for logistic supplies for long-term captivity. Unlike the Colombian jungle, Afghan terrain may allow the authorities to detect the location of hostage takers and hostages by using satellite, air reconnaissance or communication interception. Also, there are ongoing operations of the U.S., ISAF, and Afghan government forces. These forces constantly threaten the security of the hostage takers and complicate the logistics for hostages and their guards or the movement of hostage takers and hostages (Shin, 2007, August 4; Shin, 2007, August 30). Due to these situational factors, the Taliban decided to lower their demands and made a negotiation settlement within 40 days.

Meanwhile, other situational factors conditioned the Taliban to not execute their hostages. The hostage takers' specific demands for prisoner exchange guided the overall course of the negotiation. They desired something in return and thus they had a reason to preserve the hostages' lives

(Kim, 2007, July 23; Hankyoreh, 2007, August 8). Initially, the hostage takers demanded withdrawal of the South Korean military and a prisoner exchange. Responding to these demands, the South Korean government quickly promised the rapid withdrawal of the South Korean military and also expressed a strong willingness for further negotiation. Thus, the hostages had a certain trading value and this intrinsic value kept them alive.

An increased trading value also contributed to the hostage takers' decision to preserve the hostages' lives. Due to the nature of the hostage takers' demands, the South Korean, Afghan, and U.S. governments were all involved in the negotiations. This made negotiations more complicated but certainly raised the value of negotiations and thus the hostages' lives. The South Korean government had their nationals held in captivity but had no power over releasing any prisoners. The Afghan government was involved not only because the incident occurred on its soil but also it held Taliban prisoners. The U.S. government was also involved because the U.S. military held Taliban prisoners whose release the hostage takers demanded.

The high level of media, government, and public attention was another situational factor that pressured the hostage takers' decisions toward a favorable negotiation. A high-profile kidnapping usually raises the price of hostages, and thus hostage takers may expect a higher price for return. On the other hand, a high level of media attention may discourage the hostage takers from killing hostages and walking away. The hostage takers may feel significant political pressure from being seen as cruel and cold-blooded murderers. This might have been the case in the Korean incident. This incident drew great attention from the media, the government, and the public due to the fact that multiple governments were involved and a high number of hostages (including 19 females) were taken. The high number of hostages alone may protect the hostages' lives by discouraging the hostage takers from killing them all. The killing of approximately 20 hostages in total was not an easy task without taking into account significant political responsibility. Killing a large number of hostages, especially 19 female hostages, could potentially politically backfire against the Taliban (Kim, 2007, July 23; Choi, 2007, July 25; Yeonhap News, 2007, August 27).

In summary, the combined effects of the aforementioned situational factors, and possibly other factors as well, shaped the Taliban hostage takers' decision making in the negotiation stage. Thus, the following SCP measures are suggested after examining those situational factors.

- The Korean hostage incident was a "negotiation case": i.e., the authorities may need to negotiate with hostage takers to release the hostages. The authorities may anticipate the probable length of negotiations being between more than three weeks but less than two months. Due to the great media attention and involvement of multiple governments, the hostage takers may not make a deal in a short time period. This incident can be a good opportunity for the Taliban to conduct a political campaign to boost their popularity and humiliate the Afghan government. Thus, the actual negotiations could begin after the Taliban maximized their media manipulation. However, due to various aforementioned situational conditions, the Taliban could not extend this window for negotiations more than two months. In this context, the Korean government was rather rushed to complete negotiations in the beginning stages of the incident. In doing so, the Korean government had to assume unnecessary political liability and help the Taliban gain political victory through great media attention and international recognition (Jeong, 2007, August 30; Park, 2007, August 30).

- By manipulating the situational factors against the Taliban, the authorities may accomplish lowering the hostage takers' demands to save the hostages' lives. Thus, the authority may focus on lowering ransom money or releasing lower level Taliban prisoners unofficially in exchange for hostage release.

- The government may need to officially deny negotiations and work on covert negotiation through private representatives. This double standard policy can reduce the hostage takers' political rewards of being equivalent partners with the legitimate nation-state. Also, it can save the government from taking unnecessary political risks in negotiating with terrorists or of inviting more future terrorist kidnappings. In this sense, the Korean government made a significant mistake by conducting negotiations by itself with terrorists. Considering the aforementioned situational conditions, the Taliban could not refuse negotiating with private representatives in a covert manner.

- Through exhausting negotiations, the authorities could weaken the hostage takers and their demands. Talking through or ignoring deadlines set by the hostage takers, extending time, and rigorous negotiations may make the hostage takers exhausted or squander hostage takers' resources. This measure can increase hostage takers' efforts to obtain their demands in negotiations and thus possibly lower the level of hostage takers' demands.

- By utilizing the involvement of multiple governments, the authorities can "pass the buck" to other governments in meeting hostage takers' demands. The Korean government may find sound excuses by saying that they have no control over Taliban prisoners and thus could not meet the hostage takers' demands. By using this reasonable excuse, the Korean government could maintain its willingness to negotiate and at the same time "wear down" the hostage takers through this evasion of responsibility.

- The authority may arrange to disseminate the sorrow or pain of the hostages' families through media or the Internet and thus induce guilt or shame on the hostage takers. This measure may solicit local Afghani support for hostage release and thus put more political pressure on the hostage takers' decision to kill hostages (Kim, 2007, August 4).

- The authorities need to continue military operations to find the location of the hostage takers and hostages or surrounding areas of possible hideouts. This ongoing military operation may psychologically pressure the hostage takers by making them uneasy. Also, it could make the hostage takers' movements and the supply of food and other necessities more difficult. Thus, the authorities could extract more favorable outcomes from negotiations (Shin, 2007, August 30).

- The authorities could collect intelligence of the hostage taking groups for future counter-terrorism operations. Prolonged negotiations tend to handcuff the hostage taking group during an incident. The hostage taking group is usually immobilized by the presence of hostages because they need to guard the hostages and have difficulty traveling with the hostages. Also, the hostage taking group needs to make continuous negotiations, announcements, and media interviews through cell phones, radios, Internet, or face to face communications. Thus, the hostage taking groups need to expose themselves quite vulnerably for a certain period of time which provides ample opportunity for authorities to collect intelligence.

Phase IV: Post-Incident

The Korean hostage incident concluded with the release of the 19 remaining hostages. Officially, in exchange for the hostages, the Korean government promised the early withdrawal of the South Korean Army and the ban on South Korean Christian missionary activities in Afghanistan. However, it was alleged that the release of Taliban militants and ransom money were offered as a covert deal. As evidence of this, 23 Taliban fighters were later released from the Bagram U.S. military prison and the Afghan central prison in the form of a Ramadan pardon. Also, it was alleged that US $20 million was offered as ransom. Meanwhile, the Taliban militants responsible for the kidnapping were killed by Afghan forces on September 4, 2007. The casualties included Mullah Abdullah (the commander of Ghazni Taliban) and Mullah Martin (a high ranking official in the group) (Shin, 2007, August 29; Yeonhap News, 2007, September 12; Yeonhap News, 2007, September 14). No substantial follow-up study has been conducted thus far on this incident.

Based on an exhaustive review of the incident, the outcome may significantly influence hostage takers' future decisions to launch another hostage taking or kidnapping. Thus, the outcome became a new situational factor for future incidents. Based on the Korean hostages' incident debrief, the hostage takers might gain substantial success. They achieved political victory through negotiations and received global media attention while being elevated to an equivalent political entity by negotiating with a legitimate government (Park, 2007, August 30). Additionally, they achieved the release of their fellow militants and procured substantial ransom money. This substantial gain may motivate future hostage takers.

In contrast, the killing of the hostage takers who were responsible for the incident may be discouraging situational factors for future hostage takers (Yeonhap News, 2007, September 4). With their elimination, rewards which the hostage takers gained could be eventually denied and the hostage takers could be punished. Considering these negative aspects, future hostage takers may hesitate to launch a future kidnapping. By combining these positive and negative situational factors affecting future hostage takers' decision making, the following SCP measures can be considered:

- The authorities need to deny the hostage takers' gains through negotiation. The authorities may need to devalue the meaning of political or material gains of the hostage takers or treat the entire incident as an insignificant episode. An active and direct denial or devaluation may draw unnecessary suspicion or attention from the public. The indirect and covert media play may be more appropriate.

- Launching military or law enforcement operations to terminate or arrest the hostage takers is an appropriate SCP measure to influence future hostage takers' decision making.

- A meaningful evaluation of the event is required after the end of the incident. The released hostages can be debriefed to gather intelligence. All government decisions and actions during the incident can be reviewed and all hostage takers' moves and circumstantial factors can be reexamined. In doing so, a future incident may be prevented or more effectively responded to by building appropriate countermeasures.

CONCLUSION

The main purpose of this study is to propose the applicability of SCP to terrorist hostage taking and kidnapping. In doing so, the current study applied the SCP model integrated with script theory. As seen in the Korean hostage case, the current SCP model thoroughly explains the fact that situational factors significantly influenced the Taliban hostage takers' decision making in each temporal stage of the event. The identified situational factors formed scripts which eventually conditioned the hostage takers' decision making. Based on this analysis, the outcome of the Korean hostage event could be anticipated by knowing situational factors.

The current SCP model proposes a temporal mental map of the terrorist hostage takers and will eventually provide theoretical guidance to develop SCP measures. The ultimate goal of the SCP suggests workable crime prevention or reduction measures. Following the spirit of the SCP, the current study suggested several feasible situational measures in each temporal stage to prevent a current or future event, to save hostages' lives, and to punish the wrongdoers. These measures are reflections of several important situational factors identified as playing key roles in shaping the hostage takers' decision making in the Korean hostage case. These proposed SCP measures may be applicable to a future event.

The limitation of the current study lies in the research method. The qualitative case study typically raises the concerns of objectivity and generalizability, but at the same time it makes possible the implementation of a theoretical approach such as scripting that does not lend itself easily to traditional quantitative methods. Furthermore, terrorist hostage taking and kidnapping are significantly influenced by various specific situational factors which are very distinctive on a case by case basis such as political considerations, the public opinion, media presence, hostages' reactions, crisis responders' reactions, the competency of negotiators, or the hostage takers' tactical evolution. Thus, it may be very difficult to extract common situational variables from a sufficient number of cases to perform a quantitative analysis. Although these difficulties do not necessary mean the impossibility of the quantitative method, it is certainly a daunting challenge. Under the circumstances, the qualitative case study is a viable option for studying the terrorist hostage taking and kidnapping. It is to be hoped that more similar studies will accumulate enough information to provide a comprehensive map of terrorist hostage taking and kidnapping and provide the concomitant situational measures to prevent them.

Address correspondence to: minwoy@hotmail.com

NOTES

1. During the roughly two month period of the incident and the post-incident (July 20 to September 14, 2007), the author collected daily major Korean newspapers and journals including Chosun Ilbo, The Hangyoreh , Joongang Ilbo, Joongang Sunday, The Korea Herald, Munhwa Ilbo, and Newsweek's Korean edition.

REFERENCES

Abelson, R. P. (1976). Script processing in attitude formation and decision-making. In J. S. Carroll & J. W. Payne (Eds.), *Cognition and social behavior* (pp. 33–45). Hillsdale, NJ: Erlbaum.

Anderson, C. A., & Bushman, B. J. (2002). Human aggression. *Annual Review of Psychology, 53*, 27–51.

Bolz, Jr., F. A. (1987). *How to be a hostage and live*. Secaucus, NJ: Lyle Stuart Inc.

Bowers, K. J., Johnson, S. D., & Hirschfield, A. F. G. (2004). Closing off opportunities for crime: an evaluation of alley-gating. *European Journal on Criminal Policy and Research, 10*, 285–308.

Brantingham, P. L., Brantingham, P. J., & Taylor, W. (2005, April). Situational crime prevention as a key component in embedded crime prevention. *Canadian Journal of Criminology and Criminal Justice, 47*(2), 271–292.

Capotorto, G. (1985). Avoiding capture and surviving captivity. In B. M. Jenkins (Ed.), *Terrorism and personal protection* (pp. 395–406). Stoneham, MA: Butterworth Publishers.

Choi, J. (2007, July 25). *Joongang Ilbo, 13229*(43), 1.

Choi, J. (2007, July 31). *Joongang Ilbo, 13234*(42), 1.

Choi, J. (2007, August 16). *Joongang Ilbo, 13248*(43), 8.

Choi, J. (2007, August 19). *Joongang Sunday* Special Report 14

Choi, H. (2007, August 18). *Chosun Ilbo, 26951*, A8.

Clarke, R. V., & Newman, G. R. (2006). *Outsmarting the terrorists*. Westport, CT: Praeger Security International.

"Colombian hostage freed after eight years." (2008, October 26). *The Associated Press*. Retrieved Dec. 9, 2008, from http://www.theglobeandmail.com/

Cornish, D. (1994). The procedural analysis of offending and its relevance for situational prevention. *Crime Prevention Studies, 3*, 151–196.

Dugan, L., LaFree, G., & Piquero, A. R. (2005, November). Testing a rational choice model of airline hijackings. *Criminology, 43*(4), 1031–1065.

Dunlop, J. B. (2005, October). *Beslan: Russia's 9/11?* An investigative report published by The American Committee for Peace in Chechnya (ACPC) and The Jamestown Foundation. Washington, DC. Retrieved Oct. 12, 2005, from http://www.peaceinchechnya.org/

Ekblom, P., & Tilley, N. (2000). Going equipped: criminology, situational crime prevention and the resourceful offender. *British Journal of Criminology, 40*, 376–398.

Erasmus, A. C., Boshoff, E., & Rousseau, G. (2002). The potential of using script theory in consumer behavior research. *Journal of Family Ecology and Consumer Sciences, 30*, 1–9.

Fanno, C. M. (1997, December). Situational crime prevention: techniques for reducing bike theft at Indianan university, Bloomington. *Journal of Security Administration, 20* (2), 1–14.

Ghosh, A. (2006, November). The disappeared. *Time, 168*(19), 44–48.

Gioia, D. A., & Manz, C. C. (1985, July). Linking cognition and behavior: A script processing interpretation of vicarious learning. *The Academy of Management Review, 10*(3), 527–539.

Griffiths, J. C. (2003). *Hostage: The history, facts & reasoning behind hostage taking*. London: Andre Deutsch Ltd.

Guerette, R. T., & Clarke, R. V. (2003). Product life cycles and crime: automated teller machines and robbery, *Security Journal, 16*(1), 7–18.

Hankyoreh. (2007, August 8). 6062(5): 2.

Hess, P. (2008, October 13). "Iraq calmer but copycat kidnappings spread." *The New York Times*. Retrieved Oct. 15, 2008, from http://www.nytimes.com/

In, N. (2007, August 19). *Joongang Sunday* Special Report 6

Jeong, J., & Won, N. (2007, July 25). *Joongang Ilbo, 13229*(43), 5.

Jeong, Y. (2007, August 30). *Joongang Ilbo*. Retrieved Sep. 28, 2008, from http://news.joins.com/

Joe, J. (2008, October 22). *Chosun.com*. Retrieved Oct. 28, 2008, from http://news.chosun.com/

Kim, E., & Yun, M. (2008, Spring). What works? Countermeasures to terrorism: A case study of PKK. *International Journal of Comparative and Applied Criminal Justice, 32*(1), 65–88.

Kim, H. (2007, August 3). *Joongang Ilbo, 13237*(42), 5.

Kim, J. (2007, August 4). *Joongang Ilbo, 13238*(43), 5.

Kim, M. (2007, July 23).*Joongang Ilbo, 13227*(43), 2.

Kim, S. (2007, August 19). *Joongang Sunday* Special Report 9

Lee, T. (2007, August 2). *Chosun Ilbo, 26937*, A5.

Lord, R. G., & Kernan, M. C. (1987, April). Scripts as determinants of purposeful behavior in organizations. *The Academy of Management Review, 12*(2), 265–277.

McMains, M. J., & Mullins, W. C. (2001). *Crisis negotiations* (2nd ed.). Cincinnati, OH: Anderson Publishing Co.

Melbourne freeway lights go solar. (2007, Jun 17). *ABC News*. Retrieved Oct. 28, 2008, from http://www.abc.net.au/

Moreau, R., & Yousafzai, S. (2007, August 15). Pawns in a deadly game. *Newsweek Korean Edition, 17*(33), 16–17.

Musharbash, Y. (2005). How to: the Al-Qaida guide to kidnapping. *Spiegel Online.* Retrieved Oct. 28, 2008, from http://www.spiegel.de/

O'Neill, L., & McGloin, J. M. (2007, September). Considering the efficacy of situational crime prevention in schools. *Journal of Criminal Justice, 35*(5), 511–523.

Painter, K. A., & Farrington, D. P. (2001, Spring). Evaluating situational crime prevention using a young people's survey. *The British Journal of Criminology, 41*(2), 266–284.

Park, G. (2007, August 30). *Joongang Ilbo*. Retrieved Sep. 28, 2008, from http://news.joins.com/

Park, S. (2007, August 21). a *Joongang Ilbo, 13252*(40), 17.

Poland, J. M. (2005). *Understanding terrorism: Groups, strategies, and responses* (2nd ed.). Upper Saddle River, NJ: Pearson Prentice Hall.

Reber, J. R., Singer, L. W., & Watson, F. M. (1978, August). Hostage survival. *Security Management, 22* (8), 46–50.

Robichaud, C. (2005, June 9). Iraq tactics hit Afghanistan. *Afghanistan Watch: A Project of The Century Foundation*. Retrieved Dec. 9, 2008, from http://www.tcf.org/

Sater, W. F. (1985). Terrorist kidnappings in Colombia. In B. M. Jenkins (Ed.), *Terrorism and personal protection* (pp. 113–128). Stoneham, MA: Butterworth Publishers.

Scotti, A. J. (1985). Transportation security. In B. M. Jenkins (Ed.), *Terrorism and personal protection* (pp. 354–368). Stoneham, MA: Butterworth Publishers.

Seo, J. (2007, July 26). *Joongang Ilbo, 13230*(42), 4

Seo, J. (2007, August 6). *Joongang Ilbo, 13239*(40), 6

Seo, J. (2007, August 30). *Joongang Ilbo*. Retrieved Sep. 28, 2008, from http://news.joins.com/

Shin, Y. (2007, August 4). *Joongang Ilbo, 13238*(43), 5.

Shin, Y. (2007, August 29). *Joongang Ilbo*. Retrieved Sep. 28, 2008, from http://article.joins.com/

Shin, Y. (2007, August 30). *Joongang Ilbo*. Retrieved Sep. 28, 2008, from http://news.joins.com/

Terry, K. J., & Ackerman, A. (2008). Child sexual abuse in the Catholic Church: how situational crime prevention strategies can help create safe environments. *Criminal Justice and Behavior, 35*(5), 643–657.

Watkins, E. (2008, November 17). Emboldened Somali pirates hijack Aramco tanker. *Oil & Gas Journal*. Retrieved Dec. 9, 2008, from http://www.ogj.com/

Webb, B. (1997). Steering column locks and motor vehicle theft: Evaluations from three countries. In R. V. Clarke (Ed.), *Situational crime prevention: successful case studies* (2nd ed., pp. 46–58). Monsey, NY: Criminal Justice Press.

Welsh, B. C., & Farrington, D. P. (2004). Evidence-based crime prevention: The effectiveness of CCTV. *Crime Prevention and Community Safety: An International Journal, 6*(2), 21–33.

Won, N. (2007, July 23). *Joongang Ilbo, 13227*(43), 4.

Yeonhap News. (2007, August 27). *Joongang Ilbo*. Retrieved Sep. 28, 2008, from http://news.joins.com/

Yeonhap News. (2007, September 4). *Joongang Ilbo*. Retrieved Sep. 28, 2008, from http://news.joins.com/

Yeonhap News. (2007, September 12). *Joongang Ilbo*. Retrieved Sep. 28, 2008, from http://news.joins.com/

Yeonhap News. (2007, September 14). *Joongang Ilbo*. Retrieved Sep. 28, 2008, from http://news.joins.com/

You, C. (2007, August 3). *Joongang Ilbo, 13237*(40), 4.

Yun, M. (2008a). Terrorist hostage-taking and kidnapping: Using script theory to predict the fate of a hostage. *Studies in Conflict and Terrorism, 31*(8), 736–748.

Yun, M. (2008b). *Understanding global terrorist hostage taking and kidnapping: global hostage taking and kidnapping hotspots, hostage negotiation and other countermeasures, and researches*. Saarbrucken, Germany: Verlag Dr. Muller.

Yun, M. and Gho, S. (2008, September 28). *Joongang Sunday, Focus* 81. Retrieved Sep. 28, 2008, from http://sunday.joins.com/

"Zarqawi 'not leading Iraq unrest.' " (2006, April 3). *BBC News*. Retrieved Feb. 21, 2007, from http://news.bbc.co.uk/

List of Korean Newspapers and Journals used for data analysis

Chosun Ilbo (August 2, 2007; August 11, 2007; August 18, 2007) Available at: http://www.chosun.com

The Hankyoreh (August 8, 2007) Available: http://www.hani.co.kr

Joongang Ilbo (July 20, 2007 – September 14, 2007) Available at: http://www.joins.com

Joongang Sunday (July 22, 2007; July 29, 2007; August 5, 2007) Available at: http://sunday.joins.com

The Korea Herald (July 27, 2007) Available: http://www.koreaherald.co.kr

Munhwa Ilbo (July 27, 2007) Available at: http://www.munhwa.com

Newsweek Korean Edition (August 15, 2007; August 22, 2007) Available: http://magazine.joins.com/newsweek

PREVENTING DEADLY ENCOUNTERS BETWEEN LAW ENFORCEMENT AND AMERICAN FAR-RIGHTISTS

Joshua D. Freilich

John Jay College of Criminal Justice
National Consortium for the Study of Terrorism and
Responses to Terrorism (START)

Steven M. Chermak

Michigan State University
National Consortium for the Study of Terrorism and
Responses to Terrorism (START)

Abstract: *This study extends Clarke and Newman's (2006; Newman & Clarke, 2008) work that applied SCP to terrorism. Their analysis focused on international terrorists, particularly suicide attacks, and only briefly discussed domestic American extremists. The American far-right, however, also poses a significant threat to public safety. This paper applies SCP techniques to two case studies of fatal far-right attacks against law enforcement personnel in the United States. The incidents were purposefully selected from Freilich and Chermak's U.S. Extremist Crime Database (ECDB), a relational database of all crimes committed by far-right extremists in the United States from 1990 to the present reported in an open source. Cornish's "script" analysis is applied to the two cases to devise intervention techniques to prevent*

Crime Prevention Studies, volume 25 (2009), pp. 141–172.

such acts. One case illustrates the efficacy of traditional "hard" SCP techniques. Importantly, because some of these attacks were unplanned and occurred during routine incidents that escalated, recent innovations in SCP by Wortley and others are applied to a second case to demonstrate the usefulness of "soft" techniques.

INTRODUCTION

This exploratory study applies situational crime prevention (SCP) techniques to murders of law enforcement personnel[1] by far-right extremists[2] in the United States. Since 1990, 48 law enforcement officers and one judge have been killed in 37 incidents in which at least one of the suspects was a far-rightist. Over 30% of the law enforcement victims were killed in the last three years. Far-rightists murdered five agents in 2007, four in 2008, and six in the first six months of 2009. Law enforcement agents killed over 10 of the suspects, one was killed by confederates, four committed suicide, and three were injured. Besides Timothy McVeigh, who was executed for the Oklahoma City bombing, six suspects were sentenced to death for these killings (Freilich & Chermak, 2009).

American domestic political extremist crimes vary in important ways from international terrorists. Hamm (2007; see also Smith and Damphousse, 2009) found that Islamic jihadists and far-rightists differed in the crime types they tended to commit in the United States. In the last 20 years far-right extremists have been involved in more fatal encounters with law enforcement personnel than either far-left or jihadist extremists (Freilich & Chermak, 2009). Different crime types will result in different prevention strategies (Clarke, 1995).

Many deadly encounters between far-right extremists and law enforcement personnel occur during "routine/spontaneous" situations (such as traffic stops/check points, home visits and etc.) that escalate to violence (Freilich & Chermak, 2009; Pitcavage, 1998). These situations would not be labeled "terrorist" by the FBI because they involve lone-wolf perpetrators, are unplanned precipitated acts of violence, and at first glance appear to be non-ideological crimes.[3] However, far-right ideology may have influenced the suspect's perception of the encounter and the decisions he/she made as the event unfolded. Understanding the suspect's far-right belief system has important *situational implications* (Birkbeck & LaFree, 1993; Roach et al., 2005). Unlike dispositional approaches that focus on ideology to address root causes, the claim here is that understanding the far-right belief system will aid prevention strategies.[4] To paraphrase Newman and Clarke's (2006) adage to "think terrorist," the police must also "think like a far-rightist."

This chapter uses Cornish's (1994) "script" analysis, and applies Clarke and Newman's (2006; Newman & Clarke, 2008) writings on terrorism, and recent innovations in SCP (see e.g., Wortley, 1997, 1998, 2001, 2002) to two deadly encounters between far-rightists and law-enforcement. One case study illustrates the efficacy of traditional "hard" SCP techniques. These are techniques that make it impossible for the crime to be committed. In other words, the suspect desires to commit the crime but the implemented SCP strategies prevent him/her from accomplishing the illegal act. The second study demonstrates how "soft" techniques might prevent the unplanned incidents from escalating to violence. Soft SCP strategies prevent prompts and cues (that increase a person's motivation to commit a crime) from occurring during a specific event. This, in turn, prevents a crime from occurring during that incident.

First, the threat posed by the far-right to public safety and law enforcement in particular in the United States is described. Second, the terrorism literature is reviewed to demonstrate that researchers have focused on *responses* to terrorism and *why* terrorists commit their crimes, as opposed to *how* they successfully carry out their attacks. The few studies that focused on "how" have either examined international terrorism or are conceptual in nature. After Cornish's "script" method is explained, the open source information on the situational conditions of the two deadly encounters is analyzed to uncover the facilitating factors that allowed these events to turn fatal. Specific SCP techniques that could be implemented to block the opportunities that permitted these homicides to occur are outlined. The paper concludes with suggestions for future research.

IMPORTANCE OF THE PROBLEM

Domestic extremists, especially far-rightists, pose a threat to public safety in the United States (Chermak et al., 2009; Freilich & Chermak, 2009; Freilich et al.., 2009; Freilich et al., 1999; Hewitt, 2003. LaFree, Dugan, Fogg & Scott (2006) have demonstrated that in a typical year 85% of terrorist attacks in the United States are committed by domestic extremists as opposed to 15% by international terrorists. Freilich, Chermak and Simone's (2009) survey of state police agencies found that 92% and 89% of responding agencies reported the presence of far-right neo-Nazi and militia groups respectively in their states, while only 76% and 62% reported the presence of environmental and Islamic jihadi groups, respectively. Two-thirds of the responding agencies agreed or strongly agreed that elements of the far-right and Islamic jihadists pose serious threats to their own state's security (see also Carlson, 1995; Riley & Hoffman, 1995; Riley et al., 2005). Freilich and Chermak's (2009) United States Extremist Crime Database (ECDB) study has found that since 1990 far-rightists have committed over 4,000 criminal events. The incidents include over 275 homicide incidents (ideologically motivated and non-ideologically motivated) that involve more than 530 homicide victims.

Far-rightists pose a significant threat to law enforcement personnel. Freilich and Chermak (2009; see also Pitcavage, 1998) found that over 11% of far-right homicide incidents involved a law enforcement agent as the victim. More than 30% of the over 40 slain officers were killed during a traffic stop, and others were killed during calls for service, such as responding to domestic violence calls or other home visits. For instance, a far-rightist murdered two police officers in South Carolina during a "routine" visit to his parent's home about a land usage dispute in 2003. The state wanted to confiscate 20 feet of the property to widen a highway. Freilich and Chermak (2009; see also F.B.I., 1999) have identified 90 additional incidents involving far-rightists who have injured or targeted law enforcement personnel since 1990. California and federal law enforcement personnel, for example, arrested over 60 members of the neo-Nazi skinhead gang Public Enemy Number One (PEN1) in December 2006. The group had crafted a "hit list" targeting police officers. Far-right racist gangs like the Aryan Brotherhood are responsible for homicides in and out of prison. According to the Southern Poverty Law Center, white supremacists account for 1% of the incarcerated population but commit 18% of homicides inside prison, and their victims have included correctional officers (Herrndobler, 2006).

TERRORISM RESEARCH, POLICE STUDIES AND THE MURDER OF LAW ENFORCEMENT AGENTS BY POLITICAL EXTREMISTS

Terrorism research has rarely produced empirical, policy-oriented prevention studies (Hamm, 2007; Lum et al., 2006; Merari, 1991; Silke, 2001). There are no studies that devise strategies to prevent political extremists from harming law enforcement. This is surprising considering the large threat that terrorism poses, especially to law enforcement. There are two problems with existing terrorism research: (1) until recently most terrorism research was unempirical, and (2) researchers have focused on *why* terrorists commit their crimes or *responses* to terrorism, as opposed to *how* they successfully carry out their attacks. Scholars have mostly focused on dispositional issues and been uninterested in devising prevention strategies. This is a significant omission because as Clarke (2004: 57) observes, "terrorism is now a serious threat to society and merely seeking to explain and understand is to fiddle while Rome burns."

Policy suggestions generated from anecdotal evidence are unlikely to be taken seriously by policy makers (Hamm, 2007; Merari, 1991). Terrorism research has been subjected to many critiques that highlight concerns (LaFree & Dugan, 2004; Leiken & Brooke, 2006; Ross, 1993; Sageman, 2004; Silke, 2001). Lum et al.'s (2006) systematic review of over 14,000 terrorism articles published between 1971 and 2003 found that only 3% were empirical (p. 8; see also Silke, 2001). Until recently, most terrorism research used secondary data – such as the mass media, books, journals, and other published documents – in a non-systematic manner (Merari, 1991; Silke, 2001).

It is often stated that it is uncommon for scholars to "talk to" terrorists because of the difficulty of arranging access, and safety issues (Merari, 1991). However, researchers have interviewed American, Asian, European, and Middle-Eastern terrorists, as well as anti-abortion, left-wing, right-wing, Christian, Sikh and Islamic terrorists. Invariably these interviews focus on *why* individuals chose to commit terrorist acts, as opposed to *how* they successfully do so (Ekici et al., 2008).

Post, Sprinzak, and Denny (2003) interviewed 35 incarcerated Hamas, Hizbullah, and Fatah terrorists, but only examined "the social context, mindset, motivations, and recruitment of these individuals" (p. 184). One finding was that the belief that one's group/people had been humiliated played a large role in inspiring terrorist actions. Berko and Erez (2005, 2007) interviewed Palestinians imprisoned in Israel for security offenses, including seven arrested for attempted suicide bombings. One study examined the role gender played in female Palestinian participation in terrorism (Berko & Erez, 2007), while the other focused on dispositional issues related to becoming a suicide attacker (Berko & Erez, 2005). Jurgensmeyer (2003) and Stern's (2003) interviews of Buddhist, Christian, Islamic, Jewish, and Sikh religious terrorist leaders also stressed the importance of humiliation, sacredness, and the past. Kaplan (1996) examined the literature of the radical wing of the anti-abortion movement and spoke to leaders and those involved in political crimes. Again, however, the focus was on motivation as opposed to the tools necessary for successful attacks (see also Blanchard and Prewitt, 1993). Similarly, scholars who have interviewed left-wing European terrorists (see e.g., Della Porta, 1995; White, 1993) have neglected opportunity factors. For instance, Horgan (2004) interviewed and observed members of the Provisional Irish Republican Army to conduct a "conceptual and theoretical critique of the literature on the psychology of terrorist behavior" (p. 35).

Most terrorism scholars who have collected their own data have also ignored situational factors. Handler (1990) collected data from newspaper clippings of nearly 400 known terrorists from the 1960s and 1970s and provided demographic profiles of right- and left-wing terrorists. Hewitt (2003, 2005) combined information from multiple sources to create a listing of terrorist incidents that described what the attack was and where it occurred. No details about the situation itself were provided. Silber and Bhatt (2006) Sageman (2004) and Bakker (2006) studied the radicalization process of jihadists. Sageman used network analysis to study 172 persons who joined the global Salafi jihad, and Bakker replicated this study with 250 jihadists in Europe. Silber and Bhatt employed case studies. The three studies concluded that individuals joined the jihad in clusters, and that peer dynamics played a significant role.

While the creation of new terrorism databases has led to an increase in the number of empirical studies, most research examines the spatial variation of terrorist acts or prosecutorial responses to terrorism. LaFree and others created the Global Terrorism Database (GTD) from the Pinkerton Global Intelligence Services (PGIS) data that identified and coded all terrorism incidents from wire services, State Department reports, other U.S. and foreign government reporting, newspapers, information from PGIS offices, and data furnished by PGIS clients. Scholars have used these data to study the distribution of terrorist acts, trajectories, and the life course of terrorist groups (see for e.g., LaFree and Dugan, 2007), and the relationship between state failure and the number of terrorist attacks in a nation (LaFree et al., 2007).

Brent Smith (1994) and colleagues' American Terrorism Study (ATS) is an important domestic terrorism database. This study includes persons indicted federally as a result of an investigation under the FBI's Counterterrorism Program. These data have been used to investigate the prosecution and punishment of international and domestic terrorists (Smith & Damphousse, 1996, 1998; Smith et al., 2002; Smith & Orvis, 1993), examine leaderless resistance tactics (Damphousse & Smith, 2004), and profile American terrorists (Smith, 2004; Smith & Morgan, 1994).

Clarke and Newman (2006; Newman & Clarke, 2008) took issue with the "dispositional" bias of terrorism research and called for scholars to interview terrorism experts, and terrorists themselves "not to gain intelligence on terrorist organizations, but to help find ways to make terrorist actions more difficult, risky and less rewarding" (p. 233). They argued that targets that were more exposed, vital, iconic, legitimate, destructible, occupied, near and easy (EVIL DONE) were vulnerable to terrorist attack (see also Boba, 2008; Ekici et al., 2008). Clarke and Newman's work on suicide bombing used Cornish's (2004) script analysis and highlighted the resources and tools necessary for successful actions. They used this knowledge to devise intervention techniques. They acknowledged that their analysis was "speculative," however, because they had not conducted interviews or collected their own data. Similarly, most previous neo-classical terrorism works have been conceptual efforts. Taylor (1993) examined the links between rational choice theory and behavioral learning theories. Roach, Ekblom, and Flynn's study (2005; see also Ekblom, 2001) set forth the "conjunction of terrorist opportunity" (CTO) framework. They argued that their framework could prevent terrorist acts, and they called for it to be tested on case studies. Hamm (2007) applied routine activities theory and social learning theory to understanding the "criminal successes and failures" of terrorists (p. 5). He reviewed trial transcripts and interviewed terrorists and law enforcement officers to understand "the opportunities and skills that made terrorist-oriented crimes possible; and to clearly identify the events and lack of skills that prevented other crimes from occurring" (p. 13; see also: Clarke, 1980; Cornish & Clarke, 2002; Dugan et al., 2005; Ekblom & Tilley, 2000).

Although many studies have examined officers killed in the line of duty, this literature has not focused on officers attacked by extremists. Such studies rarely examine situational factors. One exception was Kaminski and Marvel's (2002) study, which compared characteristics of police homicides to those of all homicides, and found few similarities (p. 182). Interestingly, the police homicide literature did *not* account for the differences. They concluded that future research should examine opportunity factors to explain police homicide patterns.

In sum, the present exploratory study is the first to apply SCP to deadly encounters between American far-right extremists and law enforcement.

ECDB STUDY DATA

Two incidents involving law enforcement fatalities were purposefully selected from Freilich and Chermak's (2009) ECDB study. The ECDB is a relational event, suspect, victim and group database of all criminal incidents committed by far-right extremists in the United States between 1990 and the present that were reported in an open source.[5] The ECDB has identified over 30 incidents since 1990 where far-rightists killed over 40 law enforcement personnel in the line of duty. The two selected events were "ideal for getting a clear fix on the relevant empirical and theoretical issues" (Snow & Trom, 2002, p. 158; see also Creswell, 2007). One incident illustrates the efficacy of "hard" SCP techniques, while the second demonstrates the usefulness of "soft" SCP strategies to prevent such violent encounters. Brief summaries of the two cases follow: (1) *Hard SCP Case Study*: A Neo-Nazi skinhead was transported by an officer from prison to a nearby hospital for a medical appointment. The skinhead overpowered the officer in the hospital and used the officer's own weapon to shoot and kill him; (2) *Soft SCP Case Study:* An anti-government "militia type survivalist" with possible Christian Identity connections fled from a traffic stop to his home. The suspect fired at officers who surrounded his home and killed one police agent.

The two incidents were researched in 22 search engines: (1) Lexis-Nexis; (2) Proquest; (3) Yahoo; (4) Google; (5) Copernic; (6) News Library; (7) Infotrac; (8) Google Scholar; (9) Amazon; (10) Google U.S. Government; (11) Federation of American Scientists; (12) Google video; (13) Center for the Study of Intelligence; (14) Surf Wax; (15) Dogpile; (16) Mamma; (17) Librarians' Internet Index; (18) Scirus; (19) All the Web; (20) Google News; (21) Google Blog; and (22) Homeland Security Digital Library}to uncover publicly available information on them (Cornish and Clarke, 2002).

The uncovered information came from a variety of sources and increased the likelihood that there was no systematic bias either for or against the groups (Freilich & Pridemore, 2006, 2007). Close to 50 news/journalistic accounts and five watch-group publications were used to write a chronology of the "hard SCP" incident (as of April 2009 the case had not been tried). Two watch-group reports, 22 news/journalistic accounts and trial transcripts (that were purchased) of both the prosecution and defense opening and closing arguments were used to write a chronology of the "soft SCP" event.

Method

SCP is a policy-oriented approach that focuses on the criminal event to understand "how" the crime is successfully completed. Intervention techniques are then devised to manipulate situational factors to reduce crime (Clarke, 1995). Cornish's (1994) "script" approach, which examines a specific type of incident in detail, was used to uncover the full range of intervention points. Clarke and Newman (2006) argue that focusing on suicide attacks in general captures too many disparate types of attacks to be useful. A specific type of suicide attack (e.g., attacks against public transportation or pubs and bars) in a specific conflict area (e.g., Israel/Palestine) must be identified. Our analysis of the two deadly encounters between far-rightists and law enforcement agents followed this approach. The two incidents were analyzed separately to illustrate the efficacy of "hard" and "soft" SCP techniques, respectively. This insured that the correct degree of specificity required for each situation was achieved (Clarke and Cornish, 1985, p. 165).

The open source data for each incident was reviewed to create a chronological listing of the steps that were necessary for the fatal attack to occur. Cornish and Clarke (2002, p. 47) explain that "all crimes . . . involve such chains of decisions and actions, separable into interdependent stages, involving the attainment of sub-goals that serve the overall goals of the crime." Clarke and Newman (2006) found that suicide attacks could be broken down into 13 steps: step 10 focused on how the attacker successfully reached his/her target (such as a bus or a cafe). Conditions that made this easier included poorly designed buses, predictable schedules and poor venue security. They used this knowledge to devise intervention techniques such as designing doors that could be closed if the driver became suspicious and searching café patrons at the busiest times. In short, the script approach highlights the opportunities for altering the outcome and illustrates where strategies and training could be enhanced for preventing such incidents (see for e.g., Cornish & Clarke, 2002, p. 41).

Next, the open source information was reviewed and used to write narratives on the background of each case and a timeline of their key events. SCP techniques that could be implemented to block the opportunities that permitted these homicides to occur are also outlined.

ANALYSIS

Narrative and Timeline of the Hard SCP Incident

The suspect was a 27 year old male Neo-Nazi skinhead, with white suprem-acy tattoos covering his body and face. The suspect had a long criminal record and was sentenced to almost nine years in prison for being a felon in possession of a firearm 11 days before the fatal encounter. The suspect was said to be angry over the killing of his friend, another skinhead, by police a year earlier during a traffic stop. The suspect held law enforcement responsible and had threatened to attack law enforcement. The suspect had also threatened to escape and was considered a "high risk" inmate. The events that culminated in the correctional officer's murder are listed in sequential order in Table 1. This entire incident, from murder to capture, lasted approximately 50 minutes.

Application of Possible "Hard" SCP Techniques

SCP is a dynamic framework and currently there are five strategies that encompass 25 techniques to prevent crime (Cornish & Clarke, 2003). Again, they range from "hard" techniques that make it more difficult to successfully commit the crime to "soft" approaches that prevent situational cues from occurring that increase a person's motivation to commit a crime during the incident. In this case, the suspect made a rational decision to escape custody or lash back at those who killed his friend. It is unclear if he "faked" his injury and planned the escape, or if he simply "seized" the opportunity. An analysis of the narrative and timeline indicate that traditional "hard" SCP techniques could have prevented this homicide.

The slain officer violated procedure and was not wearing a bullet-proof vest. The officer also violated procedure by removing the "high risk" inmate's handcuffs during the MRI (Medical Resonance Imaging) procedure and not re-cuffing the inmate immediately after the procedure. Instead, the officer allowed the suspect to dress without restraints. If the officer had followed these two procedures it seems unlikely that the inmate would have been able to seize the firearm and shoot the officer to death. Both the vest and the handcuffs are examples of SCP's "increasing the efforts" of illegal behavior. Such policies are "hard" SCP techniques be-cause they make it harder for suspects to achieve the criminal goals of escaping or harming an officer. In the future, correctional agencies could

Table 1: Timeline of the Murder of the Correctional Officer in the Hospital

(1) *Early morning*: The 27 year old male suspect was transported to a hospital for an MRI.	(2)The suspect was transported by a single 60 year old correctional officer. The officer was not wearing a body armor/bullet-resistant vest. (This violated procedure.)
(3) *7:45 am*: 3rd floor of hospital: The suspect underwent an MRI for back pain. The suspect's handcuffs were taken off (because metal disrupts the machine) and replaced with a plastic zip-tie flex cuffs. (This violated procedure.)	(4) After the MRI procedure the suspect was left alone in the room with the correctional officer so he could change back into his prison suit. The suspect was still not wearing handcuffs. The suspect informed the officer he was leaving. The officer tried to stop the suspect and a scuffle ensued. The suspect gained control of the officer's gun and shot him twice in head and chest, killing him.
(5) The suspect fled the hospital and used the slain officer's gun to hijack a Doctor's Ford Explorer SUV. The suspect forced 2 people out of car and drove off.	(6) The suspect then called his girlfriend.
(7) The suspect drove to his girlfriend's house and dropped off his prison jumpsuit and changed clothes.	(8) The suspect left his girlfriend's house and drove off. The suspect was spotted by police who were staking out his friends.
(9) A car chase ensued that continued to a highway and continued for miles even after the suspect's car's tires were spiked.	(10) The suspect exited the highway, left his car and ran into a fast food store.
(11) In the fast food venue, the suspect pulled a gun and grabbed an employee who struggled with him. The suspect tried to shoot his gun but it jammed. The suspect pistol whipped the employee. A customer jumped into the fray. The suspect grabbed a kitchen knife and injured the employee and a patron. The patron though disarmed the suspect.	(12) The suspect ran to the back of store and hid in the manager's office. *8:35 am*: Police entered the store and arrested the suspect.

mandate that both policies are in place in all interactions with "high risk" inmates. The policies should be applied to interactions that occur off jail and prison facilities and if the officer is alone with the suspect. Mandating such policies is only the first step. Agencies must insure that their policies are carried out. In this case this agency's training programs appeared to have not been properly implemented. Agencies on all levels and in jurisdictions of all sizes should invest in and properly implement training programs on these matters to their officers.

It is important that the officer's own weapon was used in this slaying. Unfortunately, this is not a rare occurrence. The FBI found that 52 police officers (8% of officers killed on duty) were slain by their own weapons between 1992 and 2003 (Donald, 2005). An initiative that "increases the effort" and could prevent this would use biometric technology to insure "selective denial" to all law enforcement personnel firearms. Ekblom and Tilley (2000, p. 388) explain that "selective denial may render resources usable only by those authorized to do so. Technological solutions centre on biometrics – for example, a gun has been developed for police use that only fires if the rightful owner is squeezing the trigger, thereby preventing the gun being turned on the police themselves." Once such technologies are fully developed, even if expensive, they should be employed in agencies where armed personnel routinely interact with dangerous inmates. Implementing this policy would undoubtedly save lives. Ekblom and Tilley also discuss how the American military is studying the feasibility of remotely disabling weapons by radio to prevent their misuse. This technology would also aid crime prevention strategies. Relatedly, police agencies should be required to use special holsters that make it impossible to draw a gun by just undoing the snap. Instead, the gun must be pushed down and forward to release it from the holster. Because this is currently not known it would prevent most offenders – such as the Skinhead in this case – from successfully gaining control of an officer's firearm. Again, police training programs on "weapon retention," which teach officers techniques that reduce the likelihood of having a weapon taken from them, could play a helpful role.

Policies which "increased the risk" to the suspect could have prevented this tragic murder. First, the correctional agency's own report on the incident recommended that in the future two officers be assigned to transfer "high risk" inmates (see also Smith, 2005). In this event the sole officer was 60 years old while the 27 year old suspect was 33 years younger than the officer. Further, the (un-cuffed) suspect and the 60 year old officer were left alone in a room as the suspect changed. It is possible that during this brief period the suspect became aware of the lone officer's vulnerability and the opportunity it presented to escape. The suspect may have gained confidence, in other words, that an escape was doable. It is possible that "soft" SCP approaches (that seek to prevent increased motivation to commit a crime during a particular situation), discussed below, may be applicable here as well. In any case, the "hard" SCP technique of a two-officer policy for the transfer of inmates would have made it more difficult for the inmate to escape. We realize that budgetary considerations may make it difficult for agencies to require all prisoner transports be conducted by at least two officers. However, it would be organizationally feasible and effective to require such a procedure for high-risk inmates. Factors that would be used to determine high risk would include criminal record, prior/current behavior in prison, and previous charges (e.g., resisting law enforcement). In addition, having a better understanding of far-right skinhead (anti-police) ideology and sharing information between agencies would also have been useful. It is important to recall that the suspect's friend was killed by law enforcement the previous year and the suspect had vowed revenge. We will return to these points more generally in the next section.

Significantly, not only was the officer alone with the inmate after the MRI procedure (as the inmate was changing), but nobody realized what had transpired until *after* the inmate attacked the officer. Perhaps hospitals that are regularly used for inmate medical care could set aside specific wings for high-risk inmates. CCTV cameras could be installed in these locations. Hospitals that have a large and consistent volume of high-risk inmates on their premises might also make use of technology recently developed by Ohio State University researchers (Freilich and Chermak, 2009). This technology links multiple CCTV cameras to a single system so an individual – in this case a high-risk inmate – is followed automatically anywhere the monitoring computer has CCTV coverage. The benefit of linking the cameras together on one system is that an object of concern can be "seamlessly" followed. Such cameras could monitor high-risk inmates at all times they are inside the hospital or immediately outside its grounds.

For hospitals or other non-correctional facilities that are regularly visited by high-risk inmates, reserved locations could use environmental design techniques to increase safety. Here the suspect successfully fled the building. Again, interventions that could have prevented this would be limiting high-risk inmates to a specific wing. The doors to this wing –

installed at the entrance/exit points – could be designed to only open if the proper key/password/card is used. Alternatively, or in addition, security officers could be posted inside the wings or at the entrance/exit points. Finally, and consistent with the agency report on this fatal attack, communication devices could be upgraded to insure that they are accessible during these types of emergencies. It would also be helpful for the correctional facility to coordinate inmate hospital visits with local police, and especially with hospital security.

Two techniques that "reduced the reward" might have prevented the deadly outcome. Facilities with large number of inmates might install medical complexes on their grounds. Similarly, most facilities could require that physicians carry out minor procedures on their grounds. Indeed, the agency's report on this incident made this suggestion as well. Finally, law enforcement agencies could require that "high risk" inmates wear tracking devices on their garb while they are outside facility grounds. This policy would make it more difficult for suspects to successfully flee. The suspect in this case did not change out of his prison garb until he escaped to his girlfriend's house. Mandating tracking devices would insure that escaping inmates are tracked or take time to change out of their clothes. This would provide more time for law enforcement to prevent the suspect from escaping.

Narrative and Timeline of the Soft SCP Incident

The 50-year-old male suspect was an anti-government "militia type survivalist" who had threatened to kill police officers in the past. According to the defense, the suspect was paranoid and believed the police were after him and planned to confiscate his guns. The suspect had a 17 year history of non-violent drug offenses and frequently drank heavily. The day before the incident the suspect left work at 4:30 pm. He did not sleep that night. Instead, he visited friends, social clubs, casinos, and heavily consumed alcohol until the morning. Eight hours after the fatal incident occurred. the suspect's blood alcohol level was found to be .096. It was reported during the trial that the suspect's blood alcohol level was over .25 when he killed the officer. The events of the fatal encounter are listed in sequential order in Table 2.

The events from the initial traffic stop to the officer's slaying lasted a little over an hour. The entire incident, from the traffic stop to capture, lasted less than six hours.

Table 2: Timeline of the Murder of the Police Officer Outside the Suspect's Home

(1) _7:19 am_ After drinking most of the night the suspect's van is pulled over by a police officer for speeding, going through a red light & erratic driving. The officer asks the suspect for his license, insurance & registration. The suspect provides this information.

(2) The officer returns to his police car to complete a traffic citation. The officer returns to the suspect's car for additional information. When asked about his occupation, the suspect began to back up the car.

(3) _Around 7:30 am_ the suspect flees the scene in his van and drives onto an Interstate followed by the officer. A low speed pursuit (35-40 mph) ensues because of heavy traffic. The suspect exits the interstate & goes through a red light the officer does not make. A radio call is put out for the suspect

(4) Another officer responds & drives to the suspect's home address. The suspect's home is a one story bungalow.

(5) _Around 7:40 am_ the officer examines the location near the suspect's home. The officer notices & examines suspect's van parked near the suspect's residence. The van is unoccupied.

(6) The officer walks to the side and recognizes the suspect from a previous encounter where the suspect was drunk. There is a locked six foot chain link barrier (i.e., cyclone fencing) between the officer and the suspect. The officer calls out to the suspect. The suspect responds with curses, that he did not do anything and that he wants to be left alone.

(7) The suspect runs about the grounds outside his residence. The suspect is upset & it appears he was locked out of his home.

(8) Additional officers are requested & three others arrive at the scene. One of these officers had driven to the traffic stop scene & picked up the suspect's driver's license that had been dropped. The first responding officer verified that person on the license matched the suspect he just spoken with.

(continued)

(9) The officers continue to exchange conversation with the suspect, asking him to come out. The suspect refuses, curses, notes that he has weapons, and threatens the officers.

The suspect eventually breaks a back window and enters his residence.

(10) During one conversation (consisting of yelling back & forth) the agitated suspect said he could see a police officer out there & he was going to kill him.

7:59 am: the suspect fires two shots from his backdoor.
NOTE: During the suspect's trial the defense argues that the officers' comments to the suspect and their actions (i.e., displaying their weapons) "escalated" the situation and fueled the suspect's paranoia.

(11) *8:28 am:* the suspect fires a high powered rifle bullet that goes through a delivery van's engine and "center-punches" the chest of a 35 year old 302 pound male officer crouched behind it. Other officers shoot back & rescue the fallen officer who is transported to a hospital where he is pronounced DOA.

The slain officer was *not* wearing a bullet-proof vest, though it likely would not have mattered because the bullet was armored piercing.

(12) The suspect remains in his home & subsequently shoots additional rounds. The officers return fire. In total, the suspect fires 20 rounds and law enforcement fires over 80 rounds.

(13) *Close to 1:00 pm:* a SWAT team fires tear gas into the suspect's home, storms, & arrests suspect.

(The tear gas sparked a fire, and the fire department had to extinguish it.)

(14) *Aftermath*: Police find a weapons cache in the home including an assault weapon, two rifles, a shotgun, handguns, body armor, several boxes of ammunition, surveillance equipment, and anti-government and conspiracy theory videos.

The suspect is found guilty of first degree murder & is sentenced to life in prison two years later.

Application of Possible "Soft" SCP Techniques

First, and unsurprisingly, some of the hard techniques previously discussed could have been applied to this case. For example, the slain officer was also not wearing a bulletproof vest. While it likely would not have mattered, because the officer was hit by an armor piercing bullet, mandating the wearing of bullet proof vests during sieges would save the lives of officers confronting non-armored piercing bullets. Similarly, prohibiting the sale of armor piercing bullets would insure that officers wearing bullet proof vests are much better protected.

This section, however, focuses on the applicability of soft SCP, the 10 techniques of reducing provocations and removing excuses. Cornish and Clarke (2003) set forth these techniques to respond to Wortley's (1997, 1998, 2001, 2002) critique. Wortley explains that, contrary to some who assume individuals have a static motivation to offend, people have varying motivation levels depending upon the event they confront. Situations provide opportunities to offend, but in certain cases they create or supply the motivation to offend too. Wortley discusses a hypothetical pedophile observing a young naked child swimming alone. This incident provides an easy opportunity for the suspect. But, it also leads to an increase in the offender's sex drive – that could be conceived as a "situational surge" in motivation to commit a rape. The same pedophile seeing a fully clothed adult female in a crowded venue will have less of an opportunity to offend, as well as a lower sex drive and motivation to offend. Reducing opportunities fit well with the traditional "hard" SCP strategies. Focusing on "situationally induced motivation" (Wortley, 1997, p. 66) could lead to strategies to reduce provocations and excuses to insure individuals are not subject to cues that increase their motivation to offend during the encounter.

A review of this incident reveals similarities with Wortley's critique. First, this encounter consisted of two sequential scenes, the traffic stop and a subsequent siege at the suspect's home. The defense attorney argued at trial that law enforcement's actions during the subsequent siege – especially the 30-40 minutes *before* the fatal shots were fired – unintentionally escalated the event to violence. The key time frame, according to the defense, was between close to 8:00 am and 8:28 am when the fatal shots were fired. The defense claimed that the police's actions during this period were ill advised and made a bad situation worse: The officers who engaged the suspect outside his home in conversation were not trained negotiators. Further, the officers may have unintentionally fueled the suspect's paranoia by displaying their weapons and continuing to engage the suspect in conversation. The defense counsel asserted during his opening statement:

> [The suspect] sees [officer} XX bring a shotgun. [The suspect] presumably . . . sees [officer] XX with his firearm drawn when he ap-

proaches within feet of the backdoor of his residence. In fact you will hear that it was [*the suspect's*] *worst nightmare that the cops were gonna come to his front door, and here it was coming true* . . . what is really important . . . is that officer XX and officer YY continue to engage this obviously agitated [suspect] . . . [officer] XX [nominated] to be the negotiator . . . has no negotiation experience." [italics added]

The defense counsel elaborated upon these points during his closing statement:

> The interesting thing about this case . . . [is it is] one of these convergences . . . [the suspect] has this paranoia about police, about government, and then they show up at his house. He thinks [they are going to] shoot him. Of course not . . . Again, this is not to blame the police at all. . . . [officer] XX walks up . . . has his shotgun . . . They are yelling at him . . . [the suspect] is taking it in his mind . . . they are showing up to get me. . . . But more importantly, they wind up on [the suspect's] back door to talk to him, but how do they talk to him? [Officer] XX with his firearm drawn and [officer] YY with his TASER drawn . . . that would scare any of us, but in[the suspect's] mind, it's the end . . . this is before shots were even fired . . . And we have all these law enforcement officers running around in the back. . . . *it is the police that initially escalate this matter* and display deadly force which feeds right into [the suspect's] delusional impaired and vulnerable mind. . . . [italics added]

The defense counsel's argument is that police's actions during the siege interacted with the suspect's far-right anti-police ideology. This interaction of factors created a self fulfilling prophecy (Pitcavage, 1998; Wortley, 1998) that led to a situational surge in the suspect's motivation to lash back at law enforcement. First, far-rightists view the government as a symbolic enemy: the government is tyrannical and seeks to betray American sovereignty while undermining individual liberties at home, especially gun rights. Law enforcement officials are viewed as an integral part of the government's plots. The narrative shows that the suspect embraced these ideals. Second, during the initial traffic stop and the siege the suspect had personal contact with the police. In the suspect's view his abstract fears were beginning to occur in reality, law enforcement was taking concrete actions to infringe upon his liberty. Finally, according to the defense these fears were realized (in the suspect's mind) by law enforcement's continuing efforts to talk to him and displaying their weapons to him. The combination of these three factors may have increased the suspect's fears, hatred of the government and motivation to attack the police (Pitcavage, 1998; Wortley, 1998, 2002). While non-ideological extremists may also become agitated Pitcavage (2001, p. 5) notes that "extremist criminals most of whom have ideological reasons to hate or fear the government, are even more likely to attempt some act of retaliation or revenge."

Consistent with Wortley's approach (2002; see also Binder and Scharf, 1980; Fyfe, 1989; White, 2002; Wilkinson 2002), law enforcement actions (before any shots were fired) that reduced perceived provocations might have kept the suspect's fears about the government/police at bay. Such interventions are "soft" strategies because they seek to prevent the suspect's motivation to commit a crime from increasing during the specific event. In this case, if the officers had initially *not* engaged the suspect in conversation, nor publicly displayed their weapons to him they may have prevented this event from escalating. Scholars have argued that the public display of a weapon sometimes create a self- fulfilling prophecy that intensifies individual emotions and leads to violence (Birkbeck and LaFree, 1993; Wortley, 1998; Wright, 2007; see also Bayley, 1986; Fyfe, 1989). If the police had fallen back, established a perimeter and waited for a trained negotiator to commence negotiations the situation may have unfolded differently.

Similarly, if the police had paid more attention to whether the suspect was under the influence of alcohol or drugs, this incident may have played out differently. In this case it was opined that the suspect's blood alcohol level was over 2.5 (and thus the suspect was intoxicated) when he fired the fatal shot. The ECDB has identified other police killings where the suspect was drunk or impaired. Engel (2003, p. 476) found that "the strongest and most consistent predictor of resistance (to police officers) was the use of alcohol or drugs by suspects." Again, in this particular situation that involved an agitated political extremist (with anti-police views), the best solution might have been for the police to retreat and wait for the alcohol to wear off.

Such possibilities again highlight the importance of police training. Successful training programs could include various scenarios in their curricula. Training programs could alert officers to the possibility of escalation, especially when dealing with known far-rightists or others harboring animus to the police. The scenarios could include potential responses to be used in particular kinds of events. The Anti-Defamation League (ADL, 2007) stresses the importance of police making accurate threat assessments and prioritizing verbal and written threats as indicators of potentially dangerous confrontations. Patience is important and examples of standoffs that were resolved peacefully should be used (Chermak et al., 2009).

Law enforcement in certain circumstances should allow the suspect "to let off steam" (Smith, 1998, 2005). Pitcavage, founder of the militia-watchdog listserv and Director of Fact Finding for the ADL, agrees with this approach. He adds that officers could also engage in active listening and explain that he/she appreciates that the suspect is upset, understand their point of view, and ask the suspect to clarify points that they made to "to draw the [suspect] . . . out and get the speaker to slow down and consider what he or she is talking about . . . the goal is to slow the pace of the encounter down and keep the situation under control" (Pitcavage, 1998, p. 12).

This technique is consistent with the well known "verbal judo" strategy, police jargon for proactive measures to calm a situation and allow suspects to offer their views for their actions (Begert, 1998; Johnson, 2004; see also Engel, 2003, 2005). These strategies are useful for police encounters with far-rightists. Some far-rightists do not recognize the government's authority to regulate a host of issues, including guns, taxes and travel. Certain far-rightists do not use license plates, and thus tend to come into contact with police during routine traffic stops. Similar to the case here (where an initial traffic stop led to a subsequent home siege and fatal outcome), these events also have the potential to escalate.

Pitcavage (1998, 2001) endorses a variety of techniques consistent with reducing provocations to defuse such encounters. The first issue is that obviously such strategies would be of limited value if police officers did not realize they were dealing with a far-right extremist until it was too late. Pitcavage (1998) explains, however, that police officers can be trained to look for a comprehensive listing of indicators that could alert them they have pulled over an anti-government far-rightist during a traffic stop. Some signs include: strange or no license plates; objections to requests for registration or license on the basis that the subject is not driving a commercial vehicle (p. 6); peculiar anti-government (NWO) or biblical bumper stickers (p. 6); strange comments such as the driver referring to himself as a sovereign citizen and referencing "contracts"; the handing out of anti- government literature (p. 7); identification that indicates the driver as a member of a strange sounding "law enforcement" agency and/or attempts to videotape the encounter (p. 7); questions that ask to see "oath of office"; and bizarre documents produced in response to a request to see a driver's license or a fake/strange driver's license. Pitcavage (2001) also lists signs that officers could look for at residences during sieges. These identifiers include signs that contain anti-law enforcement language, unusual flags or banners (such as racist signs), and indicators of fortification, such as reinforced walls. Training officers to recognize these indicators mimics Clarke and Newman's (2006, p. 64) policy suggestion for Israel to train guards at cafe entrances to recognize suicide bombers.

Pitcavage (1998) argues that if police realize they are dealing with an anti-government extremist they must monitor the scene and determine if the suspect is armed. They should "try not to heighten tension or suspicion ... [and] they should not try to argue political philosophy" (p. 8; see also Begert, 1998). The police might also suggest that the suspect pursue his ideological beliefs at a future court hearing. But, in highly charged situations (e.g., a single officer confronting a highly agitated armed extremist), Pitcavage concludes that police should practice restraint and not pursue the incident.

A closely related strategy is for the police to remove excuses during such charged encounters by "humanizing" themselves, or in SCP's language, alerting the suspect's conscience. Again, police training should teach officers to proactively personalize themselves to the suspect. Pitcavage (2008) suggests that police "humanize themselves so that to the subject they become more than simply the symbol of an oppressive government. There are numerous ways to do so, including the time honored tactic of telling the subject, "you may be right, I don't know, but I'm just doing my job ... playing dumb can also sometimes help" (p. 8).

Posting signs on highways that reinforce that violence against the police is wrong and hurts the victim's family, the suspect's family and the wider community is another possible humanizing technique. Pictures of police officers in uniform alongside photos of them with their families – including their children – could be included on the signs (Wortley, 2001). Publicity campaigns targeting the larger community could note that previous attacks on law enforcement have backfired (i.e., led to negative consequences for the far-right movement). These campaigns should also stress that past attacks have led to the suspect's death or capture. Infamous examples like Gordon Kahl (who killed three federal agents in 1983 before being killed and whose son has served over 25 years for the slayings) could be referenced. These strategies could be implemented in locations where the state police or other law enforcement agencies have routinely pulled over far-rightists for refusing to follow traffic regulations.

Finally, building upon Clarke and Newman's (2006; Newman & Clarke, 2008) suggestions, community outreach tactics could be useful.

They discuss initiatives the police should take to break down barriers with migrant communities (which some terrorists have used to hide in) that are suspicious of the police. Interestingly, the far-right's ideology is similarly suspicious of the government and hostile to the police. The police could open a dialogue with "moderate" far-right movement leaders (Chermak et al., 2009). FBI agents Duffy and Brantley (1997) established a four category typology of far-right militia groups, that range from groups that engaged in no criminal activities to cells that plot serious acts violence. The FBI agents argued that "proactive dialogue with certain . . . [moderate] militia groups may help law enforcement agencies diffuse tensions and avert potential flash points" (p. 1). Consistent with Clarke and Newman's suggestions, the authorities could arrange to go on movement talk shows (some far- right leaders have their own shortwave radio talk shows). During these encounters the police could explain their policies and actions, humanize their officers, lower suspicion, dispel incorrect rumors, build communication, stress tolerance and their desire to avoid needless confrontations (see Roach et al., 2005, p. 18). The officers could also encourage movement members to channel their energies into legal activities like political campaigns or legal movement building activities (Freilich et al., 2009).

DISCUSSION AND CONCLUSION

This study extended Clarke and Newman's (2006) research by applying SCP to two case studies of far-right slayings of police officers. The cases were used heuristically to illustrate the potential of hard and soft SCP techniques. In most cases though, a combination of hard and soft techniques may be preferable. The research revealed a number of interesting findings.

First, international and domestic terrorists differ in ways that have implications for prevention strategies. The international terrorist strikes that Clarke and Newman (2006) focused on in Northern Ireland and Israel were planned attacks (i.e., sought out opportunities). The terrorists decided beforehand which target to strike and took actions to carry out the attacks. However, many far-right killings of police officers, like the "soft" event we analyzed, were not planned. Instead, the situation began as a routine event that escalated. Again, over a third of the ECDB's homicide events of law enforcement personnel by far-rightists began as traffic stops, and others occurred during routine calls for service. As the defense counsel in the soft SCP case here noted during his opening statement, "this was not a planned situation where he would get pulled over for a boulevard stop and go to his house and barricade himself." Instead, these attacks were "presented opportunities" (Carroll & Weaver, 1986, p. 23; Clarke & Cornish, 1985, p. 167) that may have occurred because of situational surges in motivation.[6]

Relatedly, Clarke and Newman (2006) found that the international terrorists they examined sought to keep their actions secret as they planned attacks. For example, the 9/11 attackers purposefully chose to reside and blend into migrant communities. This study, however, located an important difference with the domestic far-right. As noted, because of the far-right's ideology that claims that tax laws, gun statutes, and travel restrictions are dictatorial, some movement members purposefully violate these acts. Sometimes they publicize these acts of defiance (Hamm, 2007). It is these types of crimes that draw law enforcement's attention and commence the routine interactions that may escalate to violence. Unlike the terrorists studied by Clarke and Newman who garnered attention from the federal government, most law enforcement officers killed by far-rightists since 1990 (over 90%) were state and local police officers responding to these initially mundane events (Freilich & Chermak, 2009)

Although the study focused on the far-right, its findings have a wider resonance. The hard SCP techniques we outlined are not ideologically dependent and can be applied to all cases involving law-enforcement encounters with dangerous prisoners. Versions of the soft SCP techniques might be applicable to other types of extremist groups that are anti-government, such as the far-left, and possibly jihadists who come into contact with law enforcement personnel during routine situations (Pitcavage, 2001). For example, the far-left Black Panther's anti-government ideology is similar to the far-right's anti-government beliefs.

This study was exploratory and there are a number of issues that could be addressed by future research and policymakers. First, the soft SCP strategies of verbal judo and humanizing the officers could be examined experimentally to determine if these techniques are actually useful. Second, police departments that operate in locations that have a significant far-right presence and/or high far-right crime rate could specially train one officer to handle far-rightists. This officer could train other officers about how to proceed when confronting known far-rightists in particular kinds of situations. This officer could also be notified and consulted with about any traffic stop, home visit, or importantly a siege that involves a known far-rightist and which appears in danger of escalating. Both the FBI and

Department of Homeland Security could play a role in offering such training to state and local police agencies. Third, this study used open sources, including media accounts, watch-group materials and parts of trial transcripts to gather information for the case studies. Future research should expand data collection to include interviewing law enforcement personnel, prosecutors, terrorism experts, reporters and if possible the perpetrators. The focus should be on *how* these situations turned violent, and what skills the perpetrator needed to successfully complete the attack. Finally, future research should examine these issues using a case control design and compare unsuccessful attacks against law enforcement to fatal events. This will insure that we learn about the characteristics of the deadly events and uncover where they differ from the non-deadly incidents (Clarke & Eck, 2005; Loftin & McDowall, 1988).

Address correspondence to: jfreilich@jjay.cuny.edu

Acknowledgments: This research was supported by the United States Department of Homeland Security through the National Consortium for the Study of Terrorism and Responses to Terrorism (START), grant number N00140510629. However, any opinions, findings, and conclusions or recommendations in this document are those of the authors and do not necessarily reflect views of the U.S. Department of Homeland Security. An earlier version of this paper was presented at the 2008 Environmental Criminology and Crime Analysis (ECCA) conference in Izmir, Turkey. The authors thank two reviewers for helpful comments on earlier drafts of this paper.

NOTES

1. "Law enforcement personnel" is operationalized as local, state, and federal peace, correctional and court officers as well as security guards in the U.S.
2. There is no universally-accepted definition of "far-right" extremism. A systematic literature review on far-right extremism by Gruenewald, Freilich and Chermak (2009) centered on works that offered typologies,

definitions and descriptions (see, e.g., Barkun, 1989; Berlet & Lyons, 2000; Coates, 1987; Duffy & Brantley, 1998, Durham, 2003; Kaplan, 1993; 1995; Mullins, 1988; Smith, 1994; Sprinzak, 1995; see also Dobratz & Shanks-Meile, 1997; Weinberg, 1993). In the literature review, the domestic far- right is operationalized as individuals or groups that subscribe to aspects of the following ideals: They are: a) fiercely nationalistic (as opposed to universalistic and internationalist in orientation), anti-global, suspicious of centralized federal authority, reverent of individual liberty (especially their right to own guns and be free of paying taxes); b) they believe in conspiracy theories that involve a grave threat to national sovereignty and/or personal liberty and that one's personal and/or national "way of life" is under attack and is either already lost or that the threat is imminent (sometimes such beliefs are amorphous and vague, but for some the threat is from a specific ethnic, racial, or religious group); and c) they believe in the need to be prepared for an attack either by participating in or supporting the need for paramilitary preparations/training or survivalism. The mainstream conservative movement and the mainstream Christian right are not included.

3. The F.B.I. (1997) defined terrorism as: "The unlawful use of force or violence against persons or property to intimidate or coerce a government, the civilian population, or any segment thereof, in furtherance of political or social objectives" committed by a group. This definition systematically excludes important categories of ideological crimes, such as: (1) non-federal (i.e., state) prosecutions of ideological crimes, (2) ideologically motivated crimes committed by lone-wolf perpetrators, (3) ideologically motivated crimes where a group did not claim responsibility, (4) non-violent ideologically motivated crimes, and (5) non-ideological crimes committed by political extremists.

4. This claim is similar to Newman and Clarke's (2003, p. 9) acknowledgment that "different individuals perceive situations differently." Indeed, consistent with the argument made here about the situational effects of ideology, Newman and Clarke concede the relevance of "situational culture" that recognizes "that a situation that is bound up with deep and broad cultural values can be modified using known techniques that intervene in an individual's decision-making at just the right time" (p. 12; see also Ekblom, 2007). See also Clarke and Homel (1997, p. 18) for a similar discussion on the preventive benefits that result from inducing guilt in perpetrators during the situation, as opposed to examining the role guilt plays in longstanding criminal dispositions.

5. The ECDB identifies incidents from: (1) terrorism databases such the American Terrorist Study, the RAND-MIBT database, and the Global Terrorism Database; (2) official sources such as Congressional hearings, the FBI's Law Enforcement Officers Killed and Assaulted; and Terrorism in the United States annual reports, (3) scholarly and journalist accounts (4) watch-group reports published by the SPLC, the Anti-Defamation League, the militia watchdog listserv and other organizations, and (5) systematic media searches.

6. For example, in another ECDB case prisoners rioted and seized control of parts of a facility and took hostages. A spokesperson for the corrections authority agitated the prisoners after the riot began by implying on the news the inmates were not serious in their demands. The inmates responded by killing a corrections officer.

REFERENCES

Anti-Defamation League. (2007). Deadly domains: Standoffs with Extremists. [Online]: http://www.adl.org/Learn/safety/Deadly_Domains.asp

Bakker, E. (2006). *Jihadi terrorists in Europe, their characteristics and the circumstances in which they joined the Jihad: An exploratory study*. The Hague: Clingendael Institute.

Barkun, M. (1989). Millenarian aspects of white supremacist movements. *Terrorism and Political Violence, 1*, 409–434.

Bayley, D. A. (1986). The tactical choices of police patrol officers. *Journal of Criminal Justice, 14*, 329–348.

Begert, M. (1998). The threat of domestic terrorism. *The Police Chief, 65*, 36–40.

Berko, A., & E. Erez. (2005). Ordinary people and "death work": Palestinian suicide bombers as victimizers and victims. *Violence and Victims, 20*(6), 603–623

Berko, A., & E. Erez. (2007). Gender, Palestinian women and terrorism: women's liberation or oppression? *Studies in Conflict & Terrorism, 30*, 493–519.

Berlet, C., & Lyons, M. N. (2000). *Right-wing populism in America: Too close for comfort*. New York: The Guilford Press.

Binder, A., & Scharf, P. (1980). The violent police-citizen encounter. *Annals of the American Academy of Political and Social Science, 452*, 111–121.

Birkbeck, C., & LaFree, G. (1993). The situational analysis of crime and deviance. *Annual Review of Sociology, 19*, 113–137.

Blanchard, D., & Prewitt, T. J. (1993). *Religious violence and abortion: The Gideon project*. University Press of Florida.

Boba, R. (2008). A crime mapping technique for assessing vulnerable targets for terrorism in local communities. In S. Chainey & L. Tompson (Eds.), *Crime mapping case studies: Practice and research*. West Sussex, England: John Wiley & Sons Ltd.

Carlson, J. R. 1(995). The future terrorists in America. *American Journal of Police*, *14*(3/4), 71–91.

Carroll, J., & Weaver, F. (1986). Shoplifters perceptions of crime opportunities: A process-tracing study. In D. B. Cornish, & R. V. Clarke (Eds.), *The reasoning criminal: Rational choice perspectives on offending*. New York: Springer-Verlag.

Chermak, S. M., Freilich, J. D., & Shemtob, Z. (2009). Law enforcement training and the domestic far-right. *Criminal Justice and Behavior*. Forthcoming.

Clarke, R. V. (1980). "Situational" crime prevention: Theory and practice. *British Journal of Criminology*, *20*(2), 136–147.

Clarke, R. V. (1983). Situational crime prevention: Its theoretical basis and practical scope. In M. Tonry & N. Morris (Eds.), *Crime and Justice: An Annual Review of Research*, *4*, 225–256.

Clarke, R. V. (1995). Situational crime prevention. In M. Tonry & D. Farrington (Eds.), *Building a safer society: Crime and justice: An annual review of research*, *19*, 91–150.

Clarke, R. V. (2004). Technology, criminology and crime science. *European Journal on Criminal Policy and Research*, *10*, 55–63.

Clarke, R. V., & Cornish, D. B. (1985). Modeling offenders' decisions: A framework for research and policy. In M. Tonry & N. Morris (Eds.), *Crime and justice: An annual review of the research*, *6*, 147–185.

Clarke, R. V., & Eck, J. E. (2005). *Crime analysis for problem solvers in 60 small steps*. Washington D.C: U.S. Department of Justice. Office of Community Oriented Policing Services. Center for Problem Oriented Policing.

Clarke, R. V., & Homel, R. (1997). A revised classification of situational crime prevention techniques. In S. P. Lab (Ed.), *Crime prevention at a crossroads*. Highland Heights, KY: Anderson Publishing.

Clarke, R. V., & Newman, G. R. (2006). *Outsmarting the terrorists*. Westport: Praeger Security International.

Coates, J. (1987). *Armed and dangerous: The rise of the survivalist right*. New York: Hill and Wang.

Cornish, D. (1994). The procedural analysis of offending and its relevance for situational prevention. In R. V. Clarke (Ed.), *Crime prevention studies*, *3*, 151–196.

Cornish, D., & Clarke, R. V. (2003). Opportunities, precipitators, and criminal decisions: A reply to Wortley's critique of situational crime prevention. In M. J. Smith & D. B. Cornish (Guest Eds), *Theory for practice in situational crime prevention*. *Crime prevention studies*, *16*, 41–96. Monsey, NY: Criminal Justice Press.

Cornish, D., & Clarke, R. V. (2002). Analyzing organized crimes. In A. R. Piquero & S. G. Tibbetts (Eds.), *Rational choice and criminal behavior: Recent research and future challenges* (pp. 41–63). New York: Routledge.

Creswell, J. W. (2007). *Qualitative inquiry & research design: Choosing among five approaches*. Thousand Oaks, CA: Sage Publications.

Damphousse, K. R., & Smith, B. L. (2004). Terrorism and empirical testing: Using indictment data to assess changes in terrorist conduct. *Sociology of Crime, Law and Deviance*, *5*, 75–90.

Della Porta, D. (1995). *Social movements, political violence and the state*. Cambridge: Cambridge University Press.

Dobratz, B. A., & Shanks-Meile, S. L. (1997). *White power, white pride! The white separatist movement in the United States*. New York: Twayne Publishers.

Donald, B. (2005). Cases of officers killed by their own guns likely will not change R.I. policies. *Associated Press*. [Online]: http://www.policeone.com/close-quarters- combat/articles/100228-Cases-of-Officers-Killed-by-Their-Own-Guns-Likely-Will-Not-Change-R-I-Policies/

Drake, C. J. M. (1998). The role of ideology in terrorists' target selection. *Terrorism and Political Violence, 10* (2), 53–85.

Duffy, J. E., & Brantley, A. C. (1997). Militias: Initiating contact. *Federal Bureau of Investigation*. [Online]: http:/?www.fbi.gov/library/leb/1997/July975.htm.

Dugan, L., LaFree, G., & Piquero, A. (2005). Testing a rational choice model of Airline Hijackings. *Criminology, 43*(4), 1031–1065.

Durham, M. (2003). The American far right and 9/11. *Terrorism and Political Violence, 15*, 96–111.

Ekblom, P. (2001). *The conjunction of criminal opportunity: A framework for crime reduction toolkits*. Policing and Reducing Crime Unit. Research, Development and Statistics Directorate. Home Office. [Online]: www.crimereduction.gov.uk

Ekblom, P. (2007). Making offenders richer. In G. Farrell, Bowers, K. J., Johnson, S. D., & Tonsley, M. (Guest Eds.), *Imagination for crime prevention. Essays in honour of Ken Pease. Crime prevention studies, 21*, 41–57. Monsey, NY: Criminal Justice Press.

Ekblom, P., & Tilley, N. (2000). Going equipped: Criminology, situational crime prevention and the resourceful offender. *British Journal of Criminology, 40*, 376–398.

Ekici, N., Ozkan, M., Celik, A., & Maxfield, M. G. (2008). Outsmarting terrorists in Turkey. *Crime Prevention and Community Safety, 10*, 126–139.

Engel, R. S. (2003). Explaining suspects' resistance and disrespect toward police. *Journal of Criminal Justice, 31*, 475–492.

Engel, R. S. 2005. Citizens' perceptions of distributive and procedural injustice during traffic stops with police. *Journal of Research in Crime and Delinquency, 42*(4), 445–481.

Federal Bureau of Investigation. (1999). *Project Megiddo*. [Online]: *http://www.fbi.-gov/homepage.htm*

Federal Bureau of Investigation. (1997). *Terrorism in the United States: 1997*. Washington, DC: United States Government Printing Office.

Freilich, J. D., & Chermak, S. M. (2009, March). United States extremist crime database (ECDB), 1990-2008: Preliminary results Paper presented at the annual Department of Homeland Security University Network Research and Education Summit. Washington DC.

Freilich, J. D., Chermak, S. M., & Caspi, D. (2009). Critical events in the life trajectories of domestic extremist white supremacist groups: A case study analysis of four violent organizations. *Criminology and Public Policy, 8*(3), In press.

Freilich, J. D., Chermak, S. M., & Simone, Jr., J. (2009). Surveying American state police agencies about terrorism threats, terrorism sources, and terrorism definitions. *Terrorism and Political Violence, 21*(3), 450–475.

Freilich, J. D., Pichardo-Almanzar, N., & Rivera, C. J. (1999). How social movement organizations explicitly and implicitly promote deviant behavior: The case of the militia movement. *Justice Quarterly, 16*(3), 655–683.

Freilich, J. D., & Pridemore, W. A. (2006). Mismeasuring militias: Limitations of advocacy group data and of state-level studies of paramilitary groups. *Justice Quarterly, 23*(1), 147–162.

Freilich, J. D., & Pridemore, W. A. (2007). Politics, culture and political crime: Covariates of abortion clinic attacks in the United States. *Journal of Criminal Justice, 35*(3), 323–336.

Fyfe, J. J. (1989). Police/Citizen Violence Reduction Project. *FBI Law Bulletin, 58,* 18–25.

Gruenewald, J., Freilich, J. D., & Chermak, S. M. (2009). An overview of the domestic far-right and its criminal activities. In B. Perry & R. Blazak (Eds.), *Hate crimes: Hate crime offenders* (pp. 1–21). Westport: Praeger

Hamm, M. S. (2007). *Terrorism as Crime: From Oklahoma City to Al Qaeda and Beyond.* New York: New York University Press.

Handler, J. (1990). Socioeconomic Profile of an American terrorist. *Terrorism, 13,* 195–213.

Herndobler, K. (2006). Aryan gang thrives in prison, but its motto extends to street via ex-convicts. *The Beaumont Enterprise,* June 18, 2006. online edition: www.southeastextensive.com/site/news.cfm?newsid=16805222&BRD=2287 & PAG=461&dept_id=51288&rfi=6

Hewitt, C. (2003). *Understanding terrorism in America: From the Klan to Al Qaeda.* New York: Routledge.

Hewitt, C. (2005). *Political violence and terrorism in modern America: A Chronology.* New York: Praeger Security International Reference.

Hoffman, B. (2006). *Inside terrorism* (2nd ed.). New York: Columbia University Press.

Horgan, J. (2004). The case for firsthand research. In A. Silke (Ed).*Research on terrorism: Trends, achievements and failures.* London: Frank Cass.

Johnson, R. (2004). Citizen expectations of police traffic stop behavior. *Policing: An International Journal of Police Strategies and Management, 27*(4), 487–497.

Jones, S. M., & Libicki, M. C. (2008). *Why terrorist groups end: Lessons for countering Al Qaida.* Santa Monica: Rand Corporation.

Jurgensmeyer, M. (2003). *Terror in the mind of God.* Berkeley: University of California Press.

Kaminski, R., & Marvel, T. B. (2002). A comparison of changes in police and general homicides: 1930-1998. *Criminology, 40*(1), 171–190.

Kaplan, J. (1993). The context of American millenarian revolutionary theology: The case of the 'Identity Christian' Church of Israel. *Terrorism and Political Violence, 5*(1), 30–82.

Kaplan, J. (1995). Right wing violence in North America. *Terrorism and Political Violence, 7*(1), 44–95.

Kaplan, J. (1996). Absolute rescue: Absolutism, defensive action and the resort to force. In M. Barkun (Ed.), *Millennialism and violence* (pp. 128–163). London: Frank Cass & Co. Ltd.

LaFree, G., & Dugan, L. (2004). How does studying terrorism compare to studying crime? In M. Deflem (Ed.), *Terrorism and counter-terrorism: Criminological perspectives: Sociology of crime law and deviance*, *5*, 53–74. Amsterdam: Elsevier, JAI.

LaFree, G., & Dugan, L. (2007). Introducing the global terrorism database. *Terrorism and Political Violence*, *19*, 181–204.

LaFree, G., Dugan, L., & Fahey, S. (2007). Global terrorism and failed states. In J. J. Hewitt, J. Wilkenfeld, & T. R. Gurr (Eds.), *Peace and Conflict* (pp. 39–54). Boulder: Paradigm Publishers.

LaFree, G., Dugan, L., Fogg, H., & Scott, J. (2006). Building a global terrorism database. Final report to the National Institute of Justice, May 2006.

Leiken, R. S., & Brooke, S. (2006). The quantitative analysis of terrorism and immigration: An initial exploration. *Terrorism and Political Violence*, *18*, 503–521.

Loftin, C., & McDowall, D. (1988). The analysis of case control studies in criminology. *Journal of Quantitative Criminology*, *4*, 85–98.

Lum, C., Kennedy, L. W., & Sherley, A. J. (2006). *The effectiveness of counterterrorism strategies: A Campbell systematic review*. [Online]: http://db.c2admin.org/doc-pdf/Lum_Terrorism_Review.pdf

Matza, D. (1964). *Delinquency and drift*. New York: Wiley.

McGarrell, E. F., Freilich, J. D., & Chermak, S. M. (2007). Intelligence-led policing as a framework for responding to terrorism. *Journal of Contemporary Criminal Justice*, *23*(2), 142–158.

Meier, R. F., Kennedy, L. W., & Sacco, V. F. (Eds). (2001). *The process and structure of crime: Criminal events and crime analysis*. New Brunswick: Transaction Publishers.

Meithe, T. D., & Regoeczi, W. C. (2004). *Rethinking homicide: Exploring the structure and process underlying deadly situations*. New York: Cambridge University Press.

Merari, A. (1991). Academic research and government policy on terrorism. *Terrorism and Political Violence*, *3*(1), 88–102

Mullins, W. C. (1988). *Terrorist organizations in the United States*. Springfield, IL: Charles C. Thomas Books.

Newman, G. R., & Clarke, R. V. (2003). *Superhighway robbery: Preventing e-commerce crime*. Portland: Willan Publishing.

Newman, G. R., & Clarke, R. V. (2008). *Policing terrorism: An executive's guide*. Washington DC: Center for Problem Oriented Policing (POP) Center, Community Oriented Policing Services (COPS), U.S. Department of Justice.

Pitcavage, M. (1997). *Shootout in Ohio: A case study of the "Patriot" movement and traffic stops*. Retrieved online from: *http://www.adl.org/mwd/shootout.asp*

Pitcavage, M. (1998). *Flashpoint America: Surviving a traffic stop confrontation with an anti-government extremist*. Retrieved online from: http://www.militia-watchdog.org.

Pitcavage, M. (2001). *Officer safety and extremists: An overview for law enforcement*. Retrieved online fromnline: *http://www.adl.org/learn/safety/safet.asp*

Post, J. M., Sprinzak, E., & Denny, L. M. (2003). The terrorists in their own words: Interviews with 35 incarcerated Middle Eastern terrorists. *Terrorism and Political Violence*, *15*(1), 171–184.

Riley, K. J., & Hoffman, B. (1995). *Domestic terrorism: A national assessment of state and local preparedness*. Rand Report, supported by the National Institute of Justice and the U.S. Department of Justice. Santa Monica: Rand.

Riley, K. J., Treverton, G. F., Wilson, J. M., & Davis, L. M. (2005). *State and local intelligence in the war on terrorism*. Rand Report. Santa Monica: Rand.

Roach, J., Ekblom, P., & Flynn, R. (2005). The conjunction of terrorist opportunity: A framework for diagnosing and preventing acts of terrorism. *Security Journal*, *18*, 7–25.

Ross, J. I. (1993). Research on contemporary oppositional political terrorism in the United States: merits, drawbacks and suggestions for improvement. In K. D. Tunnel (Ed.), *Political crime in contemporary America: A critical approach* (pp. 101–116). New York: Garland Publishing.

Sageman, M. (2004). *Understanding terror networks*. Philadelphia: University of Pennsylvania Press.

Silber, M. D., & Bhatt, A. (2006). *Radicalization in the West: The homegrown threat*. New York City Police Department Intelligence Division. Retrieved online from: http://www.nypdshield.org/public/SiteFiles/documents/NYPD_Report-Radicalization_in_the_West.pdf

Silke, A. (2001). The devil you know: Continuing problems with research on terrorism. *Terrorism and Political Violence*, *13*(4), 1–14.

Smith, B. L. (1994). *Terrorism in America: Pipe bombs and pipe dreams*. New York: State University of New York Press.

Smith, B. L., & Damphousse, K. R. (1996). Punishing political offenders: The effect of political motive on federal sentencing decisions. *Criminology*, *34*(3), 289–321.

Smith, B. L., & Damphousse, K. R. (1998). Terrorism, politics and punishment: A test of structural-contextual theory and the 'Liberation Hypothesis.' *Criminology*, *36*(1), 67–92.

Smith, B. L., & Damphousse, K. R. (2009). The life course of American eco-terrorists: Informal and formal organizations. *Criminology and Public Policy*, *8*(3), In press.

Smith, B. L., Damphousse, K. R., Jackson, F., & Sellers, A. (2002). The prosecution and punishment of international terrorists in federal courts: 1980-1998. *Criminology and Public Policy*, *1*(3), 311–338.

Smith, B. L., & Morgan, K. D. (1994). Terrorists right and left: Empirical issues in profiling American terrorists. *Studies in Conflict and Terrorism*, *17*, 39–57.

Smith, B. L., & Orvis, G. (1993). America's response to terrorism: An empirical analysis of federal intervention strategies during the 1980s. *Justice Quarterly*, *10*, 661–681.

Smith, M. J. (1998). Regulating opportunities: Multiple roles for civil remedies in situational crime prevention. In L. G. Mazerolle & J. Roehl (Eds.), *Civil remedies and crime prevention. Crime prevention studies*, *9*, 67–88. Monsey, NY: Criminal Justice Press.

Smith, M. J. (2005). *Robbery of taxi drivers*. Problem Oriented Guides for Police Problem-Specific Guides Series, No. 34. Washington DC: United States Department of Justice. Office of Community Opiented Policing Services.

Snow, D. A., & Trom, D. (2002). The case study and the study of social movements. In B. Klandermans & S. Staggenborg (Eds.), *Methods of social movement research* (pp. 146–172). Minneapolis: University of Minnesota Press.

Sprinzak, E. (1995). Right wing terrorism in a comparative perspective: The case of split delegitimization. *Terrorism and Political Violence, 7*(1), 17–43.

Stern, J. (2003). *Terror in the name of God: Why religious militants kill.* New York: HarperCollins.

Taylor, M. (1993). Behavioral analysis and political violence. In R. V. Clarke & M. Felson (Eds.), *Routine activity and rational choice* (pp. 159–178). New Brunswick: Transaction Publishers.

The Officer Down Memorial Page, inc. 2009. *Honoring officers killed in the year 2009.* Retrieved online from: http://www.odmp.org/year.php

Weinberg, L. (1993). The American radical right: Exit, voice, and violence. In P. Merkl & L. Weinberg (Eds.), *Encounters with the contemporary radical right* (pp. 185–203). Boulder: Westview.

White, M. D. (2002). Identifying situational predictors of police shootings using multivariate analyses. *Policing: An International Journal of Police Strategies and Management, 25*(4), 726–751.

White, R. (1993). *Provisional Irish republicans: An oral and interpretive history.* Westport: Greenwood Press.

Wilkinson, D. (2002). Decision making in violent events among adolescent males: An examination of Sparks and other motivational factors. In A. R. Piquero & S. G. Tibbetts (Eds.), *Rational Choice and Criminal Behavior: Recent Research and Future Challenges* (pp. 163–196). New York: Routledge.

Wortley, R. (1997). Reconsidering the role of opportunity in situational crime prevention. In G. Newman, R. V. Clarke, & S. G. Shoham (Eds.), *Rational Choice and Situational Crime Prevention* (pp. 65–81). Aldershot: Ashgate.

Wortley, R. 1998. A two-stage model of situational crime prevention. *Studies on Crime and Crime Prevention, 7*(2), 173–188.

Wortley, R. 2001. A classification of techniques for controlling situational precipitators of crime. *Security Journal, 14*(4), 63–82.

Wortley, R. 2002. *Situational prison control: Crime prevention in correctional institutions.* Cambridge: Cambridge University Press.

Wright, S. A. (2007). *Patriots, politics and the Oklahoma City bombing.* Cambridge: Cambridge University Press.

SITUATIONAL CRIME PREVENTION AND NON-VIOLENT TERRORISM: A "SOFT" APPROACH AGAINST IDEOLOGICALLY MOTIVATED TAX REFUSAL

Roberta Belli

John Jay College of Criminal Justice
National Consortium of the Study of Terrorism &
Responses to Terrorism (START)

Joshua D. Freilich

John Jay College of Criminal Justice
National Consortium of the Study of Terrorism &
Responses to Terrorism (START)

Abstract: *This paper explores the applicability of situational crime prevention (SCP) to "ideologically motivated tax refusal," a non-violent crime of omission committed by far-right extremists in the U.S. as a form of political protest. Most terrorism research focuses on stopping violent behaviors by terrorists, neglecting the relationship existing between terrorism and other serious – but nonviolent – ideological crimes. All previous applications of scp have been to criminal offenses that require a proactive behavior on the side of the offender.*

Crime Prevention Studies, volume 25 (2009), pp. 173–206.

Our paper examined these issues as well as factors that contribute to the occurrence of tax refusal among far-rightists, such as the offenders' characteristics, decision-making process and resources, to highlight the opportunity structure and possible key points for intervention. In conclusion, we suggested the use of eight selected situational techniques that propose a "soft" approach – as defined by Wortley and others in contrast with traditional "hard" SCP (e.g., target-hardening, etc.) – for preventing this crime problem.

Introduction

The domestic far-right presents a major security threat to public safety in the United States (Freilich & Chermak, 2009; Freilich, Chermak, & Caspi, 2009; Hewitt 2003; LaFree et al., 2006).[1] Far-right extremists have engaged in a variety of ideologically motivated crimes over the past decades, targeting government institutions, facilities and personnel, as well as the civilian population, including actual terrorist attacks like those carried out by Timothy McVeigh and Eric Rudolph (Gruenewald et al., 2009). Contrary to public opinion and most terrorism research, however, a large portion of these crimes do not involve the use of violence.

A segment of the domestic far-right – linked to the tax protest movement – professes its ideological opposition to the government by using and advocating tax evasion strategies that range from the simple refusal to pay income taxes to complex fraud schemes. Recent investigations by the U.S. Internal Revenue Service (IRS) revealed a nationwide web of individuals who promote scams taking advantage of the beliefs of other tax protesters and the greed of ordinary citizens through the marketing of bogus trusts, "untax" kits and literature. The press has sometimes referred to this phenomenon as "paper terrorism" (Pitcavage, 1999). Although the majority of far-right tax protesters engage in crimes that are non-violent in nature, there have also been incidents of threats, harassment and violence against the IRS and other government targets (Becker et al., 2001; Hewitt, 2003; Levitas, 2002). A notorious case is that of Gordon Kahl, a fervent tax protester and state coordinator for the Texas section of the anti-tax Posse Comitatus, who was convicted of tax charges but refused to surrender to the authorities. When the marshals stopped him at a roadblock in 1983 in an attempt to bring him in, he opened fire, killing two of them and injuring several others before fleeing. The four-month manhunt ended with a second fatal shootout where he killed a local sheriff before being killed.

Some scholars hypothesize a possible radicalization process or "escalation" effect, where tax-related offenses might become a gateway to more violent forms of ideological commitment (Barkun, 1996; Freilich & Chermak, 2009). Others note that the tax protest movement is a major point of entry into right-wing fringe groups and movements (Pitcavage, 1998a). Individuals who are susceptible to the claims of tax protesters and join their ideology may be exposed to the beliefs and practices of other extremist movements, such as the sovereign militia, Christian Identity, and other racist or anti-Semitic ideologies. These arguments deserve to be studied more in depth in view of their implications for counterterrorism strategies.

This chapter explores the applicability of situational crime prevention to a tax-related crime which appears to be common in the domestic far-right, i.e., the failure to file an income return for ideological reasons, hereinafter referred to as "ideologically motivated tax refusal." What sparked the interest for this study are theoretical and practical considerations. Conceptually, ideologically motivated tax refusal presents an interesting challenge for the situational prevention of terrorism because of its nature – i.e., *a non-violent crime with a political motive* – which falls under the legal category of the so-called "crimes of omission." Most terrorism prevention research focuses on stopping violent behaviors by terrorists, neglecting the relationship existing between terrorism and other serious crime forms. Only recently scholars have started turning their attention to non-violent "antecedent" crimes that are often crucial in the preparation and furtherance of terrorist attacks (Clarke & Newman, 2006; Damphousse & Smith, 2004). In this paper we present several points to initiate a discussion on how to reduce incidents of non-violent political extremism for a more holistic approach to terrorism prevention. We also noted how, interestingly, situational crime prevention has always been applied to criminal offenses that require a proactive behavior on the side of the offender (e.g., burglary, theft, traffic offenses, etc.). No one has ever considered whether the situational approach can equally be used with crime types for which individuals are held criminally responsible as a result of their failure to act – usually in the presence of a specific duty to act established by the law.

We examined these issues as well as other factors that contribute to the occurrence of tax refusal among far-right extremists, such as the offenders' characteristics, decision-making process and resources, to highlight the opportunity structure and possible key points for intervention. In conclusion, we suggest the use of eight selected situational techniques that propose a "soft" approach – as defined by Wortley and others, in contrast with traditional "hard" SCP (e.g., target-hardening, etc.) – for preventing this crime problem.

What is ideologically motivated tax refusal and how big a problem is it?

Every year an undefined number of U.S. citizens – estimated in the hundreds of thousands – use abusive schemes to circumvent tax laws or evade taxes.[2] These schemes include various kinds of activities, which can be very simple or very complex, evidently illegal or carefully constructed to disguise the illegality of the scheme. Known cases involve the use of abusive tax shelters, exempt organizations, and strategies based on misinterpretations and distortions of federal tax obligations. The profile of individuals who use these schemes is also diversified, ranging from those who knowingly but willfully file incorrect tax returns to – most important for our purposes – those who simply refuse to file. The latter are commonly referred to as members of the "tax protest movement," one of the oldest and most active anti- government movements existing in the country (Levitas, 2001).

After World War II, two major anti-tax movements emerged. The first one was part of a left-wing movement that formed as a reaction against the Vietnam War. A number of pacifist "war tax resisters" declared the war was immoral, and consequently refused to pay federal taxes that would support what they believed was an imperialistic military strategy adopted by the American government in South-East Asia. However, the movement started to lose strength after the end of the war. Today anti-war tax resisters still exist, although in much reduced number. The second movement began in the 1950s and 1960s and has been growing steadily since that time as a key component of the extreme right-wing activism, often referred to as the "patriot" movement. Unlike its left-wing counterpart, the ideology proposed by this movement lies in the belief that either income tax laws are in some way invalid or do not apply to most citizens. Tax protest promoters have been known to make a number of claims to justify their decision not to pay taxes, including:

- Income tax is merely voluntary, because of the language used on the 1040 instruction booklet.

- State citizens are not U.S. citizens under the Constitution but "sovereign citizens," and are therefore not required to pay federal taxes.

- Labor cannot be taxed because wages are not income.

- Federal reserve notes do not count as income because U.S. currency is not backed by gold or silver.

- The Sixteenth Amendment to the Constitution concerning congressional power to lay and collect income taxes was never ratified.

- Being required to file Form 1040 violates the Fifth Amendment right against self-incrimination or the Fourth Amendment.

- Paying taxes is a form of slavery which is banned by the Thirteenth Amendment.

Both the IRS and U.S. courts have repeatedly rejected tax protesters' claims as "frivolous arguments," stating that while taxpayers have the right to contest their tax liabilities in court, no one has the right to disobey the law. The government partially succeeded in cracking down on tax protesters in the 1980s, imposing new penalties and launching prosecutions that curtailed the growth of the movement. However, the benefits of this aggressive governmental strategy did not last. As a result of a number of hearings into alleged IRS abuses, Congress reversed course in 1998, passing a legislation that weakened IRS enforcement and produced a new wave of tax rebellion. According to Levitas (2001), the number of those who simply refuse to file today has skyrocketed, and government officials have failed to address this problem decisively. Although it is hard to estimate the size of the movement, experts agree that it is growing especially as a result of the efforts of prominent tax protesters, who have been extremely vocal in their opposition to the income tax, and their ability to recruit a large number of people (Pitcavage, 1998b).

The U.S. federal budget is strongly dependent on the tax system, whose primary purpose is to raise revenues for the government to fund its operations. The problem of tax non-compliance, therefore, presents a serious threat to the integrity and security of the system and imposes a considerable and unnecessary financial burden on the part of the tax-paying population who comply with tax laws.[3] The tax gap, which is the difference between the amount of tax which should have been paid to the government and the amount actually received in a given tax year, has three major components: non-filing, underreporting, and underpayment.[4] According to IRS estimates, in 2001 the tax gap amounted to $345 billion. Although most financial losses come from underreporting of income, the tax deficit is also substantially affected by underpayment and non-filing of

Figure 1. Components of the tax gap.

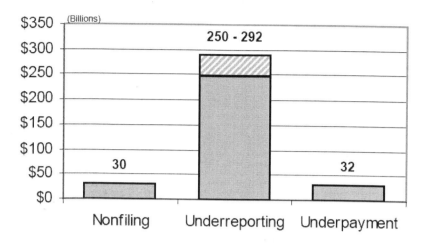

Source: Internal Revenue Service. (2005) *Tax Gap Facts and Figures*, p. 5. Available online at: http//www.irs.gov/pub/irs-utl/tax_gap_facts-figures.pdf

returns (Figures 1 and 2). In fact, the tax gap for individual non-filers (i.e., individuals who are legally required to file and for whom returns have not been filed by the due date) tripled from $9.8 billion in 1985 to over $30 billion in 2001.[5]

In recent years, the IRS has embarked on a campaign to warn American citizens against the "too-good-to-be-true" tax protest rhetoric by publishing the "Dirty Dozen" – a collection of the most popular anti-tax scams for each fiscal year. In 2003, a multi-stage strategy was implemented to bring non-filers in compliance, involving auditing procedures and administrative notices sent to identified non-filers (GAO, 2006). The IRS approach has also typically involved criminal prosecution of the most egregious anti-tax promoters. Sanctions include civil remedies (primarily civil injunctions) and criminal charges, and sometimes the imposition of additional penalties for wasting court time and money. This approach has led to some positive results – more than 190 tax preparers and promoters of abusive schemes have been shut down since 2001.[6] However, enforcement strategies have not slowed down the growth of the tax rebellion movement. On the contrary, some argue that the prosecution of prominent leaders may have had a backlash effect, and reinforced and energized the movement by

Figure 2. Individual income tax is the largest source of annual tax gap.

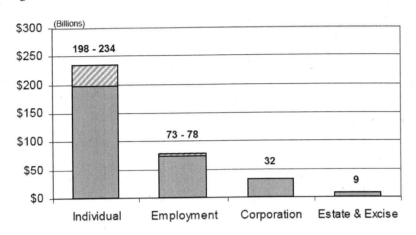

Internal Revenue Service. (2005) *Tax Gap Facts and Figures*, p. 6.

transforming them into "martyr" figures. Levitas (quoted in Sanger-Katz, 2006) points out that "for every one of those individuals who is prosecuted criminally, who publicly advocates their opposition to the income tax on the same ground – for every one person like that, there are 7 to 10 people who agree with the same philosophy," but they are simply not brave enough to admit it (Figures 3 and 4).

Factors contributing to ideologically motivated tax refusal

Individuals who refuse to pay taxes for ideological reasons share similar anti-government ideas concerning tax laws, which they believe have been made needlessly complex to keep people from investigating and finding the loopholes in the system. Tax protesters, however, have utilized different ways to avoid tax liability (Sanger-Katz, 2006). Some file bogus tax returns, indicating for example all zeros on their Form 1040 (using the so-called "Zero-return scheme"), or claiming so many exemptions that an employer does not have to withhold payroll taxes. Others say the simple act of filling out a tax return means you are entering a contract with the government. They express their refusal to comply with tax laws by not filing any income return, and instead begin sending letters filled with questions and objections to the IRS.

Figure 3. IRS individual audits in fiscal years 1996–2004.

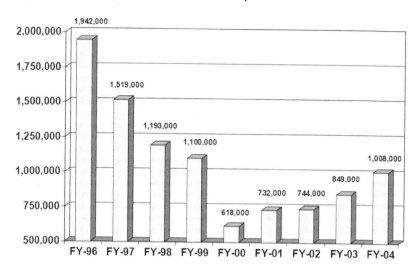

Source: Internal Revenue Service (2005). *Tax Gap Fcts and Figures*, p. 13.

In the next sections, we will examine factors that facilitate the occurrence of ideologically motivated tax refusal to highlight the opportunity structure and identify possible areas of intervention through situational prevention strategies. In particular, we will focus on three distinctive elements: (1) the nature of the crime; (2) the offenders' characteristics and decision-making process; and (3) their resources for crime.

Nature of the Crime

As noted, ideologically motivated tax refusal is unique in the context of political extremism because of two reasons: (1) it does not involve the use of violence; and (2) it is a "crime of omission," which means that a person is criminally responsible for the intentional failure to act in the presence of an explicit duty to act established by the law. Because one of the fundamental tenets of the situational approach is to be as crime-specific as possible, it is important to examine more in depth these two characteristics for devising effective preventive measures.

Figure 4. Criminal prosecutions recommended in fiscal years 1996–2004.

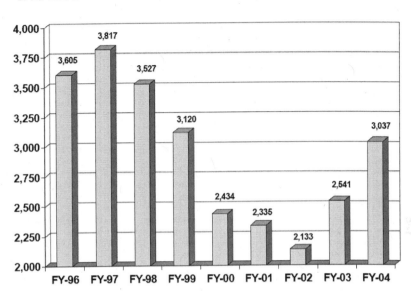

Source: Internal Revenue Service (2005). *Tax Gap Facts and Figures*, p. 15.

Tax refusal as non-violent terrorism (i.e., a non-violent crime with a political motive)

This study uses Clarke and Newman's definition of terrorism as "crime with a political motive" (Clarke & Newman, 2006, p. 6). This definition is unique because, unlike the majority of existing terrorism definitions, it does not require that an act involve "force or violence" to be included in its universe of cases (Freilich, Chermak, & Simone, 2009). Similarly, the majority of terrorism studies only examine the use of "violence" by terrorist groups to further political goals. This is a significant omission because it ignores the possibility that there may be a relationship between violent acts and other serious, but non-violent, crime forms.

Ideologically motivated tax refusal is an example of a non-violent crime committed by political extremists whose growth should be monitored as it may have serious implications for homeland security. First, anti-tax sentiments have motivated domestic terrorist attacks. Indeed, the United States Extremist Crime Database (ECDB) study has identified a number of nonfatal bombings at IRS offices as well as attacks on IRS personnel (Freilich & Chermak, 2009). Second, it is currently unknown what relationship – if any – exists between non-violent ideologically motivated crimes, and violent terrorist acts committed by the movement. Some intriguing anecdotal evidence suggests that ideologically motivated tax refusal (and other financial crimes) may act as a "gateway" to subsequent more serious criminal behavior. For instance, Scott Roeder (arrested for the May 2009 murder of Dr. George Tiller of Kansas, who had performed late-term abortions), Robert Matthews (the leader of the notorious terrorist group "The Order," responsible for five murders, in the 1980s), and Frank Nelson (the leader of the Minnesota Patriots Council, and one of first to be convicted under the Biological Weapons Anti-Terrorism Act in 1995) were all involved in anti-tax actions before their later more serious crimes (Corcoran, 1990; Flynn & Gerhardt, 1995; Hamm, 2007; McGarell, Freilich, & Chermak 2007; Tucker & Pate, 2001). This thesis is consistent with the hate-crimes literature, which argues that bias-crime perpetrators "escalate" from less to more violent hate- crimes (Shively, 2005), and the criminology literature, which finds that offenders sometimes commit crimes sequentially as shoplifting often precedes burglary and burglary precedes robbery.

Third, and importantly, non-violent tax refusal could in certain situations erupt to violent behavior. Some far-right tax protesters also stockpile weapons, and gather explosives to prepare to defend themselves from arrest and/or perceived imminent attacks from the government and other enemies. Others seem to gather weapons and explosives as a sort of "hobby", i.e. they enjoy collecting them. The ECDB has documented a number of incidents involving tax protesters possessing IEDs or explosives but where violence was prevented by careful law enforcement investigations and/or arrest (Freilich & Chermak, 2009). For example, in one high publicity case a tax protesting couple (the Browns) became involved in a standoff with law enforcement that became a cause célèbre for far-rightists. The standoff lasted for nine months before the police arrested them using an undercover officer. The police subsequently found explosive devices and manuals to build bombs in the residence (Freilich & Chermak, 2009).

Tax refusal as a "crime of omission"

The willful failure to file an income return is punishable under Section 7203 of the US Tax Code, and amounts to a so-called "crime of omission."

Unlike most criminal offenses, which require a proactive behavior and are therefore considered crimes of *commission*, with crimes of omission a person is considered criminally liable as a result of *non-action* in the presence of an explicit duty to act. Typical behaviors that constitute an omission and are punishable by the law in most U.S. jurisdictions are the failure of a parent to adequately care for his or her child – also called "child neglect" – the failure to install safety equipment in a workplace, and the failure to register a motor-vehicle.[7]

It is important to notice that situational crime prevention is not concerned with abstract legal definitions, but rather with behavioral patterns. In other words, what has meaning for the law might be irrelevant for prevention purposes. The issue of omission raises, however, interesting questions with respect to the degree of efforts needed to carry out certain criminal activities. As some have argued, the sequence of steps involved in planning, preparing and executing complex operations, such as terrorist attacks or organized crime illicit businesses, may be lengthy and multi-stage (Clarke, 1997; Clarke & Newman, 2006 Cornish, 1994). On the other hand, other crime types require much less practical effort. As a crime of omission, ideologically motivated tax refusal is an easy crime to "commit" and a difficult one to stop. Unlike conventional tax cheaters, who likely engage in additional activities to hide their criminal status and avoid detection, tax protesters often publicly display their behavior and purposefully refuse to engage in any activity. From the government perspective, the challenge is how to bring these individuals in compliance with the law. As we noted, however, traditional law enforcement approaches have proved unsuccessful in this regard, and may even be counterproductive.

In this chapter, we argue that situational crime prevention can provide a useful alternative to tough repressive approaches, although not all of the 25 techniques might be applicable. Over time situational prevention researchers have developed a variety of measures that were adapted to changing trends and different crime problems. However, most situational strategies were conceived for typical crimes of commission, aiming to restrict behaviors that are conducive to crime by, for example, devising target-hardening tools or extending guardianship to make it harder for offenders to take action. The point here is the opposite one: to reduce incidents of tax refusal, we need to find mechanisms that *induce* action. In fact, the 25 techniques already contain measures that can be used for these purposes by assisting compliance. In the following sections, we will suggest ways in which these techniques can be applied to ideologically motivated tax refusal and further expanded.

Offenders' Characteristics and Decision-Making Processes

Studies focusing on the offender's mindset and characteristics are fairly recent in the context of situational crime prevention. Traditional situational prevention strategies were modeled for the "default offender," described as a motivated and ready-to-act individual who engages in typical predatory offenses, such as theft, burglary, rape, etc. (Clarke, 1997; Cornish & Clarke, 2003). Motivation to crime was excluded from the analysis, and taken as a constant. The fear of falling in the "dispositional bias" influenced situational crime prevention scholars to the point that they isolated themselves in what Ekblom & Tilley define a sort of "self-imposed ghetto" in the criminology field (Ekblom and Tilley, 2000, p. 376).

Recently, scholars have turned their attention back to the offender's perspective and the internal and external situational factors that shape his interaction with the environment, taking into account personal belief systems, preferences, circumstances and perceptions (Brezina, 2002; Ekblom & Tilley, 2000; Ekblom, 2007; Gill, 2005; Wortley, 1998, 2001). These studies have expanded the concept of crime opportunity by examining proximal causes and resources for crime in addition to environmental factors, exploring offender-based interventions, and developing measures to prevent non-predatory crimes. As Clarke and Newman (2006) suggest in their study of international terrorism, we must "think terrorist" to identify and effectively protect vulnerable targets from terrorist attacks. Importantly, the goal is not to understand why certain crimes are committed, but rather how they are carried out. Understanding the offenders' characteristics, variety of motives and available resources can help us better understand the crime commission process and identify preventive measures that are more resistant to crime displacement (Wortley, 2001; Ekblom, 2007).

Tax protesters come from all levels of society, and include doctors, dentists, businessmen, accountants, police officers and even former IRS employees. Those who buy into these ideas are often wealthy and well-educated individuals, who are driven to the movement by a combination of ideological protest and greed. High- profile individuals include Hollywood celebrities, such as film actor Wesley Snipes, who was sentenced to three years in federal prison in 2008 for failing to pay approximately $12 million in taxes between 1999 and 2004. The most radical ones sometimes become movement promoters and engage in a variety of activities to spread these ideas. After years of vocal expression of anti-tax protest ideology and resistance even in the face of criminal prosecutions, a few have become almost martyr figures in the movement.[8] Robert Schulz, for example, the founder of "We The People" – a NY-based anti-tax organization that has had a fundamental role in the recent growth of the movement – is considered a celebrity in Patriot circles for his months-long hunger strike against the IRS in 2004.[9]

In the next sections, we will provide a closer look at far-right tax protesters, their decision-making process and resources for crime by examining the existing literature, journalistic accounts and far-right propaganda documents.

Tax Protesters' Decision-Making Processes

Situational crime prevention is based on the assumption that criminals are rational, goal-oriented individuals who seek to satisfy specific needs and desires by maximizing their personal gains while minimizing the costs (Cornish & Clarke, 1998; Newman, 1997). Considerations of risks, efforts and rewards provide the basis for the decision-making process that will possibly lead a potential offender to crime, and are essential for the development of effective crime prevention strategies (Clarke, 1997).

Ideologically motivated tax refusal provides far-right extremists with substantial benefits at relatively low costs. First and foremost, there is an obvious economic incentive from not paying taxes, which is what likely drives most tax evaders in general (Varma & Doob, 1998). Tax protesters, however, are different from prototypical tax cheaters because they pursue an additional objective, i.e. manifesting their political dissent, distrust of the government and dislike of taxation. Ideological upheaval and – in certain instances – economic sabotage are, therefore, the primary driving forces behind this crime. For example, Irwin Schiff – one of the most prominent leaders in the movement – blames the government for the current financial crisis in his book the *Federal Mafia*, and encourages people to stop filing income tax returns. The following is an excerpt from Irwin Schiff's website:

> The reason that Americans have been so deceived concerning the alleged legal requirement to pay income taxes is because we essentially have a lying and deceitful Government. [. . .] Legally, the Internal Revenue Service is only an administrative agency without any enforcement powers whatsoever. Despite the IRS having no enforcement powers, the Federal government uses the IRS to extort

income taxes from the American public. It gets away with it because of the help it gets from praetorian, federal judges, U.S. attorneys, and a legal profession that earns billions of dollars litigating a law that doesn't exist, while numerous other private sector interests earn billions feeding off the public's monumental ignorance concerning the real nature of our income tax "laws."[10]

As for the costs involved, in its simplest form (i.e., the failure to file an income return) tax refusal requires little if no effort at all by the offender. In fact, it is more time-consuming and arduous to perform the opposite task of filing income tax returns on time. Most tax protesters simply stop paying taxes when they have reached the decision to do so. This is possible because many people are paid "under the table" or are self-employed, have no interest or dividends, and do not own a house, so they can get away without filing for a while. Some do actually engage in some form of proactive behavior by, for example, sending letters to the IRS asking questions concerning the legitimacy of the fiscal system – usually after being audited. Criminal investigations and actual convictions, however, do not necessarily deter tax protesters (especially those who are more highly motivated), who often engage in long legal battles in court insisting relentlessly on their positions. The following is an example of a recent investigation involving resilient tax protesters:

Considerations of risks, efforts and rewards are, therefore, very different from those of conventional tax cheaters, although there are some commonalities. Studies on tax evasion show that tax cheaters' perceptions of risk are influenced by audit rates and the apparent risk of being audited (Varma and Doob, 1998; Raskolnikov, 2006). Audit rates for individual returns, however, are extremely low (less than 1%, according to recent statistics published by the IRS) due to the costs and time necessary to carry them out, and the penalties (civil or criminal) are not always imposed (Cords, 2005). Many may therefore not view audits as a realistic threat. In addition, publicity campaigns showing how tax protesters get away with not paying taxes decrease the perception of risk, and may encourage more people to engage in these practices.[11] For example, Al Thompson, the owner of Cencal Aviation Products, stopped withholding taxes from his employees' pay in 2000. Despite a front-page story in the New York Times, it was not until 2003 that the IRS took action against him, and although he was eventually convicted in 2005, in the meantime he was able to show many others how to avoid paying taxes.[12]

Based on these considerations, it could be argued that ideologically-driven individuals have a higher degree of motivation compared to conven-

Figure 5. Case study: Timeline of a tax-protest investigation.

Case Study: Timeline of a Tax-Protest Investigation

- Richard and Tracy Coronas stopped paying income taxes in the mid-1990s despite earning millions of dollars.
- On May 6, 1996, Richard Corona – an attorney specializing in contracts and commercial litigation – sent a letter to the government demanding documentation to prove the IRS authority to collect income taxes and threatening IRS employees with personal liability for doing their job.
- From 1997 to 2004, Richard Corona continued sending letters to the government asking questions concerning the legitimacy of the tax system and claiming to be a natural born free American National Sovereign Citizen of the California Republic, non-resident alien of the federal 'United States', and therefore not subject to taxation.
- The IRS did not answer to any of his questions and instead, in 1999, placed liens on several of the Coronas' properties and informed them they were under investigations.
- In 2004, the couple pleaded not guilty to federal tax offenses and started a "philosophical" battle in court arguing they had a good faith belief that they did not have to pay income taxes.
- In January 2008, a jury convicted the couple to more than 30 months in federal prisons but they both declared they would keep on fighting until their concerns are addressed by the courts.

Source: "The Tax Rebels" by Will Carless, *Voice of San Diego*, Monday, January 28, 2008.

tional tax evaders, as their decision not to file an income return is motivated – at least in part – by their belief system and sense of self-righteousness. Not all tax protesters, however, display the same level of ideological commitment. Research shows that individuals are sometimes drawn into the tax protest movement through some combination of greed and political protest, and may react very differently when faced with the consequences of their inaction (Freilich & Chermak, 2009, ECDB data). These variations are important and should be taken into account as they may have an impact on the effectiveness of countermeasures. This argument will be further discussed in the next section.

Tax protesters as "mundane offenders"

As noted, the level of ideological commitment varies across the tax protesters' population. Evidence of this can be found in how differently individuals react when faced with the possible negative consequences of their choices. There have been cases of tax protesters who left the movement and even expressed remorse and regret after being publicly exposed during an IRS investigation. Two Kansas businessmen, who pleaded guilty in January

2008 after willfully refusing to file income taxes between 1996 and 2001, admitted in court that they made "poor choices" and deeply regretted putting their families into such an emotional turmoil which "easily outweighed the financial burden of mounting legal fees and tax penalties."[13]

This type of reaction is probably not uncommon among tax protesters, as cost-benefit considerations vary across people depending on what is at stake for each person. Not everybody is willing to sacrifice their lives and those of their families in the name of ideology. Studies on political radicalization show that of all those who join radical action (e.g., by participating in a rally or a march), the majority gives up as a result of governmental repression, as the costs become too high to continue. On the contrary, those who have a higher level of political commitment, which is frequently accompanied by strong moral beliefs and personal grievances, are less likely to be deterred (McCauley & Moskalenko, 2008).

In this paper we argue that many tax protesters are likely to be "mundane offenders," whereas only a few will fall into the "default" offender category – i.e. the calculating criminal whose motivation never changes. The term "mundane offender" was first used in an article by Cornish and Clarke (2003), who attempted to provide a classification of offender types. The major difference from the typical predatory offender concerns the commitment to crime, which in the mundane offender is ambiguous and mutable, and oftentimes elicited by situational precipitators (Wortley, 2008). These individuals are regarded as "opportunity-takers," more susceptible to personal and social constraints compared to anti-social predators, and often in need to find moral justifications for their occasional deviance ("neutralizations").

This characterization has important consequences in terms of prevention strategies. Although we cannot expect to intervene in remote causes such as ideological commitment and political beliefs, to develop targeted situational measures it is important to acknowledge proximal factors as well as individual differences that may affect the decision-making process. In the next section, we will examine the context of resources necessary to engage in ideologically motivated tax refusal by focusing on personal factors (i.e. cognitive and moral) as well as collaborative resources.

What Types of Resources are Needed to Engage in Ideologically Motivated Tax Refusal?

Some situational prevention researchers argue that crime is not only a conjunction of motivation and opportunity; the offender will also need to own or gain access to certain resources for crime. In rational choice terms, the offender not only estimates the relative weight of anticipated efforts, risks and rewards; she will also ponder whether she is sufficiently and adequately equipped for crime (Ekblom & Tilley, 2000; Gill, 2005). Examining offenders' capacities, capabilities and resources has enormous potential for prevention research. As Gill (2005) points out: "if one accepts that there is a distinct knowledge base or skill-set for some crimes, then it is important to trace the process by which skills are acquired, not least because it provides another way of impacting upon crime. Indeed, it may be easier to disrupt the process of skill acquisition than it is to develop techniques for disarming a skilled and knowledgeable offender" (2005, 309; Hamm, 2007; Kenney, 2007).

There are various types of resources which are considered proximal factors for crime (Ekblom & Tilley, 2000; Newman, Clarke, & Shoham, 1997; Niggli 1997). As Ekblom and Tilley (2000, 382) explain: "some resources are part of the offender – whether acquired congenitally, learned through socialization or education or picked up more casually as items of knowledge. Together these could be regarded as the offender's core competences for crime. Other resources relate to facilitators – tools, weapons, etc. that the offender can pick up and down – and to the scope of collaboration with others." We will first consider tax protesters' moral and cognitive prerequisites before examining the role of collaborative resources.

Moral resources

Offenders may need to overcome moral scruples that inhibit their behavior before engaging in a certain criminal activity (Ekblom & Tilley, 2000). The role of moral resources is especially important for understanding ideologically motivated tax refusal. As noted, tax protesters who refuse to file income returns for ideological purposes have strong moral beliefs supporting them. Some disagree with the government's policy choices, others are angry because they feel the tax system is unfair and the government is taking advantage of its citizens. Some would even cite the Bible to justify the morality of their actions, like Tracy Corona (see case study above) who argued that paying taxes is not only unlawful, but also sinful: "In my opinion, it's stealing. The Bible never condones stealing the fruits of my labor."[14]

These arguments provide tax protesters with a strong moral reason that may "neutralize" feelings of guilt or shame. Situational prevention researchers have acknowledged the role of rationalizations, which may be especially important for the "mundane offender," and can be expressed by using justifications such as "he deserved it," "I was just borrowing it," and "but everybody does it" (Clark & Hollinger, 1983; Wortley, 1996; Welch et al., 2005). Certain criminal behaviors – such as stealing office supplies, drunk driving, etc. – are common among ordinary people because they can be more easily justified and morally tolerated (Cornish & Clarke, 2003, p. 62). Rationalizations and neutralization techniques may have a stronger impact on individuals' perceptions if they find support among a group of peers. In criminology, pressures to conform to a group's belief system and adopt its code of conduct are considered significant criminogenic factors (Akers et al., 1979). Importantly, immediate social settings may exert pressures "to conform to group norms, to obey to the instructions of authority figures, to comply with or defy requests, and to submerge their identity within the group" (Wortley, 2008, p. 53). A study examining how perceptions of tax evasion within a community affect community members' judgments concerning the moral wrongfulness of tax evasion found that the more individuals perceive tax evasion to be prevalent within the community, the less likely they will judge it negatively (Welch et al., 2005). For the purposes of this study, it would be useful to replicate this survey with tax protesters to understand how situationally dependent factors, like exposure to anti-tax ideology and interaction with other tax protesters, influence their moral judgment and decision-making process.

According to recent research, individuals who engage in this type of criminal behavior may be more susceptible to preventive measures that increase the incentives or pressures to comply with the law, using psychologically manipulative techniques ("soft SCP") rather than heavy-handed restrictive measures ("hard SCP"; Wortley, 2008). The following sections will explain and further elaborate on this distinction.

Cognitive resources

Cognitive resources refer to the know-how necessary to commit specific crimes, which offenders acquire in various ways (Ekblom & Tilley, 2000). Sometimes this knowledge base is essential to provide the motivation for crime, and can be associated with weighing up costs and benefits deriving from the crime (Gill, 2005). As noted, tax protesters differ from traditional tax evaders primarily because they believe they have not only a moral duty, but also a legal right not to pay income taxes. These individuals have knowledge of a variety of pseudo-legal theories that provide the initial motivation and subsequent defense of their position in court. Such theories are based on misinterpretations of the law and "frivolous arguments" concerning their tax liabilities. But how do people learn about these ideas and methods to apply them?

Tax protest rhetoric is promoted on numerous Internet websites, at expositions, through radio shows and an incredible amount of literature (tapes, books, and videos) available online and in bookstores all over the country. Anti-tax promoters have made a business selling ideas and "untax" strategies that teach tax protesters how to be freed from tax obligations and defend from government's attacks by mailing bogus forms and letters. Irwin Schiff, who is considered one of the "gurus" of the tax protest movement, has written several books that are available for purchase online as well as in his Las Vegas bookstore.[15] Anecdotal evidence supports the idea that many individuals became tax protesters after reading these materials. Christopher Gronski, for example, the coordinator of an anti-tax group in New Hampshire, said that he "was outraged" after reading Vultures in Eagle's Clothing: Lawfully Breaking Free from Ignorance Related Slavery," a book available on Amazon.com by Lynne Meredith, a prominent leader who is currently serving a 10-year sentence for tax-related federal offenses.[16] The book cover reads the following:

> Stop reading their lips and start reading this book!
> Learn How To Legally Unvolunteer! This book will expose the most intimate and well kept secrets of the IRS. It will also provide the PROVEN LEGAL METHODS others have successfully used to: Legally STOP paying the graduated income tax. Legally STOP an employer from withholding all income taxes. Apply for a refund of previous income taxes paid . . . while staying out of jail and keeping all property! [. . .]
> We The People Are Calling Their Bluff! It's time for a change. Join our INTELLECTUAL REVOLUTION to peaceably and within the framework of the law, take back our great country and make America prosper!

Conferences are also popular in the movement, where anti-tax activists can promote their ideas and profit out of them. Peymon Motthedeh, for example, an Iranian immigrant who founded the "Freedom Law School" in 1992, presented and sold his "Freedom Packages" – which range from $4,000 to $6,000, plus $2,000 a year in maintenance fees – to more than 200 people attending the "Health and Freedom" tax-protesters conference held in Irvine, CA, in March 2006. Powerful messages are sometimes used to attract people to attend these seminars, like the one advertised in a local newspaper, which stated:[17]

> Are you a jerk and paying taxes? If you are, you might want to attend our seminar, it's only $150 and we'll show you how you don't have to pay any more taxes.

Collaborative resources

As Ekblom and Tilley (2000) point out, few offenders are equipped with the necessary resources to commit crime. For many potential offenders, contacts and collaborations with individuals who can provide the initial motivation or specialized skills are often crucial (Gill, 2005). Criminals benefit from networking and organizing with specialists from whom they can pool resources and capabilities. Law-abiding citizens who turn tax protesters do not do it overnight. First, they need to get in contact with the tax protest rhetoric and, possibly, be assisted by specialized tax advisors who are part of the movement. How do tax protesters meet these contacts? Anti-tax organizations, created to spread the word and "inform" (or rather "misinform") American citizens of their "rights," and fraudulent tax preparers constitute important collaborative resources in this respect. Actor Wesley Snipes, for example, was a member of the "American Rights Litigators," a Florida-based organization of people who defy federal tax collections. One of the most prominent groups, "We The People Foundation For Constitutional Education" (WTP) led by anti-tax activist Robert Schulz, is a tax-exempt organization with many branches all over the country, including California and New Hampshire. According to the foundation's website, its mission is to educate and train American citizens on how to protect and defend themselves against the government:

> By combining highly professional research and public education programs with the penetrating analytical legal advocacy of a professional public-interest law firm, the Foundation is uniquely poised to stand as a clarion voice of Freedom and to undertake the direct challenges — popular and legal — necessary to check unconstitutional government.[18]

The organization's strategy involves a variety of means to disseminate anti-tax propaganda and provide counseling and legal advice to tax protesters. Among the activities promoted, there are nationwide gatherings that facilitate contacts and draw large amounts of people who want to know more about tax resistance. As part of a large-scale educational program to inform

Americans "about the true nature of the income tax laws, to expose operations of the IRS that are unauthorized by law, and to put an end to their illegal collection of taxes from people who do not owe them," more than 1,000 people gathered in Washington, DC, to protest against the government in April 2001. Notably, We The People Foundation was able to publicize its efforts describing the stories of various successful tax protesters in full-page advertisement messages published in The Washington Times and USA Today in 2001.[19] Unfortunately, there is a lack of empirical studies in this area. More research is needed to uncover the different methods used by tax protesters to spread their ideas and better understand the role of collaborative resources as crime facilitators.

A "Soft" Approach for Preventing Ideologically Motivated Tax Refusal

Situational crime prevention comprises measures that are designed to manipulate situational factors and reduce crime through the application of five principles: i.e., (1) increase the efforts; (2) increase the risks; (3) reduce the rewards; (4) reduce provocations; and (5) remove excuses. The original framework contained 12 opportunity-reducing techniques that applied the first three principles, which derive directly from the rational choice perspective. The fourth and fifth categories were added subsequently as a result of various critiques and suggestions to refine and expand the model, which now includes 25 techniques (Clarke & Homel, 1997; Clarke & Cornish, 2003; Wortley, 2001).

Studies on the role of rationalizations, which help potential offenders justify their choices and neutralize feelings of guilt or shame, and other situational precipitators – i.e., factors that may prompt, provoke, or pressure to crime – led to the development of a wide array of "soft" techniques aimed at, for example, reducing stress and frustration, humanizing the victim, posting instructions, and so forth (Clarke, 1997; Wortley, 2001, 2008). These developments reflected the need to depart from the stereotypical image of the "anti-social predator" as the default offender type, and to facilitate the use of the situational approach against offenses which could not be prevented using traditional "hard" strategies (e.g., target-hardening and increased surveillance). Recent situational prevention research has shown that for certain crime problems it may be more effective to use measures that act "softly" on the offender instead of trying to incapacitate her, especially if "mundane offenders" are concerned (Cornish & Clarke, 2003; Wortley, 2008).

We recommend the use of "soft" measures to reduce incidents of ideologically motivated tax refusal. As noted, the use of aggressive enforcement strategies has produced mixed results, and sometimes even backlash effects (Cords, 2005; Murphy, 2005; Varma & Doob, 1998). As the traditional governmental approach seems to have failed in its objectives, the need to introduce diverse methods for prevention appears even more urgent.

As Wortley (2008) points out, "hard" techniques (e.g., CCTV surveillance cameras, etc.) are more easily noticed, and may sometimes be perceived as provoking. "Soft" techniques, on the other hand, are subtler, and therefore more likely to have an impact on the individual without being perceived as invasive. Tax protesters already believe that the government is the "enemy." Prevention strategies should be carefully planned not to further aggravate this sentiment, and instead make an effort to play it down. A "soft" approach has the additional potential to prevent the "desire-induced contemplation of the crime in question" (Cornish & Clarke, 2003, p. 48). Considering the variations existing in the degree of motivation among tax protesters, such measures are likely to produce more positive results with individuals who are only halfway committed to the cause. Finally, soft measures may be more resistant to crime displacement. As Wortley argues (2008, p. 64), if "situations contribute to the potential offender's criminal motivation, then controlling precipitators will reduce the likelihood that she will be motivated to seek out alternative crime opportunities."

In the next sections, we propose a selection of techniques which provide an initial framework for developing a "soft" approach to prevent ideologically motivated tax refusal. Some of the proposed techniques may sometimes overlap, but this should not be considered a limitation of the study, rather an opportunity to open the debate.

1. Reduce frustration and stress: simplify the filing procedure.

According to a recent GAO study on tax compliance, the complexity of the tax code is one of the reasons why so many taxpayers do not comply with the law (GAO, 2006). The multitude of preferential provisions in the tax code, such as exemptions and exclusions from taxation, deductions, credits, etc., can become a considerable source of stress for taxpayers, who often need to resort to tax advisors in order to fulfill the process. As noted, tax protesters view this intricate system of laws as part of a deliberate strategy that the government enacted to trick its citizens. Efforts should be made to simplify the tax filing procedure, as this could help reduce taxpayers' frustration and, at the same time, undermine the tax protest rhetoric. As the GAO study suggests, "providing quality services to taxpayers is an important part of any overall strategy to improve compliance and thereby reduce the tax gap" (GAO, 2006 p. 5).

The government should develop specific initiatives for educating taxpayers about confusing or misunderstood tax requirements. Forms and instructions should be clear, easy to access and expressed in lay terms. The creation of various simplified filing forms (such as IRS Form 1040EZ, the shorter version of the long and complicated Form 1040, created for certain groups of taxpayers with more basic needs) is recommended. As almost everyone nowadays has access to the Internet, such forms should be computerized and easy to download and understand without further advice. The use of additional media instruments (e.g., pictures, videos, etc.) is also advisable, as they may facilitate the comprehension and implementation process. To further support the needs of simple tax filers, the government could even think of replacing the filing procedure with a system of annual adjustment notices. Importantly, by enabling citizens to carry out the filing procedure by themselves it will be possible to reduce opportunities that they come into contact with fraudulent tax preparers and protesters.

2. Avoid disputes: address claims and improve response system.

As discussed, individuals who refuse to pay taxes for ideological reasons are often motivated by feelings of anger and distrust in the government and the tax system, which is viewed as unfair, inconsistent and illegitimate (Cords, 2005; Levitas, 2001). A common complaint among tax protesters is that the government fails to take their claims seriously and tend to simply dismiss them as "frivolous arguments" without providing adequate explanations. This lack of responsiveness may increase perceptions of unfairness and further spread the belief that the government is "hiding something." To reduce tax protesters' anger and frustration, and avoid further disputes which may escalate these sentiments, the government should improve its response system and confront those who legitimately express concerns over the tax system in an adequate and respectful manner.

In recent years, the IRS has made an attempt in this direction by publishing various documents and press releases on its website addressing some of the "frivolous arguments" that belong to the tax protest rhetoric. Each argument is briefly explained, followed by a discussion of the legal authority that rejects the contention, an enumeration of prosecuted cases and a description of penalties imposed on tax protesters.[20] However, these documents are hard to retrieve unless one performs a targeted search over the Internet. Moreover, the language used is not always easy to understand for the layperson. As a general practice, the IRS should address any inquiry promptly and comprehensively. Importantly, in its responses, it should avoid the use of terms that could be considered unduly harsh or labeling. A study that surveyed taxpayers who had been punished by the Australian Tax Office for engaging in illegal tax avoidance scheme found that individuals who experienced stigmatization during the enforcement process (e.g., they felt the government considered them as "tax cheats") were more likely to reoffend (Murphy & Harris, 2007). On the contrary, those who felt they were treated respectfully were less likely to report having evaded taxes two years later.

3. Post instructions: outreach campaign.

Publicity is a powerful instrument for crime prevention strategies. Research on the impact of publicity-based measures found that people's perceptions and behaviors are significantly influenced by the information provided (Bowers & Johnson, 2005; Laycock, 1991). There are various ways in which publicity can be used to reduce incidents of ideologically motivated tax refusal. In this sense, the government should emulate an example from the tax protesters' activism and undertake initiatives to inform U.S. citizens on the "truth" about the tax system and the risks of falling prey of scam artists. An extensive outreach campaign should be organized, including: seminars, speeches, and workshops in local communities all over the country, focusing specifically on those areas that constitute "hot spots" for the tax protest movement: the production and distribution of informative materials, including pamphlets, books, and videos addressing tax protesters' claims in simple and clear terms; free one-on-one consultation with private tax experts; and so forth. The following techniques provide further applications of publicity for prevention purposes.

4. Neutralize peer pressure: expose hypocrites.

As noted, peer pressure and contacts with tax protest advocates and organizations play a significant role in the decision-making process of a potential tax protester. Some leaders are considered "heroes" in the movement because of their tenaciousness even in the face of civil sanctions and criminal convictions. To effectively reduce ideologically motivated tax refusal, governments' initiatives should focus on neutralizing these powerful influences. One way to do this could be to identify and isolate movement leaders using the media to expose them as hypocrites by revealing the "real" motive behind their actions, i.e., greed rather than political upheaval.

For example, Lynne Meredith, who was recently convicted to 10 years in prison after allegedly making over $6 million selling books, tapes and in seminar appearance fees, is described in quite revealing terms on an article appeared in 2003 in the Los Angeles Times:

> [She] has a perpetual tan and a lavish home in the Orange County community of Sunset Beach, lectures her followers on luxury cruises, at catered parties in hotel conference rooms. [. . .] [S]he spends most of her time at her beachside home, surrounded by a fleet of classic cars, an extensive collection of Coca-Cola memorabilia and a parrot named Thomas Jefferson. [. . .] "The gated garage of her home holds a fleet of vintage cars – a Jaguar, a Porshe, a Bentley, a 1937 Gatsby roadster, a Range Rover and a 1973 Corvette Stingray with the vanity plate "TAXREBL"[21]

By demonizing these "martyr" figures and highlighting how, in fact, they are taking advantage of other tax protesters' beliefs for their own personal profit, it may be possible to undermine their credibility and force at least some to reconsider their choices.

5. Discourage imitation: promote positive role models.

People are not only susceptible to models who convey anti-social messages; if the right model or message is used, they can also be prompted to imitate a pro-social behavior (Bandura, 1977; Loftus, 1985; Wortley, 2008). In addition to publicizing the life stories and successful convictions of greedy tax protesters, another way to neutralize peer pressure and discourage imitation could involve the use of positive role models, e.g., former movement members who eventually "repented," like the two individuals mentioned in the example provided above. The government should try to obtain the collaboration of these individuals and ask them to participate in speeches and seminars organized as part of the general IRS outreach campaign, where they would have the chance to discuss their personal experiences and victimization within the movement. Positive role models do not necessarily have to appear in person but could be presented symbolically in mass media. The impact would be even more powerful if positive messages showing support for tax compliance and discrediting tax movement tactics came from well-known individuals, such as ex-movement leaders or Hollywood celebrities (e.g., Wesley Snipes).

6. Alert conscience: humanize the government.

Research shows that there are various ways in which offenders neutralize their feelings of guilt and shame preceding or following criminal behavior (Bandura, 1977). One of these involves minimizing the victim, who is often perceived and depicted as subhuman or unworthy (Wortley, 2008). As observed, some protesters tend to justify their anti-government actions by using a variety of arguments that support their choices as morally rightful. This is accomplished in part by adhering to an anti-government propaganda that demonizes the IRS and federal authorities as "just a big money scam." To reduce the "neutralizing" effects of this propaganda, publicity campaigns should be conducted to promote a more "humane" image of the IRS and the government. In this sense, the government should take advantage of the publicity surrounding April 15 – income tax day – not only to seek injunctions or make arrests of tax scam protesters (as it has done in the past), but also to inform U.S. citizens of initiatives of public interest that were carried out thanks to taxpayers' contributions. For example, advertising spots could be passed on television showing how new schools, hospitals or other facilities were built with the money received from income taxes. By expressing concern and sincere gratitude, the government could mitigate the negative image built by anti-tax protesters and show the "good side" of paying taxes. In this regard, it would be useful to first survey residents of local communities to find out what their needs and interests are.

7. Assist compliance: make them choose!

Techniques that promote compliance are especially important for reducing incidents of ideologically motivated tax refusal – a crime of omission which involves a lack of action by definition. One method to assist compliance – and stimulate consciences – would be to allow taxpayers to choose how their income tax money will be spent. Examining data from an IRS-commissioned study on tax noncompliance, Loftus (1985) found that some individuals experience a sort of "bystander effect," i.e., the tendency to think that one's evasion behavior is not a big deal in terms of revenue lost and would not make much of a difference. According to Loftus (1985), it could be possible to eliminate the "bystander effect" and increase compliance by letting taxpayers designate which category (e.g., defense, education, health care) their taxes were to fund. The additional value of this method is that it would not only target tax protesters, but the general population as a whole. Importantly, by letting people choose where their money go to, the responsibility for certain policy decisions would be distributed between the government and taxpayers who fund them, making the people feel more actively involved in public affairs. We recognize that it might be unfeasible to implement such an approach in all circumstances (because, for example, most people would likely choose to fund a child health care program than the IRS). However, the current tax return already provides a few small choices like this, such as providing funding for elections. It would make sense to empirically investigate the feasibility of this strategy in these and other circumstances.

8. Assist compliance: create incentives and amnesties.

Behavioral psychologists suggest that compliance can be more easily obtained by creating incentives and providing rewards rather than imposing punishments (Loftus, 1985; Wentworth & Rickel, 1985). One way to enhance compliance could be to reward taxpayers who file their income tax returns early during the filing period by providing, for example, free consultation with a tax preparer or additional tax credits. In addition, the government should consider adopting specific disclosure programs and tax amnesty laws for tax protesters who decide to come forth. These practices have already been used in the past by state departments of revenues as a strategy to increase compliance among delinquent taxpayers. A more targeted strategy could be developed by the U.S. government, which should take into account the specific characteristics and needs of tax protesters, considering also the fact that some of them may be victims of fraudsters and scam artists.

CONCLUSION

This paper used Clarke and Newman's (2006) terrorism definition and extended the terrorism literature by applying SCP techniques to ideologically motivated tax refusal, a non-violent political crime of omission. Most terrorism definitions and studies have limited their analysis to violent political crimes. Strategies that prevent individuals from committing nonviolent political crimes, however, may have a positive impact on the containment of domestic terrorism. Some have speculated that nonviolent ideological tax crimes may act as a gateway to more violent forms of ideological commitment, including subsequent terrorist incidents. Our analysis indicated that "soft" approaches – recently outlined by Wortley (2002) – as opposed to traditional "hard" SCP techniques are more likely to reduce incidents of ideologically motivated tax refusal. By intervening at an early stage with targeted measures and reducing the opportunities for seemingly less serious offenses, it could be possible to stop the escalation process and discourage these individuals from turning to more dangerous behaviors. For a more comprehensive counterterrorism strategy, future studies should address these points in an attempt to shed light over the relationship between violent and non-violent political extremism, and possible radicalization processes in the context of the domestic far-right.

This paper made conceptual contributions by demonstrating that SCP and the rational choice framework are also applicable to crimes of omission – like tax refusal – where individuals are held criminally responsible as a result of their failure to act. Previous SCP studies have only examined crimes that require proactive behavior on the side of the offender (e.g., burglary, theft, traffic offenses, etc.), focusing on the use of "hard" prevention techniques (e.g., target-hardening, increasing surveillance, etc.). This is an important advance for the SCP literature, as it highlights the importance of "soft" measures that assist compliance, remove excuses and induce prosocial behaviors.

Our study opens up many opportunities for future research. In this paper, we focused on the non-violent ideological crime of tax refusal, an offense committed by individuals who do not necessarily reject violence in principle. As we demonstrated, some tax protesters have escalated to subsequent violent activity or chosen to employ force to make their point. Future studies might consider distinguishing between non-violent ideological crimes and *anti-violent ideological crimes*, intended as illicit behaviors committed by persons who openly reject violence. The U.S. civil rights movement led by Dr. Martin Luther King, and Ghandi's peaceful protests against British rule in India are examples of movements that broke the law to make their point, but which ideologically eschewed the use of violence. Future research could build upon the current study by examining and comparing anti- violent types of political activism to non-violent ideologically motivated crimes like tax-refusal. In conclusion, it is hoped that this study adds to the growing literature that illustrates the efficacy of SCP techniques to increase public safety.

Address correspondence to: rbelli@jjay.cuny.edu

NOTES

1. Frelich and Chermak (2009) defines domestic far-right members as individuals or groups who display the following characteristics: "they

are fiercely nationalistic (as opposed to universal and international in orientation), anti-global, suspicious of centralized federal authority, reverent of individual liberty (especially their right to own guns, be free of taxes), believe in conspiracy theories that involve a grave threat to national sovereignty and/or personal liberty and a belief that one's personal and/or national 'way of life' is under attack and is either already lost or that the threat is imminent (sometimes such beliefs are amorphous and vague, but for some the threat is from a specific ethnic, racial, or religious group), and a belief in the need to be prepared for an attack either by participating in paramilitary preparations and training and survivalism."

2. General Accountability Office. *Internal Revenue Service: Challenges Remain in Combating Abusive Tax Schemes*, November 2003. Washington, DC.

3. Banthome, C. and Selvey, K. "The Tax Gap: Measuring the IRS's Bottom Line." *The CPA Online Journal*, April 2006.

4. "Understanding the Tax Gap," FS-2005-14, www.irs.gov/newsroom/.

5. *Hearing on the IRS and the Tax Gap Before the US Representatives Committee on Budget, Senate Committee on Finance*, (February 2007); (see statement of Honorable J. Russel George).

6. IRS. *The Truth About Frivolous Tax Arguments*. November 30, 2007.

7. Similarly, and importantly, some far-rightists refuse to register their cars or obtain driving licenses because they also view these regulations as infringing upon their liberties. In fact, a few far-rightists have been involved in deadly encounters with law enforcement that began as seemingly mundane traffic stops for their refusal to follow motor vehicle regulations (see Freilich and Chermak, this volume).

8. As can be read in public discussions on blogs and movement-related Internet websites; see for example, last accessed on 02/27/09.

9. See *SPLC Intelligence Report*, Spring, 2004.

10. See http://www.paynoincometax.com/lyinggovernment.htm

11. The role of publicity would require a closer look, as it raises interesting issues if compared within other criminal or terrorist contexts. Unlike common tax cheaters and similarly to terrorists, tax protesters crave publicity for various reasons, e.g., to convey their message and incite fellow citizens. However, terrorists typically act in secret and come out publicly only after an attack is accomplished, whereas tax protesters are generally vocal about their ideas and activities. There may be exceptions, however, that involve individuals who – as previously noted – agree with the far-right ideology, practice tax refusal, but would not

publicly state that unless they had to (e.g., after they are brought to court). This is not the venue to discuss this sort of issues, but future studies comparing similarities and differences between violent and non-violent forms of political extremism should consider this point.

12. Johnston, D. C. "Tax cheat sentenced to 6 years for defying IRS." *The New York Times*, 04/14/2005.

13. Wagner, M. "Branson tax evaders sentenced to probation. Businessmen Martin Dingman and Shane Grady escape prison time and fines after years of snubbing IRS," 2/4/2008, *Springfield Business Journal.*

14. See Carless, W. "The Tax Rebels." *The Voice of San Diego*, Monday, Jan. 28, 2008

15. These include: "The Biggest Con: How the Government Is Fleecing You" (1977); "Federal Mafia: How It Illegally Imposes and Unlawfully Collects Income Taxes" (1999); "The Great Income Tax Hoax: Why You Can Immediately Stop Paying This Illegally Enforced Tax" (1985); "The Social Security Swindle: How Anyone Can Drop Out," by Irwin Schiff (1984); and "The Kingdom of Moltz" by Irwin A Schiff (1980).

16. See Sanger-Katz, M. "Tax Resisters," June 11, 2006, posted on concordmonitor.com

17. Carless, W. "The Tax Rebels." *Voice of San Diego*, Monday, Jan. 28, 2008.

18. See "We The People Mission Statement."Retrieved at http://www.irs-.gov/pub/irs-utl/tax_gap_facts-figures.pdf

19. See SPLC Intelligence Report, "Don Quixote of Queensbury," Winter 2001; and ADL Report "Tax Protest Movement" (2005).

20. See IRS, "The Truth About Frivolous Tax Arguments - Section I," February 1, 2009.

21. Morin, M. Lynne. "Meredith sees her arrest as part of her mission to end the government's tyranny." *Los Angeles Times* (01/05/2003).

REFERENCES

Anti-Defamation League. (2003). *The tax protest movement since 9/11*. ADL Report, May 13, 2003. Retrieved online from:
http://www.adl.org/learn/extremism_in_america_updates/movements/tax_protest_movement/tax_protest_update_030513.htm

Anti-Defamation League. (2005). *Extremism in America: Tax protest movement*. Retrieved online from: http://www.adl.org/learn/ext_us/TPM.asp?xpicked=4&item=21

Bandura, A. (1977). *Social learning theory*. Englewood Cliffs, NJ: Prentice Hall.

Barkun, M. (1996). Religion, militias and Oklahoma City: The mind of conspirato-rialists. *Terrorism and Political Violence, 8*(1), 50–64.

Becker, P. J., Jipson, A. J., & Katz, R. (2001). A timeline of the racialist movement in the United States: A teaching tool. *Journal of Criminal Justice Education, 12*(2), 427–453.

Beirich, H. (2004, Spring). Talking tough: One of the largest "Patriot" conferences in years is marked by heated calls for revolution and violent resistance. Southern Poverty Law Center, *SPLC Intelligence Report*. Retrieved online from: www.splcenter.org/intel/intelreport/article.jsp?aid=380&printable=1

Bowers, K., & Johnson, S. (2005). Using publicity for preventive purposes. In N. Tilley (Ed.). *Handbook of crime prevention and community safety*, (pp. 329–354). Portland, OR: Willan Publishing.

Brezina, T. (2002). Assessing the rationality of criminal and delinquent behavior: A focus on actual utility. In A. R. Piquero & S. G. Tibbetts (Eds.). *Rational choice and criminal behavior: Recent research and future challenges* (pp. 241–264). New York: Routledge.

Chermak, S. M., Freilich, J. D., & Shemtob, Z. (2009). Law enforcement training and the domestic far-right. *Criminal Justice and Behavior*. Forthcoming.

Clark, J. B., & Hollinger, R. C. (1983). *Theft by employees in work organizations.* Washington, DC: US Department of Justice.

Clarke, R. V. (1980). Situational crime prevention: Theory and practice. *British Journal of Criminology, 20*(2), 136–147.

Clarke, R. V. (1997). *Situational crime prevention: Successful case studies* (2nd. ed.). Monsey, NY: Criminal Justice Press.

Clarke, R. V., & Homel, R. (1997). A revised classification of situational crime prevention techniques. In S. P. Lab (Ed.), *Crime prevention at a crossroads.* Highland Heights, KY: Anderson Publishing.

Clarke, R. V., & Newman, G. R. (2006). *Outsmarting the terrorists.* Westport: Praeger Security International.

Corcoran, J. (1990). *Bitter harvest, Gordon Kahl and the Posse Comitatus: Murder in the Heartland.* New York: Penguin Books.

Cords, D. (2005). Tax protestors and penalties: Ensuring perceived fairness and mitigating systemic costs. *Brigham Young University Law Review, 6*, 1515–1571.

Cornish, D. (1994). The procedural analysis of offending and its relevance for situational prevention. *Crime Prevention Studies, 3*, 151–196.

Cornish, D., & Clarke, R. V. (2003). Opportunities, precipitators, and criminal decisions: A reply to Wortley's critique of situational crime prevention. In M. J. Smith & D. B. Cornish (Eds.), *Theory for practice in situational crime prevention.* Crime Prevention Studies, (Vol. 16, pp. 41–96.) Monsey, NY: Criminal Justice Press.

Damphousse, K. R., & Smith, B. L. (2004). Terrorism and empirical testing: Using indictment data to assess changes in terrorist conduct. *Sociology of Crime, Law and Deviance, 5*. 75–90.

Ekblom, P. (2007). Making offenders richer. *Crime Prevention Studies, 21*, 41–57.

Ekblom, P., & Tilley, N. (2000). Going equipped: Criminology, situational crime prevention and the resourceful offender. *British Journal of Criminology, 40*, 376–398.

Flynn, K. & Gerhardt, G. (1995). *The silent brotherhood: The chilling inside story of America's violent anti-government militia movement.* New York: Signet book//Penguin.

Freilich, J. D., & Chermak, S. M. (2009). *United States extremist crime database (ECDB), 1990–2008: Preliminary results.* Department of Homeland Security University Network Research and Education Summit. Washington DC: March.

Freilich, J. D., Chermak, S. M., & Caspi, D. (2009). Critical events in the life trajectories of domestic extremist white supremacist groups: A case study analysis of four violent organizations. *Criminology and Public Policy, 8(3)* in press.

Freilich, J. D., Chermak, S. M., & Simone, J., Jr. (2009). Surveying American state police agencies about terrorism threats, terrorism sources, and terrorism definitions. *Terrorism and Political Violence, 21(3),* in press.

Gill, M. (2005). Reducing the capacity to offend: Restricting resources for offending. In N. Tilley (Ed.), *Handbook of crime prevention and community safety* (pp. 306–328). Portland, OR: Willan Publishing.

Government Accounting Office (GAO). (1996). *Internal Revenue Service: Results of nonfiler strategy and opportunities to improve future efforts.* Washington, DC: GAO/GGD-96-72.

Government Accounting Office (GAO). (2006). *Tax gap: Making significant progress in improving tax compliance rests on enhancing current IRS techniques and adopting new legislative actions.* Testimony before the Committee on Budget, U.S. Senate. Washington, DC: GAO-06-453T.

Gruenewald, J., Freilich, J. D., & Chermak, S. M. (2009). An Overview of the domestic far-right and its criminal activities. In B. Perry & R. Blazak (Eds.), Hate crimes: Hate crime offenders (pp. 1–21). Westport: Praeger

Hamm, M. S. (2007). *Terrorism as crime: From Oklahoma City to Al Qaeda and beyond.* New York: New York University Press.

Hewitt, C. (2003). *Understanding terrorism in America: From the Klan to Al Qaeda.* New York: Routledge.

Internal Revenue Service. (2005). *Tax gap facts and figures.* Retrieved online from: http://www.irs.gov/pub/irs-utl/tax_gap_facts-figures.pdf

Kadish, S., & Schulhofer, S. J. (2001). *Criminal law and its processes: Cases and materials.* New York City: Aspen Publishers.

Kenney, M. (2007). *From Pablo to Osama: Trafficking and terrorist networks, government bureaucracies, and competitive adaptation.* University Park, PA: The Pennsylvania State University

LaFree, G., Dugan, L., Fogg, H., & Scott, J. (2006, May 2006). *Building a global terrorism database.* Final Report to the National Institute of Justice.

Laycock, G. (1991). Operation Identification or the power of publicity? *Security Journal, 2,* 67–71.

Levitas, D. (2001). *Untaxing America: After four decades of organizing by right-wing tax protesters, US officials have largely caved in on enforcement.* Southern Poverty Law Center, SPLC Intelligence Report, Spring 2001. Retrieve online from: www.splcenter.org/intel/intelreport/article.jsp?aid=162&printable=1

Levitas, D. (2002). *The terrorist next door: The militia movement and the radical right.* New York: Thomas Dunne Books.

Loftus, E. (1985). To file, perchance to cheat. *Psychology Today, 19*, 35–39.

Mathis, S. (2003). A plea for omissions. *Criminal Justice Ethics, 22*(2), 15–31

Matza, D. (1964). *Delinquency and drift.* New York: Wiley.

McCauley, C., & Moskalenko, S. (2008). Mechanisms of political radicalization: Pathways toward terrorism. *Terrorism and Political Violence, 20*, 415–433.

McGarell, E. F., Freilich, J. D., & Chermak, S. M. (2007). Intelligence led policing as a framework for responding to terrorism. *Journal of Contemporary Criminal Justice, 23*(2), 142–158.

Murphy, K. (2005). Regulating more effectively: The relationship between procedural justice, legitimacy, and tax non-compliance. *Journal of Law & Society, 32*(4), 562–589.

Murphy, K., & Harris, N. (2007). Shaming, shame and recidivism: A test of reintegrative shaming theory in the white-collar crime context. *British Journal of Criminology, 47*(6), 900–917.

Newman, G. R. (1997). Introduction: Towards a theory of situational crime prevention. In G. R. Newman, R. V. Clarke, & S. G. Shoham (Eds.), *Rational choice and situational crime prevention: Theoretical foundations.* Brookfield, USA: Ashgate.

Newman, G. R., & Clarke, R. V. (2003). *Superhighway robbery: Preventing E-commerce crime.* Portland, OR and Cullompton, UK: Willan Publishing.

Newman, G. R., Clarke, R. V. G., & Shoham, S. G. (Eds.) 1997. *Rational choice and situational crime prevention: Theoretical foundations.* Aldershot, UK: Ashgate.

Niggli, M. A. (2007). Rational choice and the legal model of the criminal. In G. R. Newman, R. V. G. Clarke, & S. G. Shoam (Eds.), *Rational choice and situational crime prevention: Theoretical foundations.* Aldershot, UK: Ashgate.

Pitcavage, M. (1997). *Common law and uncommon courts: An overview of the common law court movement.* Retrieved from Militia Watchdog website: http://www.adl.org/mwd/common.asp.

Pitcavage, M. (1998a). *Paper terrorism's forgotten victims: The use of bogus liens against private individuals and businesses.* Retrieved from the Militia Watchdog website: http://www.adl.org/mwd/privlien.asp.

Pitcavage, M. (1998b). *Patriots for profit.* Retrieved from the Militia Watchdog website: www.militia-watchdog.org/profit.htm.

Pitcavage, M. (1999). *Old wine, new bottles: Paper terrorism, paper scams and paper "redemption."* Retrieved from the Militia Watchdog website: http://www.adl.org/mwd/redemption.asp.

Rasholnikov, A. (2006). Crime and punishment in taxation: deceit, deterrence and the self-adjusting penalty. *Columbia Law Review, 106*(3), 569–642.

Sanger-Katz, M. (2006). Protesters see income tax as a scam. *Concord Monitor,* June 11, 2006. Retrieved online at: www.concordmonitor.com/apps/pbcs.dll/article?AID=/20060611/REPOSITORY/606110338.

Shively, M. (2005, June 2005). *Study of literature and legislation on hate crime in America.* Final Report to the National Institute of Justice.

Southern Poverty Law Center. (2001). Don Quixote of Queensbury: Bob Schulz's We The People may be tilting at windmills, but its efforts reflect a re-energized tax protest movement. *SPLC Intelligence Report,* Winter 2001. Retrieved online from: www.splcenter.org/intel/intelreport/article.jsp?aid=115&printable=1

Southern Poverty Law Center. (2003). Tax protesters: US moves against radical tax cheats. *SPLC Intelligence Report*, Fall 2003. Retrieved online from: www.splcenter.org/intel/intelreport/article.jsp?aid=110&printable=1

Southern Poverty Law Center. (2007). Tax protesters: Crackdown hits tax protesters, celebrities included. *SPLC Intelligence Report*, Spring 2007. Retrieved online from: www.splcenter.org/intel/intelreport/article.jsp?aid=744&printable=1

Tucker, J. B., & Pate, J. (2001). The Minnesota patriots council (1991). In J. Tucker (Ed.), *Toxic terror: Assessing terrorist use of chemical and biological weapons* (pp. 159–183). Cambridge, MA: MIT Press.

Varma, K., & Doob, A. (1998). Deterring Economic Crimes: The case of tax evasion. *Canadian Journal of Criminology, 40*(2), 165–184.

Welch, M. R., Xu, Y., Bjarnason, T., Petee, T., O'Donnell, P., & Magro, P. (2005). "But everybody does it.": The effects of perceptions, moral pressures, and informal sanctions on tax cheating. *Sociological Spectrum, 25*, 21–52.

Wentworth, D. K., & Rickel, A. U. (1985). Determinants of tax evasion and compliance. *Behavioral Sciences & the Law, 3*(4), 455–466

Wortley, R. (1996). Guilt, shame and situational crime prevention. In R. Homel (Ed.), The politics and practice of situational crime prevention. *Crime Prevention Studies, 5*, 115–132.

Wortley, R. (1998). A two-stage model of situational crime prevention. *Studies on Crime and Crime Prevention, 7*(2), 173–188.

Wortley, R. (2001). A classification of techniques for controlling situational precipitators of crime. *Security Journal, 14*(4), 63–82.

Wortley, R. (2002). *Situational prison control: Crime prevention in correctional institutions.* Cambridge: Cambridge University Press.

Wortley, R. (2008). Situational precipitators of crime. In R. Wortley & L. Mazerolle (Eds.), *Environmental criminology and crime analysis* (48–69). Portland, OR and Cullumpton, UK: Willan Publishing.

EXPLORING PARALLELS BETWEEN SITUATIONAL PREVENTION AND NON-CRIMINOLOGICAL THEORIES FOR REDUCING TERRORIST RISK

Joseph Clare and Frank Morgan
University of Western Australia

Abstract: *The development of the situational prevention framework to combat terrorism has broadened the traditional focus of these strategies on the immediate situation. This chapter discusses the diverse temporal and spatial focus of the set of situational techniques Clarke and Newman (2006) have proposed as a response to terrorism. As a consequence of this increased diversity, the situational prevention strategies for terrorism bifurcate to parallel the epidemiological high-risk and population approaches to disease prevention. Further, these population techniques incorporated into the expanded situational prevention framework are entirely consistent with those of theories discussed by psychologists, anthropologists, sociologists, and lawyers.*

Interdisciplinary Symposium: Why Draw Parallels?

In August 2007, a three-day symposium was hosted by the University of Western Australia, designed to enable a group of international scholars

Crime Prevention Studies, volume 25 (2009), pp. 207–227.

from a broad range of disciplines to forge an interdisciplinary perspective on terrorism and torture. Amongst the positive outcomes of this process was that experts from a range of disciplines were able to examine the complex factors that motivate terrorist acts and to discuss interdisciplinary strategies for reducing the threat of future terrorist attacks. Fittingly, the capacity for situational prevention to combat terrorism was discussed by Ronald V. Clarke, who presented aspects of the Outsmarting the Terrorists approach developed by himself and Graeme Newman (explored fully in Clarke & Newman, 2006). Although the recommendations of situational prevention were very well received by this broad range of scholars, uncertainty arose as to how these techniques related to other theoretically motivated approaches to combating terrorism. Within the context of the edited volume that arose from this symposium, we discussed some parallels between a situational prevention approach to terrorism and alternative approaches to reducing terrorist risk (Clare & Morgan, 2009).

Our original argument was presented at the 17th Annual *Environmental Criminology and Crime Analysis* conference in July 2008. As a consequence of the feedback and suggestions received at this meeting, we have decided to continue to explore the parallels between a situational prevention approach to terrorism and the recommendations for terrorist reduction that are made by other academic fields. This chapter, which reflects this continued effort, attempts to achieve two main objectives. First, we argue that, in making the transition from situational crime prevention (SCP) to situational prevention of terrorism (SPT), the framework has expanded beyond its previous boundaries: moving from a high-risk, actuarial position, focused on the immediate situation, towards a diverse set of techniques that advocate for a broad temporal and spatial focus. Second, we demonstrate parallels between SPT and the terrorism reduction recommendations made by other academic fields.

Following some brief caveats, this chapter will discuss the varying focuses of prevention, building primarily on Rose's (1992, 2001) *population* and *high-risk* approaches to disease prevention (see also Clark, this volume). The relevance of this dichotomy to crime will then be explored, and it will be argued that crime prevention strategies (including SCP) have tended to adopt a high-risk approach, with respect to both potential victims (or targets) and offenders. This will lead to a discussion of the important expansions that have occurred in the transition from SCP to SPT, and of the resulting increased compatibility between the objectives of SPT and those of other academic areas. We will argue that as a result of this transition, application of a SPT framework simultaneously promotes a high-risk and a population approach, due to the inclusion of specific techniques designed to influence risk over a longer term and from a greater distance than typically observed with SCP interventions. As a consequence of this expansion, it will be demonstrated that a SPT framework advocates certain population focused strategies that strongly parallel the recommendations of other academic disciplines. Finally, the common assumptions that hold true across SPT and the paralleled theoretical perspectives will be emphasized.

Caveats and Clarifications

Before commencing this exploration of interdisciplinary parallels, we want to briefly clarify what we are not trying to achieve. First, we are not seeking to uncover the root causes of terrorism (as Clarke & Newman, 2006, p. 187, phrased it, to "do the impossible"). Second, we are not appealing to dispositional interpretations as to why terrorism occurs. Third, we are not advocating that authorities should unconditionally negotiate and comply with extremists. Fourth, we are not developing a fully integrated theoretical perspective that attempts to "do everything" simultaneously. Finally, we are not presenting any new theories. Instead, we are simply arguing that: (a) terrorism risk reduction strategies vary in focus, (b) the SPT framework developed by Clarke and Newman (2006) already reflects this varying focus, and (c) the expansion of the situational prevention framework draws clear parallels with terrorism reduction strategies proposed by other academic fields.

Varying Approaches to Prevention

Rose (e.g., 1992, 2001) developed an epidemiological model of disease prevention and reduction that separates interventions into high-risk and population approaches. Utilizing screening procedures and with a focus on individuals within a population, the high-risk approach to disease prevention seeks to identify those individuals who have high levels of risk with respect to disease outcomes. For example, through such a process, the general practitioner routinely checks for high blood pressures as indicative of future stroke risk, and checks cholesterol levels as predictors of heart attacks. Individuals identified as a consequence of this process represent a high-risk tail of a continuous distribution. This is represented graphically in Figure 1 (a) by the area under the curve to the right of the cut-off bar. Adopting a high-risk strategy to prevention requires the health clinician to work with these individuals to reduce their health risks. Such interventions could involve variations in exercise and diet, or the use of pharmaceuticals. Over time, if a high-risk strategy were entirely successful, the resulting overall distribution would look like Figure 1 (b) – a truncated distribution with its high-risk tail removed.

As an alternative to this, the population approach to risk reduction accepts that the risk distribution of individuals reflects a property of the population as a whole. One example that Rose (2001) uses to represent this involves the considerable variation between the distributions of blood pressures in Kenyan nomads and London civil servants. Within both of these populations, the shapes of the distributions are approximately normal. However, there is a large between-population difference, with the mean blood pressure for the nomads considerably lower than the mean for the public servants. According to Rose, although the determinants of the distribution depend little on the characteristics of individuals in each population (e.g., their genetic characteristics), the differences between these distributions depend considerably on population-level lifestyle variation. This means that for the nomads, the members who are located within the tail of the blood pressure distribution still only pose a moderate adverse cardiovascular risk. The aim of a population approach to prevention, therefore, is to reduce risks of undesirable health outcomes for the whole population. Within a public health domain, successful examples of population interventions include universal wearing of seat-belts in motor vehicles, the introduction of fluoride into public water supplies, and anti-smoking campaigns for the general public. Successful operation of a population approach to lowering heart attack risk is displayed in Figure 1 (c), with intervention resulting in a significant reduction to the mean risk and a large reduction in the proportion of the distribution remaining above the high-risk cut-off level.

Rose's diverse approaches parallel Brantingham and Faust's (1976) conceptual model that identified three levels of crime prevention: primary, secondary, and tertiary. Building on work developed within a public health context, Brantingham and Faust sought to emphasize the divergent focuses of crime prevention strategies with a view to addressing confusion within the criminal justice system. The focuses of these three levels are summarized as follows:

Figure 1. Rose's representation of risk distributions for heart attack: (a) pre-high-risk interventions, (b) ideal post-high-risk intervention, truncating distribution of risk, and (c) ideal post-population targeted intervention, shifting the distribution of risk.*

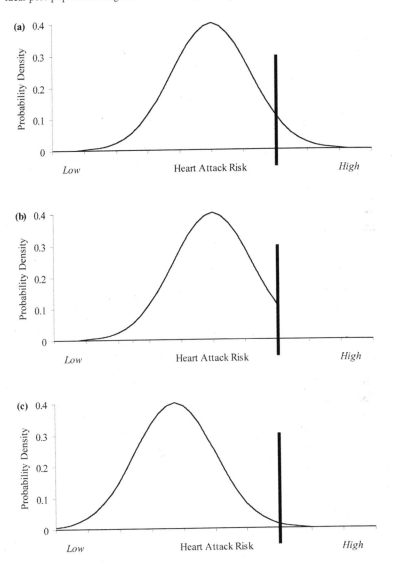

*This figure has been reproduced, with permission of the publisher, from: Clare, J. & Morgan, F. (2009), "Reducing terrorist risk: Integrating jurisdictional and opportunity approaches." In W. Stritzke, S. Lewandowsky, D. Denemark, J. Clare & F. Morgan (Eds.), *Terrorism and Torture: An Interdisciplinary Perspective*, page 330. Cambridge, UK: Cambridge University Press.

> Primary crime prevention identifies conditions of the physical and social environment that provide opportunities for or precipitate criminal acts. Here the objective of intervention is to alter those conditions so that crimes cannot occur. Secondary crime prevention engages in early identification of potential offenders and seeks to intervene in their lives in such a way that they never commit criminal violation. Tertiary crime prevention deals with actual offenders and involves intervention in their lives in such a fashion that they will not commit further offenses. (Brantingham & Faust, 1976, p. 290)

Just as Rose argues for health, this model identifies the importance of acknowledging that criminal risk emerges from multiple sources and operates at varying levels, such that a range of divergent strategies can be implemented simultaneously and all can be correctly classified as *crime reduction*. The direct compatibility of these models will not be explored beyond the suggestion that primary prevention is arguably closest to a population approach to risk reduction, while secondary and tertiary levels are more akin to versions of a high-risk approach. The benefit of considering the relationship between Brantingham and Faust's (1976) crime prevention model and Rose's (1992, 2001) disease prevention model is that the latter approach discusses the relative capacities of these different prevention methods to reduce risk.

Over all, the arguments that underlie Rose's dichotomous approaches to risk reduction transfer well to a terrorism domain. First, as some societies have a higher mean risk of terrorism relative to others, there must be scope for adopting a population approach to reducing society-wide terrorist risk. The successful implementation of such strategies for terrorism would assume that those individuals with the motivation to engage in acts of terrorism will represent a markedly smaller proportion of the overall distribution. Second, given the reasonable assumption that support for terrorism will be heterogeneous within any specific society at any given time, it follows that there will always be some members of society who hold sufficiently extreme views so as to pose a high risk of committing terrorist acts.

The following section will explore the relevance of Rose's framework for contemporary approaches to the prevention of terrorism. However, it is important to briefly explain that exploring the contribution that epidemiology can make to environmental criminology is not novel. For example, Arnold, Keane and Baron (2005) adopted an epidemiological approach to utilizing routine activities theory to reduce population risk of victimization, and Hope (2007) explored longitudinal, population differences between the majority who are able to regain their immunity from crime post-victimization and the small section of society who are chronically victimized and unable to attain this immunity. Most relevantly, Clarke and Newman (2006, pp. 198-203) explored the utility of the Haddon Matrix (e.g., Haddon, 1999) for assessing the appropriateness of anti-terrorist interventions: building on the Haddon Matrix analytical framework that separates contextual phases temporally and identifies the varying levels of factors that contribute to an event (see also, Minwoo, this volume). Application of this matrix within an injury prevention context has led to many innovative solutions to problems that do not simply "follow from what seems to be [the] primary cause" (Clarke & Newman, 2006, p. 199). As Brantingham and Faust suggest for crime, within a medical context, Jackson, Lynch and Harper (2006) recommend that population and high-risk strategies should be adopted in parallel, with the exact balance dependent on (a) the risk profile of the specific population, and (b) the amount of resources available. Just as *Quit* campaigns are unlikely to have any preventive benefit for the small section of society who suffer chronic lung disease, so too are *hearts and minds* approaches (as discussed by Clarke & Newman, 2006) unlikely to deter committed terrorists from attempting attacks. However, over a varying timeframe and with alternative implementation strategies, following the recommendations of a population approach to disease prevention (which are non-specific with respect to individuals), it is reasonable to assume that equivalently-focused strategies can have an impact on the general support for terrorism within societies and, by extension, the number of terrorists who develop. Despite this advice regarding the increased utility that can be gained from implementing high risk and population prevention strategies in parallel, it remains the case that the majority of recent terrorism prevention initiatives have adopted a high-risk approach. The next section of this chapter discusses the reasons underlying this unbalanced approach.

Utilizing a High-Risk Approach to Preventing Terrorism

This high-risk approach to managing terrorist threat is consistent with one version of a risk-based criminal justice model termed actuarial justice (e.g., Feeley & Simon, 1992, 1994). This model is supported by a number of assumptions, including: (a) offenders can be sentenced according to future risk of offending rather than past deeds; (b) statistical methods can be used to assess risk prediction; (c) the potential risks posed by unsentenced prisoners must be assessed prior to trial; and, (d) the incapacitative benefits of detention should be emphasized relative to other justice aims, such as rehabilitation, proportionality, or deterrence. Historically, actuarial strategies to crime reduction have been applied within contexts that maintain a belief that sections of the population exist (and necessarily always will) for whom traditional techniques for deterrence will not work (Feeley & Simon, 1994): the *underclass*, who cannot be deterred, reintegrated, nor rehabilitated, and as such can only be dealt with through "the specific strategies of categorically exclusionary risk" (O'Malley, 2004, p. 328). From its conception, actuarial justice has been utilized to manage a range of sections of society, from the socially disadvantaged through to persistent violent and sexual offenders.

Since 2001, the political climate in Australia has endorsed the exclusion of various sections of society, with this trend formalized when the Australian Commonwealth Government implemented the Australian Anti-Terrorism Act (No. 2) 2005. This Act gave significantly greater powers to Australian authorities in a range of areas, including surveillance, detention, and individually-focused control orders. One specific example of the scope for this legislation in Australia is the ability of authorities to detain without trial non-suspects who may have information about terrorist activities. Although there has been some opposition to these amendments, with the Australian Government Parliamentary Joint Committee (2002, Chapter 3) labeling this *Act*, "one of the most controversial pieces of legislation considered by the Parliament in recent times," in a broader domain it has largely been taken for granted that potential high-risk offenders should be targeted in this way. Although this legislation applies to individuals, there is scope to include whole groups when utilizing these laws (e.g., racial profiling at airports): an approach which directly parallels the underclass discussed previously. Ostensibly, much of the justification for this exclusionary approach to managing sections of Australian society has been provided by fear of terrorism.

As explained already, it is sometimes appropriate to implement high-risk reduction strategies with respect to terrorism. However, the application of these types of exclusionary approaches to managing terrorist risk is problematic for at least two reasons. First, to identify *at risk* sections of society (e.g., racial profiling), is to implicitly assume that (a) there is homogeneous support for terrorism within excluded groups, and (b) there is a large disparity of opinion between the excluded groups and the rest of society. This assumption is consistent with a well-understood social psychological phenomenon by which out-group members are perceived as having a much higher degree of similarity to one another than members of one's own group (e.g., see Devine, 1995; Levine & Moreland, 1995). This is not the case, as there will always be heterogeneity of attitudes towards terrorism within excluded groups, just as government-focused dissatisfaction varies across society generally. Second, exclusionary approaches ignore the fact that terrorist activity is the exception, not the norm – and is only attempted by the most extreme members of society.

The utility and necessity of exclusionary strategies is further questioned by the availability of alternative high-risk approaches. As O'Malley (2002, 2004) argues, inclusionary risk management strategies – not driven by conservative, exclusionary, punitive politics – do exist, and that for all crime the logic of risk reduction does not inevitably lead to a focus on *out-groups*. At least two other high-risk strategies are currently available. The first, traditional police work firmly embedded in rights-oriented criminal justice procedures, has been responsible for the majority of successes against terrorism post-9/11, despite the trend for individual-focused actions involving police and security agencies operating with *new* legal powers (as discussed by McCauley, 2009). The second relies on the extent to which offending can be explained in terms of opportunity, and attempts to manage opportunity by controlling high-risk situations and vulnerable targets (O'Malley, 2002, 2004, explores this idea with respect to crime generally). Neither of these strategies is dependent on categorical exclusion. Furthermore, through its reference to opportunity, the second strategy appeals to the central tenets of SCP. Given that SCP represents a viable high-risk approach to preventing crime generally, the following section provides an overview of the theoretical underpinnings and major assumptions of this framework, and also outlines the major techniques that are at its disposal.

Situational Crime Prevention

The SCP framework has a solid theoretical basis. At a macro level, SCP is informed by routine activity theory (Cohen & Felson, 1979), "that seeks to explain how changes in society expand or contract opportunities for crime" (Clarke, 2005, p. 41). Next, from a meso level, SCP is guided by the Brantinghams' (1984) crime pattern theory, which explores how offender and offence distribution is influenced by normal, everyday activity. Finally, when addressing the micro level of offending, SCP appeals to the rational choice perspective, which conceptualizes criminal behavior in terms of bounded rationality, and assumes "that crime is purposive behavior designed to meet the offender's commonplace needs" (Clarke, 1997, p. 10) within the immediately relevant temporal, physical, and logistical constraints. Clarke (2008, pp. 178-180) outlines three fundamental assumptions of SCP: (a) when crime occurs it is the result of an appropriate interaction between situation and motivation, (b) crime arises as a result of a choice, and (c) opportunity mediates the occurrence of crime.

Building on this theoretical basis and with these assumptions in mind, the SCP framework has developed over time into a set of 25 techniques that are categorized into five overarching styles: increasing effort, increasing risk, reducing rewards, removing excuses, and reducing provocations (e.g., Clarke, 2005, 2008). The most recent of these additions, reducing provocations, was "made in response to Wortley's (1998, 2001) critiques of situational prevention" (Clarke, 2005, p. 48), in which a call was made for re-analysis of the distinction between motivation (in the form of precipitators) and opportunity when assessing situations. Wortley (2008, p. 60) argued that, "The inclusion of precipitators broadens the scope of the situational approach and provides the basis for a more comprehensive analysis of so-called 'irrational' crimes,' " such as "emotionally-based or pathological behaviour such as violence and sex offending": which has direct relevance to primarily ideologically-motivated violent terrorist acts. Over all, the SCP framework provides a broad spectrum of highly malleable techniques that have relevance to the prevention of every crime.

Generally, SCP calls for careful and separate examination of different forms of crime and does not assume that offenders are pathological. Situational approaches are broadly focused with respect to potential offenders, relatively uninterested in motivation, and adopt a highly-focused perspective with respect to opportunities and potential targets. Three important factors to note about SCP approaches to crime minimization are: (a) they do not discriminate, instead impacting on all citizens equally; (b) they do not necessarily restrict human rights and freedoms under the guise of increased security, producing a "fortress" society or a Brave New World scenario (e.g., see Clarke, 1997, for a discussion of this point); and (c) they do not simply result in offenders picking the next-best target as a result of opportunity reduction (termed *displacement* within SCP).

In this form, SCP is largely consistent with the high-risk approach discussed previously, making little-to-no comment about population interventions and broader motivating factors that influence risk. However, as is discussed in the following section, in developing this framework from one focused on crime to one specifically tailored to respond to terrorism, these previous boundaries of SCP have expanded. The following section will discuss this expansion and argue that a number of techniques incorporated within Clarke and Newman's SPT framework are more consistent with a population approach to reducing risk.

Extending Beyond Crime:
Situational Prevention of Terrorism

In developing the SPT framework, Clarke and Newman (2006) compliment the structure provided by reward, risk, effort, provocation, and excuse, with an appeal to four pillars of terrorist opportunity: targets, weapons, tools, and facilitating conditions. Over all, Clarke and Newman perceive that opportunities will vary as a function of physical, technological, political, and industrial context, and they suggest that meaningful deconstruction of the terrorist opportunity structure must: (a) separately analyze the different types of terrorism, (b) view terrorists as rational, and (c) focus on how (rather than *why*) terrorists intend to attack. Just as with situational prevention in other contexts, Clarke and Newman argue that displacement is not inevitable for terrorism.

Just as with SCP previously, at first glance it appears that in the development of the SPT framework Clarke and Newman (2006, p. 70) still do not consider that reducing motivation for terrorism provides a strong basis for prevention, suggesting that, "Conflicts inherent in the terrorist group inevitably lead to the operational demands of terrorism eclipsing idealism. Understanding the ideologies of terrorist groups will therefore give little insight into their selection of targets and tactics." Although the general theoretical underpinnings for situational prevention are diverse in focus, ranging from the macro to the micro (as discussed by Clarke, 2005), the overriding principle of SCP is "that preventive measures should try to change the 'near,' situational causes of crime, rather than the 'distant' dispositional causes" (Clarke, 2008, p. 180). As with SCP previously, elements of the SPT framework are near-focused (with regards to specificity of targets, smaller-scale geography, etc.), and by extension reflect an approach to preventing terrorism that means SPT maintains a high-risk focus, concerned with immediate opportunity.

However, when crossed with the four pillars of terrorist opportunity, closer inspection of Clarke and Newman's (2006) SPT framework reveals a definite expansion of the scope of prevention techniques to instigate population changes. For example, in manipulating the fourth pillar of terrorist opportunity, Clarke and Newman (2006, Table 15.2, pp. 192-193) outline a number of techniques designed to reduce population-wide support for terrorism. These include: (a) promoting ties between local police and immigrant communities, (b) using publicity to isolate terrorist groups from the community and to portray the hypocrisy and cruelty of terrorist acts, (c) working closely with migrant communities and host communities when abroad, (d) avoiding provocative announcements, and (e) utilizing clear rules for interrogation in line with international laws and conventions which preserve the rights of non-combatants and prohibit the use of torture. This expansion of the boundaries of SCP is also apparent when the EVIL DONE acronym (standing for exposed, vital, iconic, legitimate, destructible, occupied, near, and easy) for terrorist target selection is examined, with the inclusion of factors such as *iconic* and *legitimate* that do not reflect instrumental rationality and are not proximal ("near") to the opportunity. From an iconic perspective, Clarke and Newman (2006, pp. 94-95) discuss the symbolic attractiveness of the Statue of Liberty and the Pentagon as reflective of liberty and power, and with respect to legitimacy they explain the difficulty terrorists face in "anticipat[ing] public reaction to the attack – whether it will be perceived as powerful and audacious or whether it will meet with moral condemnation." In order to demonstrate the bifurcation of these SPT techniques, we have separated the majority of the examples Clarke and Newman cited into either high-risk or population prevention approaches: as displayed in Table 1.

In addition to this separation of SPT techniques according to Rose's framework, there are also distinct groupings within the distant, population styles of terrorist opportunity reduction. For example, one type of these interventions represents the extrapolation of successfully developed, locally applied SCP interventions to such broad levels as to become essentially universal. Exponents of this group include tamper-proofing pharmaceutical products, which expanded to represent a "massive, national intervention designed to prevent a rare crime that was extremely successful at the local level" (Clarke & Newman, 2006, p. 200), and the universal (though variable) application of baggage and passenger screening at international airports, to reduce the risk of a range of criminal and terrorist acts. Another collection of these primary intervention techniques involves governmental policy, legislation, and regulating the practices of multi-national corporations. Examples include: (a) the Financial Action Task Force's (FATF)

Table 1: Examples of Clarke and Newman's (2006, pp. 192-193) Situational Prevention Techniques Applied to Terrorism, Preliminarily Classified According to Prevention Approach (either high-risk or population focused)

Situational prevention techniques	Prevention approach	
	High-risk	Population
Increase the effort	Identify vulnerable targets. Prioritize targets for protection. Security training for VIPs. High tech passports, visas, driving licenses. Reduce explosive's shelf-life.	Control dissemination of weapons technology. Hold contractors liable for stolen explosives. Tighten identity and credit authentication procedures. Tighten border controls. Disrupt recruitment.
Increase the risk	Strengthen formal and informal surveillance. Technology to identify and locate cars, trucks, cell phones. GIS chips in terrorist tools.	Track all financial transactions. Promote ties between local police and immigrant communities.
Reduce the rewards	Conceal or remove targets. Bomb-proof buildings. Swift cleanup of attack site.	Use publicity to isolate terrorist groups from community. Use publicity to portray hypocrisy, cruelty of terrorist acts. Anti-money laundering regulations.
Reduce provocations	Unobtrusive public buildings at home and abroad.	Clear and consistent rules of engagement. Work closely with immigrant communities and host communities abroad. Clear rules for public demonstrations. Avoid provocative announcements.
Remove excuses		Avoid use of controversial weapons. Avoid maltreatment of prisoners. Clear rules for interrogation.

approach to international money laundering and counter-terrorism funding initiatives, such that the "FATF specifically recognizes that the legal and financial systems of member countries differ and so identical measures cannot be adopted by each country. The FATF Recommendations set out minimum standards for member countries to implement in accordance with their own legislative and financial frameworks" (Deitz & Buttle, 2008, p. 12); (b) "international arms dealing agreements to prevent terrorists laying their hands on more [man-portable air defense systems, MANPAD] missiles"; and (c) "international agreements to prevent the use of civilian aircraft to ferry troops into theatres of conflict" (with (b) and (c) both discussed by Clarke & Newman, 2006, p. 51).

Despite expanding the SPT framework to advocate for high-risk and population approaches operating in parallel, Clarke and Newman (2006) maintain consistency with fundamental assumptions underlying situational prevention, namely: (a) terrorism is both normal and inevitable, (b) no appeal is made to converting the deviant individual, and (c) terrorism (as with all other crime) will never be eradicated. Furthermore, as with the high-risk and population approaches within a medical context, it is argued that both techniques must be applied in an ongoing manner, and be adapted with contextual variation. As Clarke and Newman explain, successful implementation of a SPT framework requires a shift in policy and practice, and ongoing, bipartisan support from governments. The SPT framework can operate effectively within existing criminal justice systems to counter terrorism in the same manner as situational prevention does for all other forms of criminal violence, and full implementation of the SPT framework simultaneously targets different time-frames of intervention, with population prevention strategies likely to take long periods of time for successful implementation, while high-risk approaches will be able to produce more immediate benefits. This said, it is important to note that, "Grateful patients are few in preventive medicine, where success is marked by a non-event" (Rose, 2001, p. 432). As such, population techniques may offer little short-term or immediate benefit and it is likely to be difficult to accurately evaluate the impact of these types of interventions.

The following section will discuss the similarities between SPT in this form and the arguments proposed by the non-criminologists who attended the previously mentioned symposium. As will be explained, there are clear parallels between some of Clarke and Newman's (2006) population techniques and the recommendations of other academic disciplines.

Parallels between SPT Population Strategies and the Advice of Other Disciplines

It is possible to manipulate the balance of opinion across society over time, as has been demonstrated by shifting attitudes towards issues such as racism, gender inequality, and environmental protection. For example, from a crime perspective, Smith (2000) has argued that attitudes and norms surrounding drink-driving, speeding, fare evasion, and graffiti, can be manipulated to reduce the overall risk of these offences occurring across the community. For the most part, these shifts have resulted from general, persistent campaigning and have occurred slowly, as opposed to suddenly as a consequence of a single, significant event. High-risk individuals have not been the focus of these interventions, but the overall behaviors, attitudes and motivations of all individuals in the general population have changed as a consequence. This is not to assert that these factors are no longer present in society, or that active prevention is no longer required. In the same way that successful anti-smoking campaigns have altered the population risk of lung disease, the magnitude of these problems has changed, meaning that targeted strategies are better able to combat the remaining examples of racism, sexism, and environmental damage.

Consistent with these previously implemented society-wide changes, the advice received from interdisciplinary perspectives has led us to believe that similar population reductions in terrorist risk can be achieved through a range of aims and strategies that address motivation (while making no appeal to pathology). Two broad categories for these types of approaches to reducing general support for terrorism within societies (as expanded in Clare & Morgan, 2009) are: (a) aligning legitimate political parties with terrorist groups and fostering a functioning political environment that allows legitimate ways for voicing dissatisfaction, and (b) acknowledging the existence of underlying factors that motivate and perpetuate terror.

Fostering a Functioning Political Environment

From a social psychology perspective, Louis (2009) argues that reducing the frequency of terrorist behavior requires a shift in the perceived utility of terrorism relative to the alternatives to terror, an adjustment that is unlikely in the absence of functioning political and social systems. To avoid exacerbating such situations, Louis suggests that anti-terror activities should target underlying belief structures that simultaneously assert: (a) alternatives to terror are ineffective, and (b) long-term, sustainable social change can be achieved as a result of terrorism. Louis suggests these objectives can be reached by defining terrorist groups as narrowly as possible to avoid treating all members of perceived high-risk groups as equivalent to terrorists, thus minimizing the likelihood of non-terrorists identifying with terrorist groups and adopting terrorist norms. In addition to this, viable, functional alternatives to violence need to be developed to achieve political change. Louis also proposes that long-term attenuation of terrorist threat will be facilitated by maximizing the amount of separation among terrorist groups (both rhetorically and socially). Furthermore, terrorist groups should be engaged by non-terrorist partners who are led by non-violent leaders: as with Sinn Fein and the IRA, where alignment between these two factions has resulted in a longitudinal reduction in politically motivated violence within Northern Ireland.

Acknowledging Legitimate Complaints

As Clarke and Newman demonstrate, it is possible to discuss underlying factors that motivate and perpetuate terror without (a) seeking root causes in terms of pathology, or (b) the expectation of being able to eradicate terrorism. To do so, however, is to challenge assertions that past and present governmental policies do not contribute to motivation for terrorist activity. There is opposition to this position, however, with the Australian Government Department of Foreign Affairs and Trade (2004) adopting the stance that "correction" or "mitigation" of terrorist threat is an impossibility (Lawrence, 2009). In response to this perspective, Lawrence (a former Federal politician in Australia) emphasizes that it is possible to acknowledge the reasons underlying terrorist motivation without agreeing with the actions of terrorists. Indeed, as Clarke and Newman (2006, p. 195) explain: "talking and negotiating with terrorists does not mean that one should give in to them, because that would increase their rewards. Rather, the aim of such talks should be to identify any legitimate terrorist complaints and offer non-terrorist alternatives to solving those complaints." Failure to do so is consistent with the findings that, "In general, economic analyses have concluded that negative sanctions such as reactive strikes or increased penalties (e.g., increased prison terms, sanctions against offending countries) do not reduce terrorism" (Clarke & Newman, 2006, p. 164).

One example of a legitimate complaint that most probably acts as a relevant motivator for terrorism is the use of state-sanctioned torture. As indicated in Table 1, one of the population techniques within Clarke and Newman's (2006) SPT framework is the importance of utilizing clear rules for interrogation. In a complementary way and operating from a legal perspective, Bellamy (2009) examines the role state-sanctioned torture plays in enhancing the motivation and support for terrorist acts. Bellamy explains that, because torture necessarily involves non-combatants, it is legally and morally wrong. Furthermore, Bellamy asserts that the reason torture and terrorism are often conterminous is because to justify employing torture justifies and validates the use of terrorism. As Clarke and Newman also argue, Bellamy posits that this cycle can only be broken through a universal and absolute application of the reaffirmation of non-combatant immunity. Further legally motivated support for this position is provided by Saul (2009), who suggests that the logic underlying arguments in support of state-based torture and those justifying terrorist action to combat excessive uses of force by governments possess a large degree of equivalence. As such, it is not plausible to utilize one of these perspectives without legitimizing the other.

Recently, within a sociological context, Moghaddam (e.g., 2005, 2009) has presented a staircase metaphor to explain how these types of legitimate motivating factors can result in the development of terrorists. Moghaddam designed this staircase to act as a conceptual model, outlining how individuals can become terrorists as a consequence of initial feelings of dissatisfaction with respect to: (a) their sense of social identity, (b) the relative treatment of the group they identify with, and/or (c) the impoverished nature of the material conditions they endure. According to this model, these factors can motivate individuals to commence an ascent from the ground floor of the staircase to terrorism, and that once the climb begins, with each incremental step, individuals are faced with ever-decreasing opportunity to avoid becoming a terrorist. Moghaddam argues that the motivation for beginning this journey is not influenced by fixed contextual or dispositional factors: instead, Moghaddam attempts to demonstrate how disaffected members of a general population can make the gradual progression to being a terrorist. Just as Clarke and Newman (2006) indicate with the inclusion of population techniques in their SPT framework, Moghaddam emphasizes that long-term risk minimization will only be accomplished by focusing attention on the metaphorical ground floor, with a view to reducing the likelihood of individuals starting to climb the staircase.

CONCLUSIONS

These parallels between the techniques incorporated into the SPT framework and the recommendations of non-criminological theorists are unsurprising given Clarke and Newman's (2006) claims that situational prevention should never be the only approach to safeguarding against terrorist attacks. In addition to SPT, Clarke and Newman outline a range of alternative strategies that can operate in conjunction with opportunity reduction techniques, including: (a) political, social, and economic policy, (b) using diplomacy to disrupt support for terrorists, (c) developing harm minimization plans should attacks occur, (d) instigating legal and judicial amendments, and (d) optimizing the impact of law enforcement, while always acting within legal constraints. According to this argument, the key to attaining the greatest benefits comes from the integration of these approaches to reducing risk. Clarke and Newman (2006, p. 171) discussed how the long-term reduction in bombings in Northern Ireland coincided with the parallel implementation of the "Ring of Steel" and diplomatic progress to address some of the motivations for the original IRA activity (see Ross, this volume, for a more detailed discussion of counter-terrorist activities in Northern Ireland). This provides good support for the holistic implementation of high-risk and population approaches, as these strategies operate on diverse levels and over divergent timeframes.

In concluding, we wish to remind readers of the two main objectives of this chapter. First has been to explore the expansions that have been made to situational prevention during its transition from SCP to SPT, and how these expansions arguably incorporate aspects of a population approach to risk reduction to a much greater extent that was previously the case. Second was to emphasize the parallels between these population techniques and the objectives advocated for within other academic disciplines with respect to reducing terrorist risk. We contend that this transition has been made while retaining focus on a central impetus of SCP (according to Smith, 2000, p. 155) in "attempt[ing] to concentrate on changing what can be changed" and focusing "on the most effective, economic, and efficient methods of reducing offending." We finish by asserting that in expanding SCP to SPT, Clarke has heeded his own warning that "the development of situational prevention has taken place in relative isolation from the remainder of criminology. This is to the detriment of both" (Clarke, 2005, p. 63).

◆

Address correspondence to: Joseph Clare, Crime Research Centre, University of Western Australia, Crawley, WA 6009, Australia; e-mail: joe.clare@uwa.edu.au

REFERENCES

Arnold, R., Keane, C., & Baron, S. (2005). Assessing risk of victimization through epidemiological concepts: An alternative analytic strategy applied to routine activities theory. *Canadian Review of Sociology and Anthropology, 42*(3), 345–364.

Australian Government Department of Foreign Affairs and Trade. (2004). *Transnational terrorism: the threat to Australia*. Retrieved September 14, 2007, from http://www.dfat.gov.au/publications/terrorism/chapter8.html.

Australian Government Parliamentary Joint Committee. (2002). An Advisory Report to the Australian Security Intelligence Organisation Legislation Amendment (Terrorism) Bill 2002, Report 1. Canberra.

Bellamy, A. J. (2009). Torture, terrorism, and the moral prohibition on killing non-combatants. In W. Stritzke, S. Lewandowsky, D. Denemark, J. Clare & F. Morgan (Eds.), *Terrorism and torture: An interdisciplinary perspective* (pp. 18–43). Cambridge, UK: Cambridge University Press.

Brantingham, P. J., & Brantingham, P. L. (1984). *Patterns in crime*. New York: Macmillan.

Brantingham, P. J., & Faust, F. L. (1976). A conceptual model of crime prevention. *Crime & Delinquency, 22*(3), 284–296.

Clare, J., & Morgan, F. (2009). Reducing terrorist risk: integrating jurisdictional and opportunity approaches. In W. Stritzke, S. Lewandowsky, D. Denemark, J. Clare & F. Morgan (Eds.), *Terrorism and torture: An interdisciplinary perspective* (pp. 325–344). Cambridge, UK: Cambridge University Press.

Clarke, R. V. (1997). Introduction. In R. V. Clarke (Ed.), Situational Crime Prevention: Successful Case Studies (2nd ed., pp. 1–45). Monsey, NY: Criminal Justice Press.

Clarke, R. V. (2005). Seven misconceptions of situational crime prevention. In N. Tilley (Ed.), *Handbook of crime prevention and community safety* (pp. 39–70). Cullompton, Devon: Willan Publishing.

Clarke, R. V. (2008). Situational crime prevention. In R. Wortley & L. Mazerolle (Eds.), *Environmental criminology and crime analysis*. Crime Science Series (pp. 178–194). Cullompton: Willan Publishing.

Clarke, R. V., & Newman, G. R. (2006). *Outsmarting the terrorists*. New York: Praeger Publishers.

Cohen, L. E., & Felson, M. (1979). Social change and crime rate trends: a routine activity approach. *American Sociological Review, 44*(4), 588–608.

Deitz, A., & Buttle, J. (2008). *Anti-money laundering handbook*. Pyrmont: Thomson Lawbook Co.

Devine, P. G. (1995). Prejudice and out-group perception. In A. Tesser (Ed.), *Advanced social psychology* (pp. 467–524). Boston, MA: McGraw-Hill, Inc.

Feeley, M. M., & Simon, J. (1992). The new penology: Notes on the emerging strategy of corrections and its implications. *Criminology, 30*(4), 449–470.

Feeley, M. M., & Simon, J. (1994). Actuarial justice: The emerging new criminal law. In D. Nelken (Ed.), *The futures of criminology* (pp. 173–201). London: Sage.

Haddon, W. J. (1999). The changing approach to the epidemiology, prevention, and amelioration of trauma: The transition to approaches etiologically rather than descriptively based. *Injury Prevention, 5,* 231–236.

Hope, T. (2007). Theory and method: the social epidemiology of crime victims. In S. Walklate (Ed.), *Handbook of victims and victimology.* Cullompton, Devon: Willan Publishing.

Jackson, R., Lynch, J., & Harper, S. (2006). Preventing coronary heart disease: does Rose's population prevention axiom still apply in the 21st century? *British Medical Journal, 332*(7542), 617–618.

Lawrence, C. (2009). I'm right, you're dead: speculations about the roots of fanaticism. In W. Stritzke, S. Lewandowsky, D. Denemark, J. Clare & F. Morgan (Eds.), *Terrorism and torture: An interdisciplinary perspective* (pp. 313–324). Cambridge, UK: Cambridge University Press.

Levine, J. M., & Moreland, R. L. (1995). Group processes. In A. Tesser (Ed.), *Advanced social psychology* (pp. 419–465). Boston, MA: McGraw-Hill, Inc.

Louis, W. R. (2009). If they're not crazy, then what? The implications of social psychological approaches to terrorism for conflict management. In W. Stritzke, S. Lewandowsky, D. Denemark, J. Clare & F. Morgan (Eds.), *Terrorism and torture: An interdisciplinary perspective* (pp. 125–153). Cambridge, UK: Cambridge University Press.

McCauley, C. (2009). War versus criminal justice in response to terrorism: the losing logic of torture. In W. Stritzke, S. Lewandowsky, D. Denemark, J. Clare & F. Morgan (Eds.), *Terrorism and Torture: An Interdisciplinary Perspective* (pp. 63–85. Cambridge, UK: Cambridge University Press.

Moghaddam, F. M. (2005). The staircase to terrorism: a psychological exploration. *American Psychologist, 60*(2), 161–169.

Moghaddam, F. M. (2009). From the terrorists' point of view: toward a better understanding of the staircase to terrorism. In W. Stritzke, S. Lewandowsky, D. Denemark, J. Clare & F. Morgan (Eds.), *Terrorism and Torture: An Interdisciplinary Perspective* (pp. 106–124). Cambridge, UK: Cambridge University Press.

O'Malley, P. (2002). Globalizing risk? Distinguishing styles of "neo-liberal" criminal justice in Australia and the USA. *Criminal Justice, 2*(2), 205–222.

O'Malley, P. (2004). The uncertain promise of risk. *Australian and New Zealand Journal of Criminology, 37*(3), 323–343.

Rose, G. (1992). *The strategy of preventive medicine.* Oxford, UK: Oxford University Press.

Rose, G. (2001). Sick individuals and sick populations. *International Journal of Epidemiology, 30,* 427–432.

Saul, B. (2009). The equivalent logic of torture and terrorism: the legal regulation of moral monstrosity. In W. Stritzke, S. Lewandowsky, D. Denemark, J. Clare & F. Morgan (Eds.), *Terrorism and torture: An interdisciplinary perspective* (pp. 44–62). Cambridge, UK: Cambridge University Press.

Smith, D. J. (2000). Changing situations and changing people. In A. von Hirsch, D. Garland & A. Wakefield (Eds.), *Ethical and social perspectives on situational crime prevention. Studies in penal theory and penal ethics* (pp. 147–174). Oxford, Portland: Hart Publishing.

Wortley, R. (2008). Situational precipitators of crime. In R. Wortley & L. Mazerolle (Eds.), *Environmental criminology and crime analysis*. Crime Science Series (pp. 48–69). Cullompton, UK: Willan Publishing.

HOW TO LOSE THE WAR ON TERROR: LESSONS OF A 30 YEAR WAR IN NORTHERN IRELAND

Nick Ross
Jill Dando Institute of Crime Science

Abstract: *Untested intuition makes for bad science, but has been our first defense against terrorism. Situational measures can mitigate damage, but typically we fail to appreciate developing dangers, over-react to outrages, and make things worse. Given the lack of scientific models in the field, this paper is mostly anecdote and autobiography; it recruits lessons from recent history to lament that in the absence of scientific rigor we fail to define objectives and repeat mistakes in tackling terror. It challenges the temptation to see terrorism as unfair, let alone Islamic. It suggests that terrorism is here to stay, that brutal countermeasures are self-defeating unless they can quickly and utterly crush the perpetrators, so parlaying is strategic necessity and must be contemplated (though not indulged in) from the start.*

INTRODUCTION

Boo.

In a word that's what terrorism seeks to achieve: fear. And aren't we suckers for it. Ever since disaffected Palestinians began to hijack airplanes in the 1960s, we've given them all the publicity they could possibly hope for – and sometimes a great deal more.

We have learned to cope with terrorism with a panoply of security measures – what crime scientists call situational, or environmental, approaches – and we sometimes underrate how productive these defensive measures are. Aircraft hijacking is a good example where, albeit at enormous cost, the threat has almost eliminated.[1] I shall describe some of these success, but only in passing, since they are covered in more detail by others in this volume. In any case they are only one part of an armory. Physical defense, like physical aggression, has tended to distract from hugely important and embarrassing intellectual deficits in the battle against terror.

Fundamentally my thesis is in three parts:

First that terrorism is full of paradoxes. A lot of them are embarrassing paradoxes for democrats in the West.

Second, that, in fighting terrorism, the good guys often tend to make things worse. I'll explain how that's a consistent pattern.

And third, that as in any war, you need total victory or compromise. Doing deals with the Devil might not sound attractive; but that's how most major terrorist conflicts have been ended.

None of this fits with the simplistic certainties which define the so-called "War on Terror."

I start with two apologies:

First, much of what I say is going to be anecdotal, even autobiographical. I am passionate about good science, but there aren't many randomized double-blind trials when it comes to terrorism.

Second, I'm going to start by defining terrorism, or rather proving it's as elusive as the Bermuda Triangle. Visitors to Puerto Rico are told that one of the Spanish forts in old San Juan is the apex of the Bermuda Triangle – and sometimes it is. But some of the Bermuda Triangle maps place it hundreds of miles outside. Every conspiracy theorist has moved the defining boundaries so as to pack in as many facts and anecdotes as fit the thesis. Terrorism is another Bermuda Triangle, open to sloppy thinking, self-serving embellishments and suspension of good sense.

Definition

Only cynical authors and credulous readers need to define the Bermuda Triangle since actuarial rates (the risks and the insurance premiums) are the same there as anywhere else in the Atlantic. But terrorism is a different matter. The U.S. alone has committed a lot of lives and cash to fight it, perhaps some $700 billion,[2] so we had better be clear about what it is we are trying to defeat.

Yet every formal attempt at defining it, and there are dozens, seems hopeless.

Is it **violence against civilians**, as the U.N. suggests[3]? Maybe, but that would exclude military targets like the USS Cole – which the Western media, and U.S. citizens and government, have always considered a terrorist act. In any case all wars kill civilians – and not just as collateral damage: throughout history whole tribes were wiped out, whole cities destroyed. We are a violent species and in the widest sense we are all combatants, and always have been. The Nazi German advance through Russia laid waste to everyone and everything. At Dresden, the RAF wiped out one of the greatest and most culturally important cities of Europe. In the infamous Rape of Nanking when Japanese troops conquered the city they slaughtered more than a quarter of a million of its inhabitants. Civilians again were the principle targets at Hiroshima and Nagasaki – and again roughly a quarter of a million died. "It shortened the war," we say, and I'm sure it did. But let's not delude ourselves: terror was the aim, and non-combatants were the pawns.

Is terrorism defined by use of **clandestine agents**, as the U.S. State Department puts it?[4] If so, it would be embarrassing for the CIA, which is a world leader in covert operations. The U.S. has armed and trained guerilla armies round the world – not least some of those in Afghanistan who are now causing us such grievous problems. See the movie *Charlie Wilson's War*.

Is terrorism **organized gangs of non-State players**, as some academics have suggested? Plainly not, if only because much terrorism is State inspired.

The fact is that terrorism has many flavors and comes in many guises, from loners to global movements, from social misfits to regular armies. It embraces individuals like Timothy McVeigh (Oklahoma, 1995, 168 dead), through little groups of malcontents like the Baader Meinhoff Gang (Germany, 1970s, 34 dead), to nationalist movements like the Kurds' PKK (Turkey, 1970 till now, 37,000 dead), to global Jihadism such as Al-Qaeda (1988, death toll hard to estimate). There are amateurish outbursts, like the Angry Brigade in Britain (1970-72, 25 bombs, no deaths) and full-scale armies like the Tamil Tigers in Sri Lanka (1975 and continuing, with untold tens of thousands of casualties).

As for **objectives**, terrorism is usually inspired by the same motives as any other conflict: mostly tribalism, religion and nationalism – the things that throughout history have been the great causae bellum or justifications for war. Thus if you're Chinese the biggest threat right now is Tibetan, Uighur and other nationalists. If you're in Iraq it is religion (sectarianism is a much bigger danger than insurgency). If you're in Spain or Sri Lanka or Turkey, it's breakaway nationalism. Elsewhere it's tribalism, caste, or any number of things which set human against human.

Does it help to go back to **etymology**, to the *origin* of the word? Not really. Its first English dictionary appearance was in 1798 referring to actions by the State in the Great Terror in France; but here's an interesting thing: in the modern sense, of violence *against* the established authorities, it was coined in 1947 to describe Jewish tactics against the British in Palestine.

Let me point up that paradox. The State of Israel, which today claims so passionately to be the prime target of terrorism and which expresses such moral outrage against terror campaigns, was forged with the help of Irgun and the Stern Gang. The immediate past prime minister, Ehud Olmert, is the son of someone the British cited as a terrorist. Some of the founders of Israel, including a future prime minister Menachem Begin, violently subverted a League of Nations mandate and blew up the King David Hotel in Jerusalem killing over 90 people. It would be today's equivalent of killing UN peacekeepers. Moreover these were the guys who killed well over 100 Arabs, mostly old men, women and children, in the notorious Deir Yassin massacre.

But it's not just the Israelis who are hypocrites. We *all* are. In truth terrorism is what *others* do, never what we do. Perhaps that's its *only* defining characteristic. That's why America sees Islamic fundamentalists as part of the Axis of Evil, and why they in turn see America as the Great Satan. We need to get away from the notion that terrorism is unfair. So is air or naval superiority. We need to accept that we have heroes who are terrorists in other people's eyes, like resistance movements in World War Two. And we need to admit that our attitudes change when terrorists win. They say: "treason never prospers, for if it does none dare call it treason." Nelson Mandela, for decades listed by the U.S. as a terrorist,[5] became president of South Africa, Nobel peace prize-winner, and perhaps the most feted man on Earth.

Moreover our attitudes change when terrorism affects us personally, rather than someone far away. As a British citizen I'm acutely aware of how many Americans, with a nod and a wink from the U.S. government, gave money – millions of dollars – to the Irish Republican Army. Are our memories so short? Are our morals so shallow or our definitions of terrorism so flexible? Apparently they are.

It really is true that one man's freedom fighter is another man's terrorist. So let's get off our high horse and be more dispassionate and more intelligent about defeating it.

NORTHERN IRELAND

Which brings me to Northern Ireland.

Forty years ago I went from my home in London to Queen's University Belfast. (I know that's hard to believe – I'm so young and debonair – but there it is.) I'm also English – but for anyone unsure of the arcane niceties of European geography, let me explain that Northern Ireland was, and is, part of the United Kingdom. Indeed that relationship between Ireland and England is what this story is about.

Why should we care about what happened in a corner of a little island which has fewer inhabitants than Philadelphia? The answer is that it played out in microcosm a problem that is now recognized as global. It is a living example of how to get things wrong and how to put things right. There was a huge and unsung role for situational approaches, which I shall come to shortly, but beyond that it shows how:

- terrorism is full of paradoxes

- we under-act

- then over-react

- before finally seeking peace.

First, a potted history.

Ireland was the place where in the seventeenth century the battles between Protestantism and Catholicism were played out by the great European powers. The Dutch, the Spaniards, the Scots, The English, the Germans, the Danes and the Irish themselves fought for the very soul of Christianity – and for succession to the thrones of England and elsewhere.

I mention paradoxes: the whole of Ireland was then part of the United Kingdom, and most Irish supported the English King, James II, who was stoutly Catholic; while the Protestants were led by a tenacious Dutch claimant to the British throne, William of Orange. When James was finally defeated (in sieges and battles still either resented or celebrated in Ireland and its diaspora) William enforced ruthless peace terms. Irish Catholicism was subjugated – far more so than elsewhere in the United Kingdom – and whereas in the years and centuries that followed religious intolerance in England began to fade, in Ireland resentment and sectarianism simmered as deeply as racism did in the United States.

After generations of unrest and occasional insurrections, Britain finally agreed to Irish independence in the 1920s; but Protestants in the province of Ulster in the north refused to join the largely Catholic south, and the island was partitioned. Six counties stayed British – though effectively quite independent – and British politicians thought that finally they'd washed their hands of Ireland. How wrong they were.

Partition provoked a bloody civil war among Irish nationalists, some of whom resented any part of the island remaining nominally British, and a tiny band of IRA malcontents conspired to sabotage the settlement. It was a hopeless cause. Over the next 40 years they caused occasional bomb outrages but that only served to justify repressive measures in the newly self-governing north. In fact it was repressive over-reaction to the IRA that eventually caused the downfall of the Protestant ascendancy there.

When I arrived in Belfast in the 1960s, the IRA was little more than the broken dreams of a few old men and a handful of young Marxists (in fact when the first violence against Catholics broke out, Catholic graffiti read "IRA = I Ran Away"). But the provincial government still retained fierce emergency powers which overrode civil liberties, and religious discrimination was almost as rife as racial intolerance in the American south. In fact what happened in the U.S. began to inspire students and middle class people in Northern Ireland. In 1968, six months after Dr King's assassination in Memphis, there was a civil rights march in Northern Ireland's second city, Londonderry. It was an unnecessarily bloody police confrontation with that march which popped the cork out of the bottle and spawned terrorism which would come to dominate world headlines for 30 years.

As so often the truth behind terrorism reveals all sorts of paradoxes.

The Protestants like to portray themselves as victims of IRA violence – but it was Protestants that planted the first bombs in the new wave of violence in the 1960s and killed the first police officer and the first British soldier. Hard-line Catholics like to portray the British as colonial oppressors – but the army marched in to the cheers of the Catholic communities and saved them from attack. The British like to think of themselves as honorable peacemakers, but they were ignorant and stupid, sometimes brutal too. The people in the south of Ireland like to think they played an admirable role – in fact they were often duplicitous and contemptuous of their neighbors and fellow-countrymen.

Perhaps most important of all is the paradox about the outcome – but I'll come to that later.

LESSONS

So what are the lessons?

First let me deal with the importance of situational approaches – those that alleviate a problem by changing the circumstances people find themselves in, rather than trying to change people themselves. To my knowledge the phrase "situational crime prevention" was never applied to British policy on Northern Ireland, and remedies were applied piecemeal with little overarching strategy. But they were fundamental to success. Indeed the "Peace Barrier" – a wall that divides hardened Protestant and Catholic communities – still stands as a, literally, concrete reminder. Most other examples have been dismantled, but police stations became fortresses with bulletproof look-out posts and high fences to catch mortar bombs. Belfast's main airport was turned inside out so that passengers and baggage could be screened before entering the terminal. Security staff were hired to protect high risk buildings, bollards were placed outside to prevent car bombings, and Belfast's shopping center was protected by a so-called "ring of steel" with vehicles and people being searched before they entered. After an IRA unit travelled to London and destroyed a building in the business district, a defensive cordon was put up there too, with chicanes and search points on every access road. All these measures were hugely successful, sometimes preventing violence altogether and generally obliging terrorists to shift to less important (and crucially less spectacular) targets. When attacks could not be thwarted the damage could be limited. For example, office buildings were kitted out with net curtains weighted at the floor to absorb blast and splinters from a bomb.

These triumphs are rarely celebrated, but they were critical to something else that is rarely celebrated in the blunt terms I use to describe it (and which I will explain shortly): an overwhelming British victory.

But that victory took 30 years, and the battle should not have happened in the first place. The conflict could have been avoided, violent passions should have been assuaged, and had the British been smarter and less visceral, had they been better students of the U.K.'s difficult and often bloody disentanglement from Empire, the so-called "Troubles" in Northern Ireland would not have caused the carnage, grief and cost they did. So beyond the importance of situational design is a suite of warnings for the future:

- Most terrorism is foreseeable.

- Its brutality is frequently triumphant in the short and medium term.

- It provokes precisely the sort of counter-violence that sustains it.

- The state security forces need to reinvent themselves.

- Liberals become drowned out and radicals are succeeded by yet more-extremist partisans.

- Those who profess abhorrence of violence and claim democratic values sometimes support terrorism – indeed, illegal quasi-state terrorism itself can be useful.

- Accordingly, terrorism has the capacity to last for many decades.

I have space only to rattle through these headlines . . .

Most Terrorism is Foreseeable

Terrorism is the pursuit of politics by other means. It happens when people feel excluded from institutions. As a young student from London, sharing none of the Belfast presumptions, I found a deeply divided place where for many of my fellow students Catholics had never knowingly met Protestants before, let alone socialized with them. I found draconian legislation, corrupt local politics, and what passed for a democracy where one party always ruled and where the only legislative success of the Opposition since the 1920s was an amendment to the Wild Birds Act. It was a recipe for unrest – and I wrote to the newspapers at home warning that this place was a tinderbox.

The trouble with our free press is that it is enslaved. It is walled in by the prevailing culture. It shares a news agenda. It panders to the prejudices of its owners and readers and viewers. Each country tends to get an eccentric, homogenous and above all, self-regarding, view of the world. The result is remarkable ignorance among a sea of newsprint and a blizzard of news bulletins.

Which is why when Northern Ireland exploded the media were as dumbfounded and as ignorant as everyone else.

On the other hand, the liberal media are almost designed to trumpet the worst excesses of terrorism. If you want to make your grievance known, bomb something, kidnap somebody or hijack a plane.

Its Brutality Is Frequently Triumphant in the Short and Medium Term

There are four main motives for terrorism. One is to harry an enemy during a conventional war – as with the Resistance movements who took on the Nazis. Another is to attract attention – that's why the PLO hijacked planes, and it's what attracted Nelson Mandela to violence in the days of apartheid in South Africa. But neither of these can win a conflict on their own. One way is ethnic cleansing – to frighten people so much that they give up or run away – and we saw that in the disintegration of Yugoslavia. But the main one, and we need to learn this lesson, is to provoke the enemy into over- reaction – as happened in Northern Ireland and, of course, that's what Palestinian militants have been trying to do with Israel.

Terrorism Provokes Precisely the Sort of Counter-Violence that Sustains It

Perhaps this is the most important lesson. But apparently one we never learn.

Where did the moral advantage lie in the days and weeks after 9/11? Unequivocally with the United States. Where does it lie now? Well, whatever your politics, you surely won't deny that the world is not as well-disposed to America as it was then. A great power wounded by a terrorist incident sought revenge – a crusade, no less. You can judge the effects for yourself. So far it has cost the lives of over 4,000 American and British military personnel, at least 150,000 Iraqis,[6] and perhaps $3 trillion to U.S. and British taxpayers – and it has savaged America's global reputation.

Or look at Israel's bloody lashing out against the Palestinians. If terrorism is asymmetrical warfare, the asymmetry in the Middle East is that 10 Arabs die for every Jew. Shelling from Lebanon into the north of Israel led to the disastrous invasion: 17,000 Arabs killed and 700 Israelis. The second Israeli incursion killed about 1,500 Arabs, two-thirds of them civilians, for the loss of 200 Israelis. The kidnap of two Israeli soldiers led to another invasion which killed hundreds – and so it goes on. Each outrage against Israel provokes a more lethal response from the Israeli military. Has it worked? Is Israel now safer? Have Arab militants been silenced? It seems not. Nationalist Palestinians were pushed aside by the more militant PLO, and in the West Bank they too were outflanked by Hamas. Meanwhile Iran is bristling with more and more animosity to Israel, and perhaps with nuclear technology too.

In Ireland there was a small rebellion against British rule in 1916 at the height of World War One. Most people in Ireland saw the Easter Uprising as a stab in the back and there was little sympathy when the ringleaders were caught. But they were hanged: traitors one day, martyrs the next. The British did something similar in 1971. A crude policy of internment turned the whole Catholic population against the British – and took world opinion with it.

Far too often we react emotionally to terrorism and allow the tail to wag the dog. It is a pattern repeated again and again. We overreact and lose the high ground.

But it is not just official policy – it is official blindness to the harsh realities of conflict.

We all know about Abu Ghraib. The image of a hooded and wired man being tortured in 2004 could not have been more repellent if it was from the archives of Saddam Hussein. We liked to think of it as an exception, but it was a stunning indictment of our naivety. More and more pictures came to light. Not many incidents are photographed and only blatant examples surface, but put young people into conflict, give them power over prisoners, and brutality is par for the course. At first we feel duty bound to support "our brave men and women who risk their lives on our behalf." Then we blame individuals rather than systemic poor management, but we never accept that excesses by our enemies are anything less than systemic.

The British, who seemed to have clean hands when the scandal broke in Iraq, subsequently acknowledged their own troops had indulged in mistreatment and even murder. With classic gullibility the armed forces minister blamed a small minority of soldiers rather than the Army or his officials, let alone himself. Nothing was learned, no new safeguards were put in place.

All policymakers should all remember the horror of Mai Lai – 500 women and children butchered by U.S. soldiers – one of hundreds of massacres by French and U.S. forces in Vietnam. It is sobering today to go to Ho Chi Minh City and see the American Museum in Vo Van Tan.

It happened in Northern Ireland: on Bloody Sunday 13 civilians were shot dead by British troops. It turned out not one of the demonstrators was armed, though for over three decades the British authorities persuaded themselves otherwise, covered up and prevaricated rather than blame their own troops. Soldiers too, and perhaps above all, rationalize their own failings. When once, as a reporter for the BBC, I asked a commander why a detainee had been badly beaten up he told me the man had been hit by a swinging door. I think he actually believed it.

We should hardly be surprised. There is any number of experiments by social psychologists that show how ordinary people – even academics – become vile and bestial in circumstances soldiers and guards are placed in.[7] *Cruelty* is as much default behavior as is kindness.

In the U.S., cruelty has been formal policy. Torture such as "waterboarding"[8] – the inhumane behaviors we associate with totalitarians and psychopaths – was authorized and even routine at the Guantanamo (Cuba) prison and elsewhere that "enemy combatants" were held. What sort of message does that send to our enemies? How can we be outraged when the "bad guys" behave with cruelty to us?

If you want to win hearts and minds, stop being naïve. Behaving *better* than our adversaries has to be at the core of the training and control of every combatant, every police officer, everyone who's on your side.

If there's one lesson above all others I would urge on civilian and military leaders fighting terrorism it is this: hang a placard above your desk which reads, "Any brutality, official or individual – the buck stops here!"

The State Security Forces Need to Reinvent Themselves

Countering terrorism needs intelligence and finesse, not a clodhopping army. When British troops marched onto the streets of Northern Ireland they were quickly out of their depth. They had been trained to fight the Eastern Bloc in a formal military campaign, not police the streets and take tea with the locals, and not how to deal with the change of heart as the army of liberation overstayed its welcome and became a force of occupation. You could respond to the Soviets with artillery and machine guns, but how do you react to youths pelting you with insults, stones and petrol bombs?

The Americans discovered a similar unpreparedness when they went into Iraq. They were crude. They imposed their own untutored assumptions, riding roughshod over local sensitivities and dismantled critical parts of the infrastructure. They made enemies of the very people they had come to set free.[9] They regarded their own, American, lives as more valuable than those of the citizens they were there to serve. It was the inverse of policing, where officers are expected to take high personal risks in protection of the community. There were shocking scenes where soldiers shot wildly at cars killing whole families rather than risk a suicide bombing. The results were predictable: as in Northern Ireland the saviors became seen as imperialists. Only recently have U.S. commanders learned that you have to make friends, and forge alliances.

You need enough troops. You need to keep control. But locals need to see the army is protecting *them* – rather than itself.

Radicals are succeeded by yet more extremist fanatics while the religious or political causes that sustain it can become peripheral or even hard to identify.

Over-reaction and brutality inflate the conflict. We have seen it in Palestinian politics – I watched it in Northern Ireland. If you don't find accommodation quickly, the moderates become drowned out and are overtaken by extremists and the extremists by fanatics. Northern Ireland protests began with middle-class campaigners and moderate politicians like Gerry Fitt and John Hume who only asked for civil rights; but when they failed and their followers were beaten down they were swept away by a resurgent IRA. Similarly the conservative Protestants were pushed aside by ultra-conservatives, finishing up with the arch-bombast of all, the Reverend Ian Paisley.

Those who profess abhorrence of violence and claim democratic values sometimes support terrorism – indeed, illegal quasi-state terrorism itself can be useful.

In calling for a restraint I am not necessarily endorsing a liberal agenda. Facts don't always fit political paradigms.

In May 1974 a series of car bombs went off south of the Northern Ireland border leaving 33 dead and almost 300 injured. Those were the worst casualties of any single day in the Troubles. Blame was laid on northern Protestant fanatics, though there may well have been unauthorized British collusion. At any rate it was effective. People in the south who had supported the IRA suddenly went quiet when they got a taste of terrorism themselves. After the Dublin and Monaghan atrocities attitudes in the south would never be quite the same, and the government started to work for a rapprochement with the British.

Never let it be said that violence doesn't pay. It can.

If we get it right

So there are many ways to lose the war on terror. Most of all, if we are to avoid defeat, we need to understand that we have to fight it with much more subtlety than in conventional war. As Mao Zedong, one of the greatest guerilla fighters of all time, said, "The people are like water and the army is like fish."[10] At all costs we must avoid turning the water toxic if we want to go on swimming in it.

But in the end we often get it right, and sometimes, by heading off trouble before it gets out of hand, we are scarcely aware of just how successful we have been. I close, therefore, on an optimistic note.

If we get it right:

1. Terrorism can often be nipped in the bud.

2. "Situational" measures such as target hardening are effective.

3. Tough military countermeasures are highly beneficial when precisely targeted.

4. Intelligence is king.

5. But compromise is emperor.

Again, through shortage of space, I can not go into all of these, but will pick out one because it is so infrequently discussed by academics – and is to some extent politically counterintuitive. Frequently the key to winning is something hard-liners find very hard to swallow. Indeed, it is something we all find hard to swallow when faced with callous violence: flexibility.

Compromise

Of course asymmetrical wars can sometimes be ended by the authorities securing complete victory, as with the British defeat of communists in Malaya in the 1950s or India's crushing of Sikh extremists in the 1980s. In fact military counter-terrorist campaigns are often more successful than they are given credit for. But whereas in conventional warfare an army can be crushed and its leaders can be obliged to order complete surrender of their forces, in terrorism the fighting is sporadic and the enemy is organized in clandestine cells rather than open military formations, so there are almost always pockets of resistance and it is hard to force all the rebels to sign up to an armistice. Accordingly hostilities can drag on and on, with the authorities maintaining the upper hand but never eliminating the terrorist threat. The British have had more experience than most, holding their own in Kenya, Cyprus, Aden and other quarters of their crumbling empire after the Second World War until – back home in the United Kingdom as more and more body bags arrived – people questioned whether it was worth it.

And that is the danger – erosion of public and political support – much more so than that guerilla forces vanquish a professional army. War-weariness is what usually ends terrorist campaigns. In time the language of conflict becomes less acrimonious, there are secret and tentative feelers for peace and, usually after a number of false dawns, one side or another quietly backs down.

Occasionally it is the rebels themselves who give up most. This is the pattern with ETA Basque movement in Spain, where violent excesses by Marxist separatists have, over four decades, eroded their social and political foundations. And this is what happened in Northern Ireland too.

Such reconciliation can only be achieved when tough and tender measures work in unison, when terrorists face military stalemate and when moderates reassert themselves and seize the opportunities for peace. The result to aim for might well be that the terrorists can claim victory, while in reality they achieve nothing. It is a difficult outcome for everyone to swallow – imagine the U.S. accepting any compromise with Islamic fundamentalism; or Israel allowing Hamas to claim any sort of victory – but look at Northern Ireland, now at calm after thirty years of mayhem.

The Provisional IRA likes to think it won – and a lot of Protestants agree, many of whom fulminated against the peace accord. But that is what's so clever about the settlement. Instead of getting something for nothing the IRA got nothing for something. No one seems to say so, and perhaps that is just as well, but the IRA was comprehensively defeated. In fact they abandoned every single one of the policies on which they ever fought.

A united Ireland. But it's still partitioned.

A socialist republic. But it's as capitalist as anywhere.

No truck with British institutions. But their former chief of staff is now joint First Minister of the Crown.

Terrorism is out of the bottle and won't ever be put back. Our interconnected world and porous communities have done for asymmetrical warfare what removing store counters did for shoplifting. *Homo sapiens*, that most belligerent, often irrational and most dangerous animal on Planet Earth, is in for a long struggle.

We need to carry a big stick. We need to be systematic about situational defenses. But we must always be ready to parley.

◆

Address correspondence to: PO Box 999, London W2 4XT, UK; e-mail: nickross@lineone.net

Acknowledgments: Nick Ross, a U.K. broadcaster, is Chairman and visiting professor at the Jill Dando Institute of Crime Science, University College London. The text of this chapter was originally delivered at an international conference on Justice and Policing in Diverse Societies, held in San Juan, Puerto Rico, in June 2008.

NOTES

1. Even the most effective situational defences can – as with an antibiotic – be overcome in time because of complacent management or mutating threats.
2. Source: US Congressional Research Service Report for Members and Committees of Congress, 11 April 2008.
3. UN Ad Hoc Committee on Terrorism: Informal Texts of Article 2 of the draft Comprehensive Convention on International Terrorism, prepared by the Coordinator, UN Doc. A/C.6/56/L.9, Annex I.B.
4. 22 United States Code, Section 2656 (d)] - cit. *United States Department of State: Patterns of Global Terrorism*, 1999. Dept. of State Publ: Washington D.C., April 2000, p. viii.
5. Nelson Mandela's African National Congress was banned in 1960 and he spent 27 years in prison. He was banned from the U.S. except for attending the UN headquarters in New York and was not removed from the U.S. terror watch list until in 2008.
6. World Health Organisation figures.

7. See the famous and oft-repeated Milgram experiments, for example.
8. Waterboarding is a euphemism for repeated near-drownings, a technique that was popular with the Gestapo.
9. *On Point II: Transition to the New Campaign*, the US Army's study of its campaign in Iraq in the 18 months following the overthrow of the Baathist regime, US Dept of Defense, 2008.
10. Mao was describing China's struggle to throw out the Japanese (1948).